SCENE WITHIN A SCENE

Scottish Independent Music 1992-2001

SCENE WITHIN A SCENE

Scottish Independent Music 1992-2001

Grant McPhee

OMNIBUS PRESS
London / New York / Paris / Sydney / Copenhagen / Berlin / Madrid / Tokyo

(A Division of Wise Music Limited)
14-15 Berners Street
London W1T 3LJ
England

Cover designed by Amazing15
Picture research by the author

ISBN 978-1-9172-7425-8

A catalogue record for this book is available from the British Library.

Typeset by Palimpsest Book Production Ltd, Falkirk, Stirlingshire

Printed in the Czech Republic.

www.omnibuspress.com

Contents

Contributors

Marc Baines (Vesuvius)
Sandy Black (Poison Sisters)
Stuart Braithwaite (Mogwai)
Jan Burnett (Spare Snare)
Jim Byrne (Kazoo Club)
Pat Byrne (Kazoo Club)
Tracyanne Campbell (Camera Obscura)
Paul Campion (ac acoustics)
Jane Chalmers, aka Jane Strain (Pink Kross)
Steven Clark, aka Sci Fi Steve (bis)
Alan Cormack (Spare Snare)
Pat Crook (Melody Dog/Vesuvius)
Pete Dale (Slampt)
Stuart David (Belle and Sebastian)
Gordy Davidson (The Stanleys, F&J)
Richie Dempsey (dawson/Stretchheads)
Gavin Dunbar (Camera Obscura)
Phil Eaglesham (Stretchheads)
Keith Farquar (The Male Nurse)
Cameron Fraser (The Cateran)
Vic Galloway (Huckleberry)

Graham Gavin (Subliminal Girls, Ganger and Lugworm)
Chris Geddes (Belle and Sebastian)
Barry Gibson (Spare Snare)
Simon Alexie Grant (Z28s)
Jade Green, aka Amanda Doorbar (Lung Leg)
Stewart Henderson (The Delgados/Chemikal Underground)
Stuart Henderson (Fenn/Ganger)
Saskia Holding (Sally Skull)
RM Hubbert, aka Hubby (F&J Records and various bands)
Alex Kapranos (Kazoo Club/The Blisters/The Karelia/Franz Ferdinand)
Colin Kearney (Eska)
Paul Kearney (Guided Missile Records)
Graham Kemp (Urusei Yatsura)
Stevie Jackson (Belle and Sebastian)
Elaine Lawrie (Urusei Yatsura)
Fergus Lawrie (Urusei Yatsura)
Kid Loco
Brian MacDougall (The Yummy Fur/Vesuvius)
Jason MacPhail (V-Twin)
Steve Mason (Beta Band)
David McArthur (Distemper)
Michael McGaughrin (V-Twin)
Jane McKeown (Lung Leg)
John McKeown (The Yummy Fur)
Gus McPhee (Glue)
Amanda MacKinnon, aka Manda-Rin (bis)
Felicity Macreath (friend of Ben Wallers and Steve Mason)
Malcolm Middleton (Arab Strap)
George Miller (Country Teasers)

Andy Milne (The Cateran)
Aidan Moffat (Arab Strap)
Stuart Murdoch (Belle and Sebastian)
Andrew Loog Oldham
Emma Pollock (The Delgados/Chemikal Underground)
Alan Rankine (The Associates/Electric Honey/Stow College)
Mark Raine (ac acoustics)
Jer Reid (dawson)
Caz Riley (ac acoustics)
Paul Savage (The Delgados/Chemikal Underground)
Annie Spandex (Lung Leg)
Craig Tannock (13th Note)
Tracy Vandal (Dick Johnson)
Ben Wallers (Country Teasers/The Male Nurse)
Lawrence Worthington (Country Teasers/The Male Nurse)
Tom Worthington (Hee Haw, Starstruck, Bosque Records)

Introduction

Splash One, Glasgow's scene-defining club mecca, opened in 1985. It was an important melting pot of influences that eventually led to the sort of music that populated the *NME*'s C86 cassette. Bands from the Creation roster played at Splash One and many Glasgow bands travelled south to play at Creation events in London, each importing and exporting new advances in indie music, attitude and fashion. Independent and indie were now practically interchangeable terms: what had originally started as a means of releasing records had become a genre in itself.

Scotland's 'indie' music scene of the mid eighties was vibrant and rich; it was a rebirth of the glory days of Fast Product and Postcard and, against all odds, became even more successful and influential. The culmination of this was perhaps Nirvana's public advocacy of The Vaselines. But like all musical scenes it was cyclical and transitory. It was never meant to last. The advent of dance culture had a huge impact on independent guitar music in Scotland. Some bands, such as The Soup Dragons, The Shamen and Primal Scream, embraced this revolution while others stuck to their guns. One such band was Teenage Fanclub, who arrived in 1990 and thrived, influenced and steadfastly affirmed the electric guitar. But in the main, as raves and dance labels prospered, local indie guitar music was on the retreat. When Fast Forward Music released their final record in 1990, it certainly felt like the end of an era. The most significant event, which might be seen as the final curtain of C86 and indie, was the spectacular collapse of Cartel and Rough Trade Records. Yet this made way for a new beginning and a new kind of music in Scotland, one that, with a few exceptions, drew a firm line in the sand. The next generation of Scotland's indie music determinedly distanced itself from C86 even though, ironically, they drew their influence from the 'other' side of the cassette: they began with contradictions. This is the story of the alternative C86.

John McKeown (The Yummy Fur): We were the indie Taliban.

Jane McKeown (Lung Leg) For me, Lung Leg, we're the children of the no-wave movement in New York. Kim Gordon and Thurston Moore are my mum and dad.

Stewart Henderson (bass, The Delgados; Chemikal Underground): For me personally, it's hard to overstate the influence or the importance of Teenage Fanclub.

Alex Kapranos (Kazoo Club, later; Franz Ferdinand): There was a connection to that scene. . . what I was doing in the nineties had been very much more about bringing everything together and having this open approach.

For some, bands such as Teenage Fanclub and Captain America, who took their influence from the past with their cross-Atlantic pollination and US Underground affiliations, held solid credibility.

As with most new scenes, however, some in the nineties began by disregarding their immediate past. They took an entirely different view: that the new decade would be another Year Zero moment.

Many in this new generation found inspiration in the compilation that helped define 'indie' as a distinct style in the minds of readers of the weekly music press – the NME's *revered* C86 *compilation.* C86 *has become a synonym for a certain style of 1960s guitar-inspired band, often with hints of The Velvet Underground or Postcard Records. The Pastels are a prime example. But the compilation had another distinct sound that may have been forgotten: the short, discordant, Beefheartian blasts of energy and experimentation brought to the cassette by Ron Johnson Records. For many years a shadow Glasgow Underground scene, generated from this 'other side' of* C86, *had been running concurrently with their more celebrated pop contemporaries. Ironically, this scene was also hugely influenced by the 'other' acts who played at the Splash One club, particularly bIG*fLAME Much of this shadow scene arose from those sounds, mixed with a US hardcore influence and a strong, left-leaning political stance.*

The Scottish band The Mackenzies were one of the Ron Johnson bands that appeared on the original C86 *tape and were a huge influence on this co-existing scene.*

Paul Turnbull (drums, The Mackenzies): We were big fans of the *C81* tape, so I was really pleased when we were invited to contribute a track to the *C86* tape. The album's a pretty good snapshot of the independent scene at the time although it is not as diverse as the *C81* tape. All the bands were on independent record labels in the UK and were playing out live at the time.

I suppose it hints at what would become known as the 'indie' genre. The description used by the press doesn't really convey the variety of music on show. We wanted to create music which had danceability with an edge to it, an uptempo groove. We sounded like a jazz-punk version of The Meters, the 1960s/1970s New Orleans funk group – the drummer of which, Joseph Modeliste, was an influence on me. Other influences were Captain Beefheart & The Magic Band, The Pop Group, James Brown, Funkadelic and Curtis Mayfield. *While a large section of Scotland's new indie youth was distancing itself from the preceding independent scene,* Select *magazine, tiring of the cultural tsunami brought by Nirvana's* Nevermind, *began its proto Britpop push. Britpop essentially became a synonym for London pop and as will be seen, this London-centric musical scene was not fondly welcomed in Glasgow or the north-east of England. The success of Oasis meant that Manchester was included but in general the London weeklies seemed uninterested in what was happening elsewhere. There were a few hugely supportive labels south of the border that were to play a significant role in this next step of Scottish independent music, however, among them Slampt in Newcastle and Guided Missile in London.*

Perhaps the most significant aspect of the new generation's musical evolution was rooted in the past – anarcho-punk and collectivism, American no-wave and the Edinburgh and Glasgow Music Collectives.

CHAPTER ONE

Scene Within a Scene

The beginnings of Scotland's 'shadow' independent music scene

Scotland's 1980s music scene has been celebrated worldwide. Postcard Records bands such as Orange Juice are often associated with it, and this sound later evolved into what can be heard on the C86 compilation. This itself became a genre, and the scene included The Soup Dragons, The Pastels, The Vaselines, Shop Assistants and Primal Scream. But running concurrently with this was another equally vibrant scene.

*In Glasgow, while one part of Splash One and the C86 compilation were custodians of the past, combining 1960s jangle with DIY energy, the other part embraced the diversity and experimentation of bIG*fLAME and Sonic Youth. This was hugely responsible for sowing the seeds of the nineties scene.*

However, the most important element for the indie youth of the nineties was the influence of the eighties shadow Underground scene, from which emerged the hugely important Glasgow Music Collective, formed by Splash One regulars including Jer Reid and Richie Dempsey.

Jer's band, dawson (with an important lower-case 'd') and

Richie's band, Stretchheads, were initially inspired by that 'other' side of the C86 compilation, as well as anarcho-punk and the US hardcore scene. They hadn't been made particularly welcome in Glasgow, almost certainly due to the weekly music press's fascination with all things jangly, so opportunities to play were limited. This 'shadow' scene was firmly rooted in the anarcho-punk collectivism that began with Crass. In Scotland, it was exemplified by Aberdeen's Toxik Ephix and Dunfermline's Alternative. Toxik Ephix came out of Aberdeen's punk scene, centred on the 62 Club, and was built upon collectivist ideals. There were no promoters, and fans wrote directly to the bands. Neil 'Marsh' Marshall and Adam Sanderson (previously of Aberdeen's first punk band, Enormous Snakes, later The Jasmine Minks) were regulars at both the 62 Club and Crass's farm and undoubtedly led to Toxik Ephex's subsequent releases on the Crass label.

Alternative, whose collective space, 'the Pad', was in Dunfermline, followed a similar path. They, too, were heavily associated with both Crass and Poison Girls, and went on to have a release on the Crass label. The label was later hugely important to Glasgow's nineties scene, especially via John Loder and his association with it via his Southern Records studios, label and distribution network, SRS.

Future Hardy Boys frontman David McArthur was a part of Scotland's small but vibrant anarcho-punk scene. Based in Greenock, his band helped create an infrastructure that future bands were able to build on, allowing the sound of a new scene to emerge in the area.

Distemper

David McArthur (vocals, Distemper; later Safe Houses and The Hardy Boys): From the moment I heard Crass, I knew I wanted to play in an anarcho-punk band. One problem: I couldn't play a note/I couldn't sing a note. My parents had bought me a cheap, steel-strung acoustic guitar, but I craved *noise*. I filled school jotters with lyrics about 'the system' and 'society'. I was ready. What I needed was a band.

Every Saturday in Greenock, the town's youth tribes gathered in 'the toon', hanging around outside shops or browsing record racks, if you had a few bob. I met the three guys who would become Distemper hanging around outside of Marks and Spencer. They needed a singer. I needed a band. Quid pro quo.

Of course, forming a band means locking yourself into relationships with people you barely know and are likely to be spending an extraordinary amount of time with. Tommy, our guitarist, played loud but knew little more than barre chords. He was aggressive, often drunk, and manically depressed. Liam, on bass, was brooding and prone to sudden violence, but keen to improve as a musician. Ian, the drummer, was the real talent: tight, energetic and hilarious offstage. A beautiful man. He and I would later play in Safe Houses and The Hardy Boys. He died in October 2019. He was a drunk. Sometimes I feel like I still haven't processed it, at least not properly. Back then, I was 14 and 15, drinking in pubs with older bandmates. Alcohol in Distemper was ever-present.

Our first gig was at the same youth club where I first heard Crass, two-and-a-half years earlier. Local skinheads '*sieg heil*-ed' in front of us throughout our set. It was fucking tense. That version of Distemper lasted less than two years, but it *felt* longer. It felt *much* fucking longer. We recorded a four-song demo at Pattern Studios in Greenock in March 1984. Word spread through the network of UK punk fanzines. Soon I was receiving 30 to 40 letters a week – kids from Widnes to Warsaw asking my views on veganism and the monarchy, sending blank tapes to copy our demo. We soaped stamps so that the postmark could be wiped off and the envelopes reused. I loved it. We protested the Orange Walk in Greenock by playing an outdoor gig. Rumours began that the police broke it up before we had it out with the Orangemen: this became known locally as 'the Battle of Broomhill'. The truth is that the police saved us, and our equipment, from an absolute beating that evening.

By autumn 1983, I had started work as an apprentice in the Greenock shipyards, so buying records and the ubiquitous black uniform of the anarchist punk were no longer a problem. We were invited by Craig Ireland of *No Visible Scar* fanzine to record a track for a split EP with Glasgow's Last Rites and The Condemned, and Edinburgh's Oi Polloi. Craig had championed Distemper from when he heard the Pattern Studio Tapes. However, by then, my lyrics had evolved. I felt I was stepping back in time singing something I'd written when I was 14. I'd joined the Young Communist League, a hilarious mistake, and had little patience for 'hippy anarchists' or 'skinhead boot boys'. Liam and I took over songwriting, and we veered towards a more poppy sound, albeit with our one-chord guitarist in tow. Tommy became increasingly unstable, and useless as a member.

We recorded 'Insane Society' for Treblinka Records – punk

labels always had awful names – at Centre City Sound Studios in Glasgow on a pissing wet Friday night in February 1985. I contributed 50 quid to the project and became a joint 'owner' of the label, along with Craig, Alan Curry from Last Rites, and my Liverpool gig buddy Vinnie McMenemy. I hated every minute of the recording session. Tommy turned up with a heavily bandaged left wrist after a visit to hospital; one can only guess at what happened. He once tried to slash his wrists in my bedroom of my parents' house. He wanted a fight. The Condemned almost got us kicked out of the studio due to their drunken skinheads act. They wanted a fight. It was fucking bleak. Everyone wanted a fight. I wanted out.

Our second cassette, recorded in May 1985, had six songs and a much poppier feel. We managed to persuade Tommy to leave out distortion on the introduction to one song! The fanzine-letter cycle repeated, and I even had a four-page interview in the doyenne of punk rock magazines *Maximum Rock and Roll,* straight out of Berkeley, California. I waffled on about animal rights and working-class revolution: it must have been obvious that I didn't have a fucking clue what I was talking about. It was great exposure. We were asked to play in the US. I had hardly left Scotland. The band told me to fuck off when I suggested it. What I didn't know as a just-turned-18-year-old is that the left can politically always be outflanked by the left. Oi Polloi's frontman had deemed our £1.50 price tag for the cassette a 'rip-off' and as a result I was a 'capitalist'. He would tell his followers to boycott the release. I would discover later in life that he was right. I *was* a capitalist. I had factored in recording and production costs and priced the cassette high enough to pay for those and leave a bit left over to fund future recordings.

By June 1985, I was done. Sick of Tommy's moods. Sick of Liam's threats. Sick of punk's dogma. Sick of its crushing conservatism. It felt stifling. The band, except for Ian, were listening to an awful noise. I was listening to The Membranes, The 3 Johns, Yeah Yeah Noh. I was discovering techno and clubs. That summer, as part of 'International Youth Year', we headlined an all-day festival at the same youth centre where it had all begun. We were good. The band was tight. There were no Nazi skinheads. But my heart wasn't in it anymore. I decided after that gig that Tommy had to go. Problem was, I still couldn't play guitar.

So, I started learning. How hard could it be? By the end of 1985, I was writing the first Safe Houses songs and Liam had emigrated to Canada. I was free at last.

The night of the final Distemper gig in June 1985, The Hardy Boys played just before us. I knew Alan, their guitarist, from hanging out in 'the toon'. He went to the same gigs in Glasgow that I did. If I'd just said, 'Fancy forming a band?' I could've skipped two years of chaos.

The largest influence on Glasgow's nineties scene was probably the Edinburgh Musician's Collective and associated bands Archbishop Kebab and the Dog Faced Hermans, who were themselves heavily influenced by Manchester's Ron Johnston bands. Its approach was inspired by the Crass Collective's concept of direct DIY action in which promoters were excluded and bands put on their own events, in this case centred on Edinburgh Art College's Wee Red Bar. In addition to supporting local bands, the Collective also brought in acts from further afield, including The Ex from the Netherlands – another band to have a huge influence on the later scene. Of course, the music scene in Glasgow, then in the thrall of C86, *was pretty compressed and in need of a similar collective for their similarly 'outsider bands'.*

Jer Reid (guitar/vocals, dawson): It's interesting, it was so long ago, actually when I think about it now, I don't think of Splash One in terms of the culture. I mostly think of me being very young – 17, 18 – and the hassle, including violence, there was, being a weirdly dressed teenager walking about Glasgow. Splash One was a club in the city centre where you could go and hang out with your pals and be able to relax. Of course, the reason it was safe was because it was people who had different priorities from folks who usually ran clubs. Those priorities were, of course, music and non-mainstream cultures. It was great to be in a room of 'weirdos' of various kinds.

In terms of *C86*, me and my friends were into a lot of the bands on it. I liked the more straightly melodic bands like The Shop Assistants and The Bodines and I really liked McCarthy – partly because of their explicit politics. But it was the Ron Johnson bands that we really loved: A Witness, The Shrubs, The MacKenzies and especially bIG*fLAME. Also, not a Ron Johnson band, but Bogshed! What a singular band. It's interesting that those bands didn't get the same coverage afterwards as bands like Primal Scream but written histories often bring a retroactive notion of the importance of certain bands that become better known afterwards. That hierarchy wasn't the feeling at the time. Definitely not between me and my friends, anyway.

Richie Dempsey (drums, Stretchheads): At that time, it wasn't easy for wee bands to get gigs in Glasgow. We didn't really know anybody. The only gigs Stretchheads played in Glasgow were at Rooftops, supporting Happy Mondays, Wonderstuff etc. . . All thanks to my good friend Tam Coyle who was the main man for gigs in town. Unfortunately for us, these gigs proved to be mismatches and we felt the need to play gigs with like-minded bands. Also, I think we were the only 'noisy' band that was getting such gigs. It's all about who you know, right?!

Glasgow itself wasn't a very friendly place towards any musicians who weren't blue-eyed soul and many of the venue owners had unsavoury reputations. As Jer noted, the beauty of Splash One was the relaxed attitude and safety net afforded by the promoters. After Splash One, Glasgow needed a safe haven for the outsiders. And a place where the outsiders didn't have to pay.

The Cateran

The Vaselines, BMX Bandits and Teenage Fanclub have been celebrated in the press for their connections to Nirvana. There's another Scottish band associated with the Seattle behemoths who, unfairly, have received less attention. The Cateran were a fantastic band and in many ways acted as a direct link between the Scottish Underground scene of the 1980s and what came later in the 1990s.

Cameron Fraser (vocals/guitar, The Cateran): The band initially formed up in Inverness when I met Sandy (Macpherson, original vocalist), who was working in The Other Record shop at that time. Sandy introduced me to the delights of Black Flag and Iggy Pop's post-Stooges albums. We then headed off to the Market Bar where we decided to form a band. We'd both played in bands previously: Sandy in Inverness and me in Perth and Edinburgh. Kai (Davidson, bass) and Murdo (McLeod, guitar) joined shortly after. I can't really accurately remember the chronology back then but I do recall we had a really good drummer, but he got into big bother and went to jail for quite a while. The move south was brought about mainly with jobs or study and it just seemed to fit with everyone's plans to head south. . . we also needed to find a new drummer. Sandy moved to Glasgow and the rest of us to Edinburgh where Murdo introduced us to Andy Milne who just seemed like a great fit right from the start. . . if you discount the mullet.

Andy Milne (drums, The Cateran): I joined the band in late 1985, in Edinburgh. It had formed for a couple of years earlier, up in Inverness before coming down to Edinburgh. Murdo and I had been in He's Dead Jim together up in Aberdeen (I was living in Edinburgh, but used to travel up for our local gigs there) and so he thought of me as a potential drummer for The Cateran.

Murdo, Cameron and Kai turned up at the door of my tiny top floor bedsit in Manor Place one evening to see if I was interested. They were very persistent. I was cooking some sausages at the time, and after we'd talked for a bit I realised the smell of forgotten burning sausages had become overpowering. I abandoned the sausages and we headed off to their rehearsal space in Niddry Street. Sandy turned up and we tried some of their songs out, and it sounded good. I don't think I actually gave a definite yes to joining until after we played the first gig together as a five-piece – at an old cinema or something like that in Abbeymount. From what I remember, at this point we were called The Fabricators. I'm pretty sure the other band playing was We Free Kings. That went well, so I thought I'd stick with The Fabricators. I think the name change to The Cateran came very soon afterwards.

Cameron Fraser (vocals/guitar, The Cateran): I worked with Sandy McLean for about five years at Fast Forward (distribution) (Fun fact: latterly, Sandy persuaded me to take over as Managing Director of Fast Forward, a role I was as thoroughly ill-equipped for as Sandy was himself.) So I worked alongside Stephen McRobbie and regularly met all the 53rd & 3rd and DDT bands. However, nothing that was happening there was inspiring me to get involved. I liked loud, fast and furious but also melodic. Sandy liked what we did so did include us on the DDT label, and that was a vital first step for us.

There wasn't much around in Scotland, or across the UK really, that I felt like I related to. We were lucky that European audiences were more into what we did. We also had a decent core of support in and around London. I think what's often overlooked is how much being from the Highlands made us seem a bit different to our peers in the Central Belt. It also took me quite a while to understand the impact of Edinburgh and Glasgow's private schools on the music scene in Scotland. Growing up in Inverness it never occurred to me that people you knew didn't just go to the same school as everyone else. It's such an Edinburgh thing, and Glasgow too but maybe to a lesser extent. So I think a combination of geography and naivety around background and class both contributed to us deciding to do our own thing. Also, fundamentally, compared to strumming some twee pop songs, being in a hardcore band intent on playing faster and louder than anyone else was fun as fuck.

The US Underground was a huge influence on the band, and this distanced The Cataran from their Edinburgh contemporaries at the time. But, alongside The Dog Faced Hermans, The Cateran were hugely important to the development of Glasgow's 'other Underground scene'.

Cameron Fraser (vocals/guitar, The Cateran): For me, it was US punk. I'd always liked the usual punk stuff: Clash, Ramones, etc., but I think liked less obvious stuff too, Television and Pete Ubu spring to mind and Josef K too. Hüsker Dü were an early influence too but less so than Dinosaur Jr, fIREHOSE or Squirrel Bait. And anyone on SST or Homestead Records. But mainly American punk or hardcore bands. I think being up in Inverness meant it was as easy to relate to bands from the American Midwest as it was to London, Manchester or even Glasgow bands. . . they all felt like they were a world away.

One of the best-known bands on US indie record label SST was Black Flag. (Bizarrely, Craig and Charlie Reid of The Proclaimers had an earlier but completely unconnected band of the same name.) The Reid brothers' later punk band, Reasons for Emotion, which featured and was managed by Kai Davidson, was also briefly associated with The Cateran.

Andy Milne (drums, The Cateran): We did a few gigs with Craig and Charlie Reid at this point. They had been in a band with Kai and the two of them used to come with us in our van and open for us sometimes. Which sounds an odd combination, but it really did work.

The earlier incarnation of the band changed, and they progressed in the direction of the US Underground.

Andy Milne (drums, The Cateran): On the first album, *Little Circles,* I played very straightforward drum parts to sort of keep out of the way of the other guys. When Sandy decided to leave in late summer 1987 we rethought what we were doing. I'd been introduced to 'Skag Heaven' by Squirrel Bait – by Cameron I think – and liked their full-on drumming, which got in everybody's way but sounded really exciting. So I tried that out live and on the second album, *Bite Deeper.* The guys were very encouraging to me regarding that approach. And it was a bit *Kick Out The Jams,* in my head, at least.

The new direction led to The Cataran becoming heavily involved with Nirvana, eventually leading to a full tour with them.

Cameron Fraser (vocals/guitar, The Cateran): I was working at Fast Forward when I bought the first batch of Nirvana 7-inch singles from Calvin Johnson at K Records. I loved it and sent them out to people like Keith Cameron, Alastair McKay and our agent, Russell Warby. Russell loved them too and set up that first tour with Tad. Russell has said to me that receiving that single completely changed his life. I suppose he's right. I can't give you any great insight from back then. I thought they were pretty good, but to me they were a bit too poppy, and as far as

I was concerned, weren't anywhere near as good as Squirrel Bait, Dinosaur Jr, fIREHOSE, Mudhoney, etc. So, honestly, I wasn't thinking these guys are going to change the face of music. So what did I know?

CHAPTER TWO

DIY Veganism

Enter Craig Tannock

Venue owner and entrepreneur, Craig Tannock, is one of the most important figures in Glasgow's music history and without him this book may not have been written. To understand the nineties Glasgow music scene requires an understanding of the context in which the city found itself during the late eighties. In order to present this accurately I think it is necessary to include this extended interview with Craig. The series of venues he owned and offered to young musicians is absolutely fundamental to this story and the success of the nineties scene in Glasgow, most especially the 13th Note venue, famously home to the Kazoo Club.

Craig's interview begins with a discussion of 'pay-to-play', a self-explanatory policy promoted by many other venues. It was the antithesis of what Craig believed was necessary for a healthy industry and was seen by aspiring musicians as a roadblock to performing.

Craig Tannock (Glasgow venue owner): I think pay-to-play largely came out of the fact that some of the places you could play didn't have a love of music at the heart of it. Very often they were pubs who'd have a meeting in the summer and they'd say, how are we going to get the place busier? And someone says I know, so-and-so had a band on and the place was busy, so let's get bands on. It's all from the point of view of getting money in the till. If that's the whole idea behind pubs starting to do gigs, then it's not going to be band-centred in any way. Generally these people are business people so they look at it as another kind of business transaction. From that perspective you can see the logic, because it minimises the risk and investment of the venue. Really, it's more than just pay-to-play, it's unpaid labour as well. Because they're getting the band or bands who are playing to basically promote their place.

Say there was a basic cost for the pub to put on the gig – whether that's PA hire or whatever – one way Pay to Play would work would be to give the band some tickets for them to sell to their pals, and then they keep anything over and above the cost. Completely putting the onus on the band to make the night a success, and not really doing much as a venue to promote it. There wasn't one pay-to-play model; it was more of a general approach, which is about not really investing in live music, more just getting more punters into your pub in an economically safe way.

That's how I always saw it. We evolved into what we did from a completely opposite direction.

Craig's epiphany had started with his own attempts to become a musician and later, band manager.

Craig Tannock (Glasgow venue owner): I've always been that wee guy in a band, just trying to get gigs. In a bar venue culture, which was most of the case in Scotland at the time, bar venues that had anybody who was actually interested were few and far between. And you tended to play these places a lot.

I was in bands, player-managing my own band in '84, '85 in Glasgow. We were a five-piece originally and then the drummer went down to Manchester, so we were a four-piece with a drum machine. Two of us were long-term unemployed, and the other two were at the start of careers. Me and Lachlan McQuarrie, who were the unemployed members, used to rehearse in a really lovely studio called the Hellfire Club. [It was run by] David Henderson, a wonderful man, and a generally unsung guy. I don't think he even realises how important he was for the scene. One thing I always felt about the Glasgow eighties scene was that it was very macho. It was all leather jackets and very male, very testosterone, just unpleasant from my perspective.

Eventually we were thinking of forming the band into a co-op, and started talking to the SCDC, the Scottish Co-op Development Committee, about doing that. It didn't work out but we then realised maybe we could get some funding – in those days, you could actually get funding to do stuff: things like the Enterprise Allowance Scheme, which I managed to get on twice. We thought of getting our own studio, primarily as a resource for the band to use, but it would also give something for me and Lachlan to do that wasn't just being on the dole. We could go onto the Enterprise Allowance Scheme and hopefully, not make loads of money but make enough money to live on by having a studio. It was a very sweet, naive idea because we had no concept of what work would be involved in doing such a thing. Also Lachlan and I were the last people that anybody who knew us thought would even remotely get anything like that together! We were natural deadbeats, but proud of it as well.

The Enterprise Allowance Scheme allowed Craig to set up a hugely important part of Glasgow's music infrastructure, Tower Studios, a low-cost recording facility within the city. This would be the first of Craig's venues – and it was where many of the later stars of this story would first record.

Tower Studios was a place that was affordable and, most importantly, it set the template for the ethical and philanthropic aspects that weren't just a characteristic of future venues but also trickled down to the musicians who would themselves carry on that philosophy.

Craig Tannock (Glasgow venue owner): We opened Tower in March '87. Up to that point, I have to say that even though I'd been at university and whatnot, I'd had a very gentle, relaxed life. I'd spent most of my time either doing music stuff, which was just fun, or shopping for nice food. I went veggie in 1980 and I went vegan in '82. Veganism and vegan food became a passion as well.

My whole life changed in five minutes at St Andrews University in October 1980. I'd had a dog, who had sadly passed by then. I always liked animals but I'd never seriously thought about how our culture exploits animals. It hadn't hit me. I was sitting in a psychology lab, and we were about to do an experiment. (A quick thing to say is that up to that point, I don't think I'd ever made a proper significant decision in my life. I just sailed through things. The only reason I went to St Andrews was, I was desperate to leave Greenock. I ended up doing first and second year psychology in the one year, to try and stay on an honours potential course.) They brought out a piece of paper which described what the experiment was going to be. It was about a psychological process called imprinting. One of the things it described is how when young chicks when they're are born they get imprinted normally, on their mother. Supposedly the reason for this is because when the chicks (particularly chickens and hens) are born, they're totally precocious. Out the shell, like, hey what's happening – they're ready to go. The exact opposite of humans. So obviously it's important to have this process so that they bond instantly with their mother. That's why you'll see whole crowds of them just following their mother around, because they just have to. It keeps them safe, and it helps their mother keep them safe.

The experiment was to take an object, any object – it could have been a glass – and introduce the glass into the box and see if you can imprint the chick on the glass. The way to show if you'd successfully done this or not was to now and again remove the glass, put the glass back in, remove it again, and use the frequency of the chick's distress calls to establish whether you had imprinted the chick on the glass. You were given numbers, so if the stress calls reached a certain frequency – a number of calls per 30 seconds or whatever – then you had successfully imprinted the chick on the glass. And once you had successfully imprinted the chick on Object A, then you'd take that away and pick another object, maybe a small plastic brick or something. You'd try to see if you could change the imprinting from the glass to this next object using the same process. Once you've successfully done the second one, you'd then see how far you can go, see how many different objects you can have the chick imprinted on.

The first paragraph of the instructions described what imprinting was. It said we were going to be supplied with a tray, with edges, and a whole bunch of different random items. We were also going to be given a very recently hatched male chick from a local farm.

And then there was just one sentence at the very end that explained that there'll be a natural end to the experiment because there will come a point – I always get really emotional when I talk about this – there will come a point where you can no longer distinguish the frequency of the chick's distress calls related to the removing of the item, over and above the background level of distress calls. I read that, and I'm sitting in a lab in St Andrews University. And for the very first time in my life I thought, for fuck's sake! This is fucking evil. This is wrong. What the fuck is going on? So I stood up, walked out, I thrust the paper at the professor and said, 'No way'. And I walked out.

That started everything. I just opened my eyes and looked into absolutely everything. I looked at what the university were doing in general. Within a couple of weeks I started an anti-vivisection group; made myself extremely 'popular' in the department, and in the university in general. They were very sensitive because they'd had a big problem, all over the tabloid press two years before, with primate experiments. And also some postgraduate students had done some research on whether killing birds is innate in kittens or not by putting kittens and small birds in the same place to see what would happen. After a few weeks I was arguing vociferously with anybody who'd listen about what we did to animals, and then eventually I realised, fuck, I'm eating them. I looked more at how they get to our plate, so within two months I went veggie.

I didn't know about veganism, I didn't even know it was an option then. It was only about a year and a half later that I overheard the term being used by somebody in a derogatory way. I found out what it was. I found out how the dairy industry and the meat industry are basically two sides of the one coin, and there's all sorts of reasons why that's the reality. Once I found that out, I had no choice. It wasn't like going veggie was a decision for me. I just had no choice. I was the last person that would have gone veggie, I absolutely loved my typical west of Scotland diet. I didn't eat much in the way of vegetables, it was just any sort of meat, fried potatoes, bit of fish, eggs, cheese, I loved it all. I'm also not naturally a disciplined person. The only way for me to make changes is to have no choice but to do it. That's how I see it.

Tower Studios was born with a fundamental principle behind it that embraced veganism, respect and co-operation. And to this day, all of Craig's venues have been strictly vegan.

Craig Tannock (Glasgow venue owner): We didn't really set up Tower with a big agenda, as to the vibe. It was me and Lachlan and also somebody we met through our former drummer in the band, David Garrett. We became a three piece – a three-person workers' co-op. We worked on it for two years, and got it open. Out of the three of us I think I was maybe the only one that had quite a shock realising how much work it was actually going to be. But I totally loved it. Opening a studio was another thing that changed my life because up to then I'd been a bit of a dreamer. Always having lots and lots of ideas, never quite having the confidence to realise you could actually do them. We opened the studio and started getting bands in rehearsing. It became a recording studio as well but that was a few months later. The thing that changed for me was when you picked up the phone or you phoned somebody and said, 'It's Craig from Tower Studios' – something clicked in my brain. All of a sudden there was a vehicle that I was part of that was bigger. I wasn't just the wee guy in a band, phoning up saying, 'Hey it's Craig from (my band) News from Nowhere, can I have a gig?' Somehow I felt the extra respect that you could get from whoever it was you were talking to, just because you're calling from a studio, rather than just a wee band. Slowly, ideas came and I just started doing them. And they worked. It was a wonderful change in my life.

Tower proved to be a small success in the late eighties but it was its relocation and an unfortunate event that would cement its soon-to-be significant impact.

Craig Tannock (Glasgow venue owner): We moved location because the rent was going to double. We started looking for somewhere to move to and there was a place which had opened up in 1988 and was called The Shelter (now The Flying Duck). It'd been opened by a guy called Larry Diamond, the brother of Jim Diamond the singer. Larry was an architect, and him and an accountant from Rutherglen opened it up together. What they did was pretty good but they made a really bad mistake. They opened up a café-bar venue, three rehearsal rooms, a duplicating facility and they had an office. They also had a lot of loft space at the back of the building, which eventually they were going to develop into a recording studio. They did a huge PR job for the launch of it. Danny Wilson played the opening. They announced to Glasgow that this was now going to be the centre of the grassroots music scene. And it wasn't! You can't just tell Glasgow what is, or what isn't. . . It just flopped. There was a lot of razzamatazz, a lot of money. The place itself was cool, but it flopped. We were looking for somewhere to move the studio to in '91. It had been closed for a while and the accountant, who'd kind of been left holding the baby, tried opening up again in the summer of that year. They just called it by the address: 7 Renfrew Court. I went to see a gig there so I knew about it. But I also knew they still hadn't done anything with their back space.

We started talking to this accounting guy about moving our studio to the back space. As we started talking to him we got more of a sense that he was going to be out of business again pretty soon, so we put it to him that he let us take on the whole thing. It took a while to persuade him because we'd not got a track record, no money to pay for a premium or anything like that. I think he was probably desperate. He said he'd give us a year to see how it went. We got in there, I think it was Sunday 24 November 1991, and we opened the next day. Almost instantly we got the rehearsal rooms filled. They'd been nowhere near full. And then we were just piling in the gigs. We changed up the menu – not overnight because there was still lots of stock and also I was the only vegan or even veggie on our general team, so I didn't have the confidence to say we were going veggie or vegan.

That was all going fantastic, the brewers were very happy, we tripled the barrelage. We were getting to grips with how to run the place better, looking forward to the autumn when the students came back and the touring bands came back. We had a good programme in the place, global acts as well, plus local bands obviously. And then there was a major fire, at the end of August, in one of the artist's studios in the buildings above. We were completely destroyed by the water damage.

Just before the fire, things were going well and we thought there was opportunity for gain and benefits of scale. One of the places we'd run the Devil Disco in was a place in Glassford Street called Traders. It was going through a very rocky time, changing management and just not going anywhere. I had a similar conversation with the owner there, about us taking over. Again it took a while to persuade them – we weren't making any money up front. He did charge a premium that we had to pay back over a couple of years. The original idea was for it to be more of a folky place, and that was partly because the guy helping us with the bar management was more of a folky guy. It had taken a while to do the work there and we'd opened just a few weeks before the fire. The folk thing wasn't working and effectively we moved what was The Apollo down to Glassford Street. We gave it a new name, and that name was the 13th Note. I think that was 1 December 1992, the 13th Note launch.

The 13th Note was the central hub where this story really begins. Glasgow now had an artist-led recording studio, a vegan café and a venue willing to break the pay-to-play cartel. It also had a number of bands who operated on similar principles and would prove to be a significant and important influence.

CHAPTER THREE

Splash Two

dawson, Stretchheads, Badgewearer, Glue

Jer Reid (guitar/vocals, dawson): dawson's first gig was upstairs at 46 West George St in 1988. Me, Tom (Graham Thomson) and Ali (Begbie) played seven songs in eleven minutes. We know it was short because a pal went for a piss when we were coming on and by the time he was back we had finished. It made a lot of sense that our first gig was at 46 West because in the downstairs room me and Ali had gone to Splash One Happening gigs there, seeing fIREHOSE, Sonic Youth, The Jesus and Mary Chain, 23 Skidoo and then a bit later we saw the Ron Johnson bands that were a big influence – excitement.

Richie Dempsey (drums, Stretchheads later XXX): Me, Andy and Mac (Stevie Dreads) had all been playing in daft wee bands in Erskine in 1985 under the guises of Mutant X, The Marsoupeals (actual spelling – seriously) and Spongé (pronounced spong-gay). Graham from Ganger and Craig McNally from Dewy Lester and the 603 were also in Spongé. We were all school pals that happened to be the only ones in our school that were into the same kinda music. Bogshed, Membranes, The Fall, Mary Chain etc.

Yep, we were bored in Erskine. We played a disastrous gig at the Park Mains High School youth wing on Friday night in 1986. It was sooooo bad. We hired a PA from a local guy. He just set it up and left it up to us to make it work. Fuck sake. . . We made early Mary Chain gigs sound like Rush in comparison. The saving grace of that night was the support band, City Gents. Some local guy called Stevie Jackson on guitar. Chances are he may have moved on to better things since then! Round about March 1986, we hooked up with Phil Eaglesham. Phil was actually at that gig that night, wearing a 'stookie'. He knew Andy and only lived down the road. We all lived about five minutes' walk from each other in fact. Pretty sure it was the first time I met him, although it was very brief. I had to pack up the PA for the guy to come and collect. He had the best goth hairdo. His hair was fucking huge. I was pretty jealous of that. Phil broadened our musical horizons with his fucking mental record collection. Throbbing Gristle, PTV, Tools You Can Trust, SPK, Pop Group etc. were all new to us. We'd be fed all this insane industrial stuff.

Phil Eaglesham (vocals, Stretchheads): We all lived in Erskine, I'd dropped out of uni, split up with my girlfriend and was on the dole. We had a mutual friend in Andy's big sister who was the year below me at school (with Dougie Vipond). There was a gig at the local community centre, I swung by and these wee Jesus and Mary guys had hoovers up against their guitars and amps: it was hilarious – noise and pisstake. I'd also spotted them at the Splash One, Richie in particular, with his ghetto blaster, he used to bootleg gigs. Graham Gavin/Jas was another mutual friend through his big sister who was in my year at school. We just started hanging out in Erskine, there was NOTHING happening, but I was really into all sorts of weird music and art and cinema (thanks to my ex-girlfriend) and we started jamming in Richie's bedroom, I think maybe Andy's garage once? Then shortly after, I'd started my nurse training in Paisley, so we were going through there to rehearse at Sunset studios. We did a terrible *C86*-ish demo under the name Spongé, it's just awful. The sheer embarrassment of that, then seeing Dog Faced Hermans, going to FSD and seeing them in the BBC Studio, the Splash and Fat Pig shows at Daddy Warbucks – we gelled pretty quickly as a three-piece (Andy had moved to Glasgow by then) and called ourselves Gewalt after the DAF song and played one show in Bennetts, essentially forming to put on the Dog Faced Hermans there. It went down so well and Andy wanted back into the band and provided a Glasgow base, Dog Faced Hermans asked us to play again and by then we'd agreed a new name as Stretchheads.

The Stretchheads

Paul Kearney (Guided Missile Records): I can't remember exactly how I discovered Badgewearer and dawson but I think it was a pal of mine I shared a house with called Dave Radford. We had bonded over a shared love of jerky guitar eighties 'John Peel bands' like Bogshed and bIG*fLAME and I seem to remember Dave lent me Badgewearer's *FTQ* album and dawson's *How to Follow*. I had already started the Guided Missile label and released a single by a band in Amsterdam named Donkey (whose bass player had been in another band I loved, Dandelion Adventure). Once I heard Badgewearer I knew I wanted to release stuff by them too.

These lads knew Donkey already. Along with Stretchheads, Dog Faced Hermans, The Ex, Whirling Pig Dervish and others there definitely was a 'scene' – or a 'movement' if that doesn't sound too wank. I don't know what it was called but you'd see the same people at all these bands' gigs.

Most of these gigs were promoted by the Glasgow Music Collective.

CHAPTER FOUR

The Glasgow Music Collective

The GMC was formed as a result of disappointment at the lack of venues willing to promote local bands, and a distrust of venue promoters.

Dawson / Glasgow Music Collective poster

Richie Dempsey (drums, Stretchheads; later dawson/Fenn): The GMC was formed after a conversation between me and Jer one day in RAT Records, a record shop in town where I used to work. I was friends with the Dog Faced Hermans, who were heavily involved with the Edinburgh Musicians Collective. They had put on the Stretchheads quite a few times that year (1987, I think).

Jer Reid (guitar/vocals, dawson): Glasgow Music Collective was originally started by Joyce Monaghan of We Are The Men/Tower Studios, Jim Kavanagh of Egg Records and me but I was the only starting member who stayed until we put on our first gig. As part of the Glasgow Music Collective I put [dutch band] The Ex on (with dawson on the bill). I think it was the first time they came to Scotland and it was a night so full of possibility, connection and fun that it felt like a 'the time before and the time after' event.

Phil Eaglesham (vocals, Stretchheads): It was through The Ex's camaraderie with the Dog Faced Hermans, particularly, and Donna and The Kebabs that the Dog Faced Hermans had started going over to Europe. That breadcrumb trail to Holland is really significant for a lot of our bands and our comrades: it showed a completely different way of going about doing your music, DIY collectivism. And so many of our bands went over. Badgewearer went over quite early doors, I think dawson went over to stay with The Ex and they would sort out a tour for you basically, they would start you out with a 15-day squat tour of Holland, Belgium, sometimes straying into Germany.

Richie Dempsey (drums, Stretchheads; later dawson/Fenn): We decided it would be a good idea to round up a bunch of the bands we knew and find out if they were interested in forming a collective, helping out putting on shows. There were loads of bands that were up for it so it looked like it was going to happen. Jer pretty much took the bull by the horns and was a real driving force behind it from that point.

Jer Reid (guitar/vocals, dawson): The Glasgow Music Collective started out with various intentions – to open rehearsal space and maybe start a collective record label but it ended up being a collective putting on gigs, starting in 1990. We often mixed bills, so that there was a variety of types of music – noisy guitar music with free jazz, more melodic guitar bands with noisier US touring bands and occasionally putting on hip-hop and bands like Nyah Fearties. We put on a lot of touring bands and paid them and fed them and put them up so there was some money involved but the focus was on making connections with each other and the music. The GMC was a spoke in the wheel of the non-profit music support networks that were all over the UK and Europe and USA. There was more at stake than just the music – as important as that was – an ethos of doing things collectively, without bosses, a culture not based around money or career but focused on helping each other out. For me it was about building a culture that set itself apart from capitalism and where we built connections, friendships and ideas that could sustain and support us in managing living in capitalism.

Angus McPhee (bass, Glue): The GMC really ended up being a wee organisation to help you be responsible for your own entertainment. The 'promoter' side of things maybe strayed away a bit from the original intention of allowing bands/musicians to do stuff that it was hard to do all by yourself. I think it was originally more about self-help, sharing equipment, finding places to play, which wasn't so easy back then, generally helping each other out just like many another collective.

Richie Dempsey (drums, Stretchheads; later dawson/Fenn): The venues the GMC used were Traders in Glassford Street and a cool wee place called the Clyde Cavern, next to Calton Place railway arches, on the south side of the river, a hideous-sounding room made of metal, stone and ceramic floor tiles. That's where the first GMC gig was. Blyth Power, We Are the Men and Badgewearer. Ironically, Jer and I missed it as we were on tour with dawson. I think we were actually doing a Peel session that day.

Annie Spandex (guitar, Lung Leg): The Glasgow Music Collective was a bit more of the hardcore side of the music. I lived in the Gorbals and went to the Barras every Sunday and there was a really good second-hand record stall and a guy who sold bootlegs, from the Barras basically. So if you went to a gig at the Barrowlands you'd get your bootleg there eventually. I migrated to working on the stall. . . I went to Splash One where you'd see The Pastels and that kind of stuff. The Music Collective formed after that. It was more the hard edge of stuff, more male, I guess. . . I was always fascinated with The Raincoats and a couple of girls were at the stall and they were looking for a violinist for their all-girl punk band. They'd lost a violinist so I joined them and they were called We Are the Men and they were part of the GMC scene.

Annie briefly joined We Are the Men, which also featured Joyce Monaghan who had been involved with both Tower and GMC.

The collective was proving very successful, inspiring a series of new bands to form in its wake.

Annie Spandex (guitar, Lung Leg): So you've got things like dawson. All that stuff that came out of the music collective and again it was DIY, putting on gigs before 13th Note existed. They'd put a gig on in a restaurant, there was a place down at the Clydeside, which is now a big Asian restaurant, and they put gigs on for people coming up – Leeds bands, whatever. So it kind of started from there and I was in that band and then joined another band with Jane (Mckeown, Lung Leg) at the same time, called Snagglepuss. A bit more hardcore, and we got our first gigs and all that through the music collective.

Richie Dempsey (drums, Stretchheads; later dawson/Fenn): The GMC grew arms and legs and more people got involved long after I took a back seat. To be honest, I booked my back seat pretty early on so I can't take any credit for any of the shows they put on. I was just happy enough to help plant the seed.

Jer Reid (guitar/vocals, dawson): Our bills often reflected the diversity of aesthetics and subcultures that co-existed and cross-pollinated in Glasgow at the time. We knew Richie from the mighty Stretchheads and he had been at a lot of the 46 West gigs

Richie Dempsey (drums, Stretchheads; later dawson/Fenn): I loved dawson and I'm not going to lie that I was also very jealous of them as well. I met Jer in RAT Records (before I worked there) and he handed me a demo. I took it home, listened to it and immediately want to join them. I was in the Stretchheads at the time but I honestly couldn't see past what dawson were doing. Loved it. Went to see them at Pharoes in Great Western

Road one night. The place was packed and five minutes before they were due to go on, there was a power cut! So, the gig was pulled. But, I met tons of brilliant people that night. During a sort of drunken conversation in the pub a few months later, I told Jer that if their drummer was ever to leave, to gimme a call. I'm glad he remembered.

CHAPTER FIVE

Another Edinburgh

Tom Worthington: Hee Haw, Starstruck and Bosque Records

In the late 1980s Edinburgh music scene, Tom Worthington began playing in bands that would quietly influence a new wave of Scottish DIY music. From his early group Hee Haw to his founding of Bosque Records and his later move to Glasgow, Tom's story follows a familiar path for independent musicians in that period: enthusiasm, struggle, and a stubborn refusal to wait for anyone else's permission.

Tom Worthington (Hee Haw, Starstruck, Bosque Records): I'm from Moray, up north, and for me The Cateran were the beacons. They showed that you could do punk rock on your own terms – appreciate where you come from while ripping the piss out of it.

Those mid-eighties Scottish punk bands gave Tom a sense that independence was possible. By the late eighties he had moved to Edinburgh, where Hee Haw began to take shape among friends connected through art school, small gigs and record shops. The atmosphere was still charged with the spirit of the late-seventies post-punk energy, but the infrastructure that supported new bands brought in with Fast Forward had started to fade. C86 *had moved on, dance culture was emerging but there were still groups politically charged with that original punk philosophy of anarchy, and exchanging ideas and attitude.*

Tom Worthington (Hee Haw, Starstruck, Bosque Records): Around that same time, Dog Faced Hermans were blazing a path too. Those near-contemporaries were getting their music into the right hands around the world. It was a revelation: you could connect globally from here.

Hee Haw (Tom Worthington and Mark Gibbons) followed that example. Rather than chase a deal, they decided to make and release their own records. The first step was to come up with a name: Bosque Records. It wasn't yet a formal label, more a practical idea to get their songs pressed and circulating.

Tom Worthington (Hee Haw, Starstruck, Bosque Records): Hee Haw started because the obvious thing was to put the records out ourselves. We set up Bosque Records as a simple vehicle – box up the 7-inches, send them out, write the letters, answer the letters back.

Their first small release, 'Splash Your Head', gained some traction. John Peel played it, and the band began performing more regularly around Edinburgh and beyond. But like many groups of that time the excitement of making a record didn't translate into longevity.

Tom Worthington (Hee Haw, Starstruck, Bosque Records): John Peel played it and we got some gigs, but we were never that stable as a band. Everyone had other things on, and the label quietly outlived the band.

Hee Haw's connection with Sandy McLean's Fast Forward distribution network seemed promising, but that relationship also showed the limits of outside advice for a small DIY group.

Tom Worthington (Hee Haw, Starstruck, Bosque Records): Fast Forward were helpful up to a point, but we got terrible advice. We were talked out of two 7-inches in favour of a 12-inch EP – nonsense for a band at our level. They [Fast Forward] seemed together in a sea of untogetherness, but it didn't fit how we worked.

As Hee Haw came to an end, Tom and bandmate Mark started a new project called Starstruck. The emphasis shifted from live shows to recording, often on basic equipment in flats and shared spaces. Around this time, Tom became involved in the international cassette-trading network, which linked small musicians and experimental artists around the world.

Tom Worthington (Hee Haw, Starstruck, Bosque Records): The cassette was our natural habitat. You'd hear about a great tape, write an actual letter, and two weeks later Kramer or Daniel Johnston or Eugene Chadbourne would write back. Connections bloomed if you were doing it for the right reasons and you weren't an arse.

Those exchanges were about more than swapping music. They gave people a sense of community across countries, long before email or social media. It confirmed Tom's belief that he didn't need anyone's approval to keep releasing music.

Tom Worthington (Hee Haw, Starstruck, Bosque Records): We tried to push forward technically – Mark was early into computing – and with Saskia Holling we ran an internet café on Bread Street. Total fiasco. Another reason to leave Edinburgh – it destroyed us financially and emotionally.

Bosque would begin to look west for their next move as there was soon to be a monumental shift of energy.

CHAPTER SIX

Veganism Meets DIY 2

The Blisters and Me, Hubby & Thom

Many budding musicians were completely unaware of the existence of the Glasgow Music Collective scene. One of these bands was The Blisters, which would share members with a similarly minded group, Me, Hubby & Thom. They were both based in Bearsden, a small suburb of Glasgow. This story goes back to before their stewardship of the Kazoo Club, and (Blisters singer) Alex Kapranos' time in the Scottish Highlands.

Alex Kapranos (guitar/vocals, The Blisters later Franz Ferdinand): I got a job as a dishwasher in Fort William. And one day one of the chefs didn't turn up. The head chef threw me this guy's dirty whites and said, right you're a chef now. I started cheffing up there in a place called MacTavish's Kitchens. I won't go into the full story of that but one of the waitresses there was a girl from Bearsden who lived pretty close to where I was staying, called Katie Falls.

We started going out with each other, and then she said her brother was a drummer. He was still at school and I was like, me and my pal Glen are getting a band together, do you think your brother might be up for it? And she was like, oh yeah sure, I'll introduce you. So we start playing with Thom, and it was particularly appealing because Katie's dad had some big job; I think he was like, governor of the Bank of England in Scotland, if that's a thing? It was something to do with the Bank of England, like the Bank of England representative in Scotland. And as part of the job they gave him this massive house. The basement of that house was Thom's practice space. And it was amazing for us. We suddenly had this place where we could just practice. And Thom played with these other people. He played with two other bands. And I got to know them as well.

RM Hubbert (Hubby) (guitar/vocals, Me, Hubby & Thom): In my first real band, Me, Hubby & Thom – Thom was the drummer. His parents had a big house in Bearsden with a basement where we would rehearse. Thom was also in The Blisters. He was also in a band called Tarot Marrow, who turned into The Fortune Cookies, who are relevant to El Hombre's history because Ben from El Hombre was in that band. It's all very incestuous. I met Alex and Glen, the bass player in The Blisters, through Thom because we were all hanging out in that basement.

Alex Kapranos (guitar/vocals, The Blisters; later Franz Ferdinand): One of the bands Thom played in was another three-piece called Me, Hubby & Thom. And that was Hubby who ended up becoming RM Hubbert. I became particularly good friends with Hubby actually. I really hit it off with Hubby, and Gary who played bass, so there'd been that connection with these guys at that particular point; we'd hang out together a little bit in this basement. Then we wanted to play gigs, and we booked a gig. First gig I ever played was supposed to be at Nice N Sleazy. There was a guy called Hugh Reed. Hugh Reed was the original booker at Nice N Sleazy. I brought down a demo tape that me and the other guys, The Blisters, had made and he was like, oh this is amazing, this is great, I love it. And he booked it. We turned up at this gig at Nice N Sleazy. Hugh Reed was nowhere to be seen. He'd been fired, and this guy called Mig had taken over. Mig now booked the bands.

Mig says, oh listen, Hugh got the sack. I booked another band for tonight. I'm sorry you can't play. We didn't play and the guys from Tarot Marrow went to King Tut's. They'd booked King Tut's. It was horrible, I hated the experience. At that time in the early nineties it was a pay-to-play-type thing. You had to give a venue a certain amount of money to book it. I get it from the venue's perspective, you can't just give some unknown band a gig and pay the staff and just lose money. I guess that's their perspective. From our perspective, it was a horrible, horrible position to be in. Finding money to put up front to play your gig. It was a bit weird; it felt weird to us and it had a big impact on my approach to booking bands after that.

Craig Tannock's new venues were opening at the same time as the Glasgow Music Collective was beginning, and together they were the anthesis of what had come before. They were responsible for creating an infrastructure in Glasgow that prepared it for a new generation.

The Apollo Café and the 13th Note: New beginnings for Glasgow

Glasgow's new generation of indie outsiders were drawn like moths to Craig Tannock's chain of venues (which included the Apollo Café and The Bogle Stone). The Glasgow Music Collective had been putting on a lot of gigs at Craig's operations, breaking the pay-to-play rule that had previously been the norm. Craig's next venue was soon to host the night that would change Glasgow's indie music scene forever.

Jer Reid (guitar/vocals, dawson): Finally, there was a place that bands could play where it was run by people who weren't low-level gangsters or folks who saw you as an annoyance that had to be put up with to get bar takings. For the first time ever there was a place you could play where the people would enthusiastically support you in whatever way they could.

RM Hubbert (Hubby) (guitar/vocals, Me, Hubby & Thom): I was young, I shouldn't have been in the Apollo, I must have been about 15 or 16 when I was sneaking into those gigs. I definitely shouldn't have been there. I remember that my first band, Me, Hubby & Thom, handed in our first demo to the Apollo, like, two days before it burned down or something. I remember thinking it was not a great sign for my burgeoning music career.

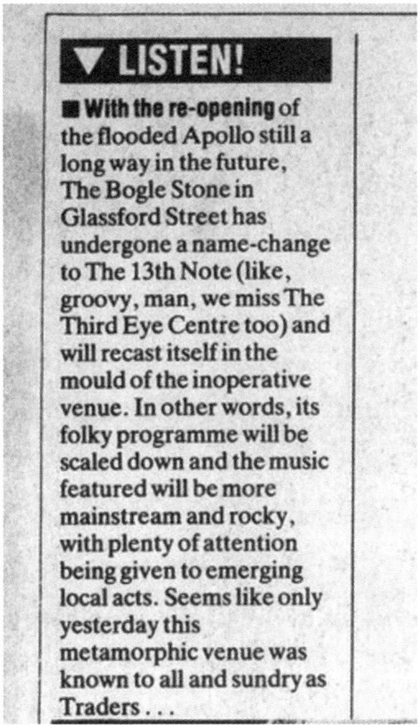

▼ LISTEN!

■ With the re-opening of the flooded Apollo still a long way in the future, The Bogle Stone in Glassford Street has undergone a name-change to The 13th Note (like, groovy, man, we miss The Third Eye Centre too) and will recast itself in the mould of the inoperative venue. In other words, its folky programme will be scaled down and the music featured will be more mainstream and rocky, with plenty of attention being given to emerging local acts. Seems like only yesterday this metamorphic venue was known to all and sundry as Traders . . .

The List advert for the Kazoo Club

RM Hubbert (Hubby) (guitar/vocals, Me, Hubby & Thom): The Blisters had gotten a gig. . . at this time in Glasgow, it's important to know there wasn't really anywhere doing tiny gigs for bands that weren't playing covers, or blues. It was all pub gigs, or Barrowlands. There were medium-sized venues and people like Glasgow Music Collective and Splash One were doing stuff but that was just far away from us. We didn't know how to access that. I don't know how Alex heard about it but he got a gig at The Bogle Stone, at the Kazoo Club, on a Tuesday night. It was run by a guy called Jim Byrne, who was in a band called 'The Hemmingways.

The Kazoo Club

The flooding of The Apollo Café, one of Craig Tannock's other venues (not to be confused with the infamous 1970s large venue of the same name) created a chain of events that heralded a new era in Glasgow's music. In late 1992, the building across the road from the Apollo, The Bogle Stone, changed its name to The 13th Note. The 13th Note was a place for bands to play every night, free of the constraints of pay-to-play. Jim and Pat Byrne ran a night there called the Kazoo Club, which was eventually taken over by Alex Kapranos and RM Hubbert. It would further galvanise this new Glasgow scene.

Jim Byrne (founder, Kazoo Club; musician): Along with Pat [Byrne], we started a live music club called the Kazoo Club. This was in the basement of what became the 13th Note in Glassford Street in Glasgow city centre. We started it so that there would be a regular place to play for my band (the dying days of a band I had called The Hemingways), but after the very first gig Bruce our drummer said he was never going to play it again because it was too smoky and it wouldn't be good for his health. I was very upset about this at the time, as the club was part of my grand plan to make the band successful. We had big 'artistic' ideas, mixing artists with musicians. The idea was to have live music and live painting on the walls. Sadly the artistic aspect only lasted about a month as the more middle-class artist types didn't mix well with the more working-class musicians. The art aspect drifted away, leaving it as a live music venture.

The opening night of the Kazoo Club, featuring Dexter Slim (aka The Hemingways)

Pat Byrne (founder, Kazoo Club): Craig [Tannock] had a small recording studio in Glasgow (Tower) and also managed some bands. This included Jim's band Dexter Slim and the Pickups. Alex [Kapranos] came along looking for somewhere to play. Alex had his first gig at the Kazoo with his band The Blisters.

Alex Kapranos (guitar/vocals, The Blisters; later Franz Ferdinand): Jim used to play in a band called The Hemingways and I saw a notice somewhere saying: 'Bands wanted to play, music and art jam'. That's the way he was imagining it in the beginning, a music and art jam. We were like, great, and I gave Jim a call and he said, yeah come down, come down, it'll be great. It was in this place called The Bogle Stone. And The Bogle Stone was at 90 Glassford Street. We went down, really excited. Jim's band The Hemingways played, and we played. It was literally just us and a couple of our pals. I don't think we'd even told anybody about it – I think we played to pretty much an empty room. Jim seemed kind of mortified, he was really apologetic. He said it's just the club starting off, we'll get it going. And we were like, fuck no, this is amazing. We're getting to play and nobody's telling us to stop. We're getting to use microphones and a PA for free. We love this, can we come back and do it again? I was 19 and totally full of enthusiasm. And Jim was like, oh really you want to come back? Aye, fucking right! And I was like, listen, have you got any other bands booked? And he said, well no, nobody's really come back to us yet. And I said, listen there's a couple of bands that I know, could I invite them down?

RM Hubbert (Hubby) (guitar/vocals, Me, Hubby & Thom): Jim [Byrne] said I don't want to do this any more, do you want to do it? At which point we were kind of sitting there going, aye, aye. Actually it might not have been the first night, it might have been a few nights in. Very early on anyway. I remember The Blisters played, and then the next week Me, Hubby & Thom did our first show.

Alex Kapranos (guitar/vocals, The Blisters; later Franz Ferdinand): So the next week Me, Hubby & Thom came down and we had a great time, we played for each other. And maybe at that one, a few more of our friends had come down. We started hanging about and thought of other bands we knew. Word got around. We'd started inviting more and more people that we knew, and everybody who came down knew somebody else in a band. Gary from Me, Hubby & Thom knew someone else who was in a band. I think it was through him that I met The Savilles. I met the guys early on from The Stanleys, with Gordy who started the Amphetameanies, for example. They came down, it was all completely word of mouth. So we kept it going for three or four weeks.

RM Hubbert (Hubby) (guitar/vocals, Me, Hubby & Thom): I think maybe Urusei Yatsura did their first gig around that time as well. They were great. I think Jim had been doing it for a while and just nobody came to these gigs, it was a Tuesday night. . . we jumped at the chance to take this night on. I think we were all booking stuff for the first few weeks. But I do remember early on there was one night where Alex, myself and Glen had all booked two or three bands each for the same night. It ended up being fucking chaos. It was very quickly decided after that that Alex should do the booking.

Jim and Pat handed the Kazoo Club over to Alex and Hubby, whose stewardship would become a defining moment in Glasgow's music scene. It was like an extension of the Glasgow Music Collective. Not only was it a place where brand new bands could play, it was a place to make mistakes, gain valuable experience and have fun.

Alex Kapranos (guitar/vocals, The Blisters; later Franz Ferdinand): Craig [Tannock] and I just hit it off straight away. We got on really well. He was great. And I said to him I thought this was really exciting. I told him what I thought was missing in Glasgow, how there isn't really a place where bands that are starting off can play. I think I described the King Tut's experience to him. In my head I had this very strong idea that when you start making music, you're not particularly good. You need to do it to become good, like anything in life, you've got to go through the period of not being good at it. And I had this idea of this club as being the place where people could start off not being good, and then become great if you have that environment. I could already see it when bands would come back a second time, their second gig, they were more confident. I liked this idea of a place that would nurture people and allow people to become what they could become. I was also explaining about how difficult it was – because most bands that start off are skint. And you don't have things like amplifiers or drum kits, never mind microphones and PAs.

What made the Kazoo unique was that, not only was this now a place where a new band could play, Craig Tannock's offer of a free PA and instruments meant that bands didn't even have to own their own kit.

Alex Kapranos (guitar/vocals, The Blisters; later Franz Ferdinand): The Apollo had been flooded. And in the basement of the Apollo were all these rehearsal rooms. Everything had been written off by the insurance company. Everything was written off as destroyed by the flood. But somebody still had the keys for the Apollo rehearsal rooms. And somehow, all of the amplifiers that were just slightly flood damaged – a drum kit, a PA and microphones, and basically everything you needed to perform as a band – suddenly appeared in this new place, the 13th Note. And Craig said to me, listen, there's all that gear that was written off: you guys use it, and use it for the club. Craig had this very open attitude, like, just do it, do it your own way.

RM Hubbert (Hubby) (guitar/vocals, Me, Hubby & Thom): I would do the sound, having never done sound before. The deal with the venue was, and this is why it was so amazing for bands like us, they didn't charge us anything. We didn't get paid for doing it either. But there was a PA, and a full back line. It was all fucked, but there was a drum kit and bass amps, guitar amps, a vocal PA and we just needed to figure out how to work it all. That's how I started my illustrious sound engineering career, just figuring out what those knobs and faders did.

Alex Kapranos (guitar/vocals, The Blisters; later Franz Ferdinand): And if it hadn't been for Craig's adventurousness and open-mindedness, none of that club would have happened. And none of that scene would have happened. He gave us the instruments and he gave us the gear, which meant that a bunch of reprobates who just had a bunch of ideas and had been practising in their bedrooms or whatever, could suddenly turn up and have a band situation in which to play in.

RM Hubbert (Hubby) (guitar/vocals, Me, Hubby & Thom): There were a couple things that made it so creatively successful. The first was that there was an active booking policy that if someone wanted to play they could play, as long as they weren't dicks. There was no musical gatekeeping. If you were cool to be around you can come and play, and we'll come and watch, and we'll get drunk. I joke about it sometimes but it gave us all a place to go and be shit at being in a band. And the opportunity to get good at it. We'd be playing to other bands constantly, who would be understanding. There was friendly competition but it was very supportive. It felt like we'd been given the keys to the sweet shop where we could go and learn how to be in a band, how to present yourself on stage, how to do it. It fed off this energy that as I've gotten older and seen a lot of DIY scenes come up and disappear, it's made me realise that the absolute key to a successful DIY scene is having the belief that you're the first one to have thought of it. You're going to lose money, it's going to be a depressing experience quite soon but you've got that energy of saying 'fuck the system', this is a much better way of doing it.

Alex Kapranos (guitar/vocals, The Blisters; later Franz Ferdinand): My manifesto was: there is no manifesto. Everything that I booked in that place was based upon my instinctive reaction to the people. Whether I felt excited about it, and whether I felt there was some, more than anything, some kind of potential. That was what excited me more than anything. It was seeing the way the bands evolved and the way that the band developed. It was astonishing to see it, seeing how people set up these domino rallies, it felt a little bit like that, where you would just set something off and watch it unfold. It was like being part of a beautiful and unpredictably scripted drama. It was like imagining a great boxset about a subject that you find truly enthralling and fascinating. And not just watching a big part of it in the middle, and not knowing where it's going, but having a certain degree of being able to bring in these characters and watch them.

RM Hubbert (Hubby) (guitar/vocals, Me, Hubby & Thom): There was a core of bands early on that played the Kazoo Club that were still going every week by the end of it. They were really supportive of everyone and not defensive of the scene, but kind of protective I suppose. There was ourselves, The Blisters, The Stanleys, Poison Sisters, Pink Kross, bis, Urusei Yatsura, Super Slinky, Glen or Glenda – I'm sure I'm missing hundreds to be honest.

Gordy Davidson (The Stanleys, Amphetameanies, F&J Records): We were The Stanleys, and I suppose we were one of the foundational bands of the Kazoo Club scene that sprang up at the old 13th Note in Glasgow's Glassford Street, alongside a dozen or so others who always seemed to be there or thereabouts, plus a vast cast of occasionals. Before I get into the boring detail, I can assure you of two things: one, it was fucking great, and two, we all took it totally for granted. OF COURSE there was a place where we could go every Tuesday night (later extended to Thursdays) where we could watch a cavalcade of entirely original, diverse, edgy, imaginative bands playing, for free, and sometimes play for a wee half hour ourselves, also at no cost. Then all hang around, coolly assessing each other's trousers. It was a given thing. Just part of our landscape, and for what felt like the longest time, the Kazoo Club was just there every time you went looking for it, like the sky or the sea.

Stuart Braithwaite (Deadcat Motorbike, Eska; later Mogwai): Someone said there's a place in Glasgow that will book your band. . . you just send Alex a tape. I just phoned him up and said, 'Did you listen to the tape, can we get a gig?' He was very supportive. He felt that the old guard of Scottish music were not inclusive and were quite competitive and a little bit snobby. I think he wanted to do something completely different. He was just totally up for helping out a band and he had his own band. Obviously, Alex went on to be in a huge band but for quite a long time he was just in local bands and doing his own thing without breaking out of Glasgow that much. He was super. . . it was very much a DIY scene. It was a lot of fun. I don't think you got paid for the Kazoo Club but you got some beers. A lot of people would just make bands up on the spot just so they could get beers that night.

Sandy Black (vocals/guitar, Poison Sisters): Up until this point, every time Poison Sisters played anywhere, everyone looked a bit shocked and we never got asked back. This was because I hadn't understood the difference between a pub that puts on bands, that actually mainly wants bands who play cover versions, and a venue that wants bands who play their own songs. The 13th Note was one such venue. The first time we played at the Kazoo Club in the 13th Note, at the end of the set, Alex rushed up to us and exclaimed, 'You're the type of band that we want! Can you play again next week?' To which, we replied, 'Really? Aye, we can do that!' And that was that. We'd finally found somewhere to play that would tolerate (and actively encourage) our shenanigans.

Graham Kemp (guitar/vocals, Urusei Yatsura): The 13th Note was just a place we liked hanging out in, and Alex Kapranos was booking bands for the Tuesday night Kazoo Club. Fergus (Lawrie, Urusei Yatsura) had got talking to him and realised that the booking policy was really loose, and you would get a couple of cans for your trouble into the bargain. We had only played at a house party in a deconsecrated nunnery previously, so we basically learned how to be in a band by playing Tuesday nights there, thanks to Alex's bemused tolerance. His own group were playing there regularly, plus Hubby's band, The Stanleys, Poison Sisters. Lots of great groups like Pink Kross, REID and The Yummy Fur would turn up.

Colin Kearney (guitar/vocals, Eska): It was one of those things that you can only properly appreciate in hindsight. I think that part of the point of difference is that many small venues were in the basements of pubs, but the majority of the punters in the pub would be a completely different demographic from the kids that would be putting on/playing the gigs down the stairs. The Note was staffed by musicians (not exclusively, of course), who might finish a shift only to go downstairs to soundcheck, and the people who drank/ate there were more likely to be an artist, a punk, a fanzine editor, what have you, rather than an old boy poring over the racing form. The Blane Valley and The Steps Bar were right there for those lads, and absolutely essential to Glasgow's illustrious pub culture, but Craig Tannock had hit upon something that Glasgow was obviously ready for: vegan burgers and cheap beers slung by local, and not-so-local, young creatives, and an inclusive policy to booking gigs.

Alex Kapranos (guitar/vocals, The Blisters; later Franz Ferdinand): Even when I think about it now, I'm getting chills on my back thinking about it. Seeing bands like Urusei, remembering when they came down and played the first gig, and seeing how they improved over the years. The new ideas and hearing songs for the first time. . . quite often it didn't come to anything. Quite often the guy you'd been speaking to about his band, came and played and were shite, and they came down three weeks later and they were shite again. There were a lot of bands that didn't meet the potential that you thought. The one that everybody's probably mentioned is Trout. Willie Rogan's band. Trout were kind of the stars of that scene, really. They were the greatest band of that time. And nobody really knows them apart from the people who were there at that time. It felt genuinely, genuinely exciting.

Urusei Yatsura beginnings

Urusei Yatsura very quickly established themselves as one of the most promising early bands from the 13th Note scene. They seemed inevitably set for success.

Graham Kemp (guitar/vocals, Urusei Yatsura): Me and Fergus started playing music together because we had a shared love of Galaxie 500. I had a small Peavey amp in my flat and the first thing we played together was our version of their cover of the Jonathan Richman song, 'Don't Let Our Youth Go To Waste'. We took that to heart and decided to actually start doing something with our time. I had a fanzine called *Kitten Frenzy*, which was also the name of a band I was going to start with my girlfriend. Jenny never did learn the bass, so I joined Fergus's theoretical band and he joined mine. We were both going to see bands like Ride and Slowdive and clubbing a lot, so either dancing sarcastically to Dee-Lite or gazing at our shoes in King Tut's. We both got into the more abrasive rock bands coming out of the USA like Dinosaur Jr and Sonic Youth, and loved the primitive approach of Beat Happening. Calvin [Johnson from K Records]had a 7-inch out of 'Make It Fucked Up' and we took that as a motto of sorts.

Fergus Lawrie (guitar/vocals, Urusei Yatsura): Haha! Why does anyone form a band? You probably need something wrong with you, right? I had my first drink at 18 months old when I managed to grab my dad's full wine glass at a party. I drained it. We were from the north but we lived in the south and I never felt like I fitted in. I always had difficulty deciphering social situations and communicating effectively. I came to Glasgow to study and had vague ambitions to be a writer or journalist but probably would have ended up a teacher or something. . . Musically I was a typical early nineties indie kid into Galaxie 500, MBV, Pixies, Throwing Muses, The Wedding Present, The Cure, Velvets, Bowie, Leonard Cohen, whatever was flavour of the month in *NME*, never particularly sophisticated music taste or very interested in curating a music collection but loved going to gigs and playing guitar. Graham and I met through Glasgow University and started playing together pretty much straight away. He was quite a strategic thinker in terms of putting the band together, while I had an excess of kind of happy floppy-dog enthusiasm to socialise and make things happen. We started to work out how to go about being a band, we had no idea how to write a song or find a rehearsal room or get a gig so there was a lot of trial and error.

Elaine Lawrie (bass, Urusei Yatsura): In the late eighties and nineties you could see bands every night of the week, it didn't cost loads of money and there was a good mix of Glasgow, Scottish, UK and American bands doing the rounds. I grew up in Glasgow and so the Barrowlands, Nice N Sleazy and King Tut's were regular haunts. I spent most of my time at gigs and at indie discos, and was a regular at student unions like the QM and Strathclyde. I would go and see bands like Throwing Muses, Pixies, Sonic Youth, Pavement, Dinosaur Jr, The Lemonheads, Sugarcubes and Nirvana. We were absolutely spoiled. Around this time I bumped into Fergus and some of his friends at the QM and we hung out.

Graham Kemp (guitar/vocals, Urusei Yatsura): We were initially playing with acoustic guitar and one electric but Fergus met Elaine in a nightclub and she foolishly mentioned she played guitar, so he invited her to come to a rehearsal if she was interested in trying bass. She came along and that was our first time playing in a rehearsal room and the proper beginning of the band.

Elaine Lawrie (bass, Urusei Yatsura): When I saw Fergus again at Strathclyde Union he told me he and his friend had started a band, and I told him I played guitar, which I did, but only barely. He asked if I wanted to play bass, they had a loan of one from a friend. So, the next week I went to his flat, met his pal Graham, and we took a taxi to a freezing rehearsal studio in Scotstoun, a railway arch on Curle Street. We started rehearsing every week, and moved to another rehearsal studio in Maryhill.

Fergus Lawrie (guitar/vocals, Urusei Yatsura): Obviously at this point we were absolutely shocking as a band but we were having a lot of fun hanging out. We all shared the same sense of humour and soon it was like family. We would spend half our rehearsals sitting around drinking coffee and laughing our asses off, and then go to the pub. We settled into a basic rehearsal room called Babelfish Studios in a converted office in the middle of a scrapyard. Gradually we started to pull it together. The fact that we never really played with anyone else and were learning together meant that we really became a proper band, forming our playing style around each other at an age where brains are still plastic enough to adapt. A real privilege to experience and something that can only happen once in a lifetime. Although we were never remotely technical performers, in time we became a tight and ferocious live band.

Graham Kemp (guitar/vocals, Urusei Yatsura): Sometime in 1993 we were in the 13th Note at the Kazoo Club. We had played once or twice due to the lax gatekeeping policy of Alex Kapranos so he asked if we wanted to play a few tunes as one of the bands hadn't made it. Our regular drummer wasn't there, but Ian [Graham, Elaine's brother] was, so we dared him to do it. He must have been just drunk enough, so he sat in despite never having played drums before. How hard could it be, right? He did great, so we got a brother/sister rhythm section which I think is pretty cool. We had no aims apart from continuing to hang out together and maybe having a few laughs along the way. We had crazy dreams like doing a Peel Session, getting a record out and going to Japan, but we never thought any of those were a serious possibility. Later we did two out of three of those, but at the time we had no money and were playing with borrowed gear.

The 13th Note was a great education and provided us with a bunch of like-minded people to hang out with, but also was great as a guide of what not to do. Every band passing through seemed to use some combination of the words 'baby', 'head', 'radio', 'gun' or 'honey' as a name and we were determined to avoid that. Also to be avoided was the sin of 'trying too hard' and 'taking it all too seriously'. You don't hit the stage of the 13th Note shouting 'Hello Glasgow' and do three encores, because you just look like a dick. I was really into comics like *HATE* and *Eightball* and *Dirty Plotte* [and] was quite interested in manga and Japanese art. You didn't see much around in the early nineties, but I had been buying the colour reprints of *AKIRA* from Forbidden Planet on Buchanan Street, and one day I chanced on the eight-issue run of Rumiko Takahashi's *Urusei Yatsura*. I was just really depressed and it cheered me up. We needed a name and *HATE*'s Buddy Bradley rant about bands named after comics being losers led me to suggest Urusei Yatsura, in a spirit of awkwardness. One translation of the name was 'noisy stars' so it seemed to fit. Obviously with hindsight this is a crazy decision, but I used to enjoy John Peel being possibly the only person in Britain who pronounced it right, including us. I have a series of photos in a box somewhere of Fergus looking pissed off in front of misspelled show posters from across the UK.

Urusei Yatsura

The Stanleys

Gordy Davidson (The Stanleys; later F&J Records): The Stanleys were an all-boy four-piece, which had formed out of the fragments of two sketchy wee bedroom bands I'd been in during the mid- to late eighties. . . a very studenty thing called Professor Salamander (and the Visual Imposters), which involved a bunch of town-planning students from the art school (the lowest subject in the GSA pecking order, with close to zero arty-points) and a power pop band called Uptight, which had formed within the Glasgow Vespa Club, of which I had become a member after buying a second-hand scooter with summer job wages when I was between school and college.

I'd drifted into leading a bit of a double life, with pals in both these camps. They didn't mix well.

At that time, the students were all about seated-round-a-bedsit table sarcasm, spliffs, the reggae end of The Clash and the wanky end of the Floyd, while the scooterboys were all about physical tomfoolery, Buckfast, and leaping about unselfconsciously to ska, soul and mod. On the occasions these two crowds met at parties in various basement hovels around the West End, it never went well.

However, after both my bands had split, I brought together Shane Connolly, the very gifted and energetic drummer from Uptight, and my old school pal Rat, the guitarist from Prof Salamander, with me playing bass as before, and we managed to agree on a kind of post-punk agenda that often veered into territory that would soon emerge elsewhere dubbed as 'Britpop'.

This was helped along by a young Maryhill postman called Gerry Callaghan, who Shane found somewhere. He voiced a desire to be a frontman, and talked his way past me by gushing about The Housemartins.

However, Gerry's real deal was The Smiths (whose cultural impact I'd largely ignored, having been too busy pursuing my scooterboy social life around a variety of dilapidated English seaside towns in the summers, and cut-price Lanarkshire miners' welfare clubs in the winters) so I didn't really clock quite how much Stephen Patrick he was bringing to the table as he flailed his arms, singing about Catholic guilt and slapping his own arse.

ANYWAY, The Stanleys started on stony ground, getting gigs at the aforementioned scooter club dances, playing covers of Jam, Housemartins and Billy Bragg songs, and throwing in a few things of our own, which somehow came out a bit more Madchestery, 'cause Shane could do the funky drummer well, and Rat was all about eight-to-the-bar scratching of half a diminished chord, that was never entirely in tune with my rather bog-standard major scale power pop basslines. The best reception we ever got was a pair of Coatbridge skinheads standing right at the front of the stage chanting, 'You're shite you're shite you're shite', but then asking for a Stanleys badge each to prove they'd seen us, in case we got famous despite being shite. (Rest In Peace, Caldo and Goody.)

Deadcat Motorbike, Eska and Mogwai

Still selling out huge venues today, Mogwai were one of the earliest bands to arrive on the 13th Note scene. Like many of his friends in Glasgow, Stuart Braithwaite was from one of the city's satellite towns, Strathaven (pronounced Straven by the locals).

Stuart Braithwaite (drums, Deadcat Motorbike/Eska; later guitar/vocals, Mogwai): Mogwai was my second band. I had a band at college called Deadcat Motorbike and it was with that band I met Alex Kapranos, and he was a big supporter of both my bands. Through playing gigs in the 13th Note we got to know other bands like Trout (one of my favourite bands) who we played with a lot, The Yummy Fur, Eska (who I played drums with for a bit), Pink Kross and Lung Leg.

Alex Kapranos (guitar/vocals, The Blisters; later Franz Ferdinand): I remember Stuart coming down originally with Deadcat Motorbike and thinking, this guy's like a pop virtuoso; also he plays like nobody I know, it's totally incredible. . . then the Mogwai thing comes around. Those kind of moments, they're great, truly, truly spine-tingling, because you felt like it was all coming from that one principle of openness, and trust in your instincts.

Stuart Braithwaite (drums, Deadcat Motorbike/Eska; later guitar/vocals, Mogwai): I definitely think the kind of Scottish – American connection was really, really big and almost like a conscious choice, because. . . the London music scene seemed really unwelcoming. Whereas the Olympia [Washington State] music scene was very welcoming and very willing for a lot of those musicians to collaborate with Scottish bands. You would probably hear more about The Pastels or the BMX Bandits in American fanzines than you would in the *NME*. It was almost like an alternative route. We definitely found that when our band started we were always keen to play with American bands. And I guess because America is so big it's not quite as fashion-led as Britain was, certainly at that point with the weekly music press. It was always about what was in and what was out and that never really appealed to me. I like the idea of music being permanent, not like a fleeting, fashionable thing.

Colin Kearney (guitar/vocals, Eska): In 1993, I met Chris Mack while on work experience at the old Guitar Store, which was on Hope Street at the time; there wasn't meant to be two folk doing work experience at the same time, but destiny dealt us a double booking. While the majority of our schoolmates were getting high on photocopier ink fumes, Chris and I were sharing our love of the burgeoning US indie-rock scene, playing renditions of Pavement cuts in the acoustic section of the shop and really experiencing work, you know? A kid called Callum frequented the place over the week we were there, and proposed we all start a band together – being a socially imperfect teenager, I was delighted with this suggestion as it provided an opportunity to continue hanging out with Chris, as asking for a phone number and proposing hanging out beyond our time together at the guitar shop seemed too bold somehow. Chris and I started writing songs and would cobble them together in his attic bedroom. His songs were much better than mine, not to mention his guitar playing, but the obvious talent gulf gave me a kick up the arse to get better, and fast. I think at our first gig (at the basement venue of the old 13th Note on Glassford Street, natch), we played about a 50/50 split of covers and originals, and the latter was another even split of primarily Kearney- or Mack-penned jams.

Deadcat Motorbike and Mogwai quickly differentiated themselves by mostly playing noisy instrumentals rather than the short, vocal-led sets favoured by many of their contemporaries.

Stuart Braithwaite (drums, Deadcat Motorbike/Eska; later guitar/vocals, Mogwai): There were other contemporaries doing noisier stuff – ac acoustics were really noisy and around about the same time. Ganger were a fully instrumental band – a really great band. There was lots of stuff, bands like Fenn and (later) Long Fin Killie, Luke Sutherland's band, doing interesting, weird music. For a while there were all these bands who seemed to be 'diet' Teenage Fanclub, being very similar to what they were doing. And I think what I liked, looking back, about the 13th Note scene was that none of the bands were like each other. None of the bands wanted to be like any other band. There were some really idiosyncratic, interesting, weird people doing pretty unique stuff. It wasn't cool to have your band sound like other bands, which I think is a great place to get to.

As mentioned, Stuart also played drums for, Eska.

Stuart Braithwaite (drums, Deadcat Motorbike/Eska; later guitar/vocals, Mogwai): I played drums when I was at school, I had a drum kit. I think drums were my second instrument when I did my Higher music, so I can kind of play the drums. I'm not going to be in Led Zeppelin anytime soon but I can get away with it. Me and Dominic [Aitchison] started Mogwai – his high school best friend was Colin, the singer from Eska, who I knew, because his big brother went out with my sister's best friend – they were some of the first people I met. I met those guys before any of us were in bands. We weren't close pals but I kind of knew them so when I started playing gigs in Glasgow; I knew Colin because we'd met years ago. And they were like Spinal Tap, their drummers were always quitting. And I guess I'm never one to turn down an opportunity, especially back then, I would have been like, 'Yeah, I'll play drums in your band'. I played with them for a while. We went and did a Steve Lamacq session. I played on one of the 7-inches and had a lot of fun. Kenny who played bass in Eska does Mogwai's live sound now, so I still see those guys a lot and we're still really good friends. That was a lot of fun. . . I was in both for a while. And it would have been round about the time that Mogwai started. So I was probably in Eska for a large part of that first year of Mogwai.

Colin Kearney (guitar/vocals, Eska): First of all, can I assure you that none of the drummers died! Our first sticksman was Thom from The Blisters, and he left when they were getting bigger. My pal Martin Donnelly filled in for a short spell, which just happened to coincide with our first forays into recording, but I think we were maybe a little too punk rock for his tastes in the end; I mean, he shared my and Kenny's love for The Replacements, but if pushed I think he would've preferred slow-coring it in a Galaxie 500-type band. Stuart warmed the seat after that. I think I first met Stuart via my older brother's girlfriend at the time, as she was good pals with Stuart's big sister, and we'd met up at gigs at the Barrowland, probably featuring Ned's Atomic Dustbin or similar. Dominic Aitchison was my best pal since primary school, so I guess we all came into orbit around the same time, leading to the formation of Mogwai. I think Eska pre-dates Mogwai, but not by a whole lot. Anyway, Stuart was on the tubs at the same time as playing in Mogwai, but they blew up pretty quickly, so it was a brief affair. Nevertheless, we recorded the 'III Spike' single with Stuart, and also did a session for Radio 1's Evening Session, where famously the engineers couldn't give two fucks about us because Garbage were due in Maida Vale studios the next day and they were running about soldering stuff while roundly ignoring us. We had a small element of revenge, however: we were doing a song of mine called 'Struts' but balked at the very end of the song after an otherwise good take, so we suggested dropping in as a full band just for the end section – the engineer said it couldn't be done, but we persuaded him to give it a try, and we nailed it. It only elicited a raised eyebrow of acknowledgement, but that felt like a lot, given the context.

For Stuart, Mogwai soon took priority as their trajectory ascended.

Colin Kearney (guitar/vocals, Eska): Mogwai quickly climbed the indie leagues, so Stuart parted ways with us by way of necessity. Our last gig with him was supporting Rocket From The Crypt at The Arches, where Stuart had to play on a chair from the bar as nobody would let him use their drum stool, which kinda hampered his ability to play a bit, and my guitars were all out of tune because we'd smuggled a pal into the show disguised as a guitar tech – he did a great job tuning my guitars to equal temperament, which was a shame because we routinely tuned down a half step, so I was out by a good semitone. I noticed pretty quickly, but it was a bad start to a show with one of my favourite bands and my already-jangled nerves frayed entirely. So, I guess Stuart was probably glad to leave that chickenshit outfit in the end! It was a bit weird to see Mogwai blow up and it definitely prompted some pangs of jealousy at points because, hey, I was young and ambitious and thought my band were brilliant too. But mostly I was concentrated on what we were doing and we got to do a lot of cool stuff. Our next drummer, Willie Mone, really meshed into what we wanted to do. He was a drummer's drummer, not a guitarist cosplaying as one (something I did myself for many years in bands like Empire-Builder, Pro Forma, The Royal We, Bricolage etc.), and he wasn't clicking the sticks for other acts. It makes me laugh to think how ancient we all thought he was! Poor guy, he was only like ten years older than us. Having him in the band helped us kick on, as we were gradually becoming more intricate and complex and, some might say, pretentious.

The Kazoo Collection recorded live at the 13th Note

A compilation album, The Kazoo Collection, *was the first vinyl offering from the nascent new scene. It was recorded live at the 13th Note on 13 October 1993, compiled by Alex and Hubby, and released on Glass Records in 1994. Featuring The Stanleys, The Blisters, Me, Hubby & Thom and Urusei Yatsura, among others, it marked the beginning of a revitalised Glasgow indie-label scene, with much that came after it indebted to this compilation.*

Back of *The Kazoo Collection* LP

Alex Kapranos (guitar/vocals, The Blisters; later Franz Ferdinand): I got it pressed up. I remember doing loads of research trying to find a place to press up records. And I found this place in the Czech Republic called Gramofonové Závody. They pressed it up and I know that they were used by a lot the folk that came afterwards doing 7-inch vinyl. Urusei used it for a 7-inch, I think maybe Mogwai did too. Flotsam & Jetsam did. Anyway, I didn't really know what I was doing. I had no idea how to put a record out or the organisation involved or what distribution was or anything. We recorded it using Jim Brady and some of the guys in the music shop over the road where there was a studio downstairs. They came in and set up and they recorded it. The release was just around about that time that I first met Jane and John (Mckeown) and all that lot. They weren't playing in the first year of the club.

RM Hubbert (Hubby) (guitar/vocals, Me, Hubby & Thom): Gramofonové Závody was hugely important to everything that happened after this. Alex had the idea to do the album, which we were all obviously really into. We thought it was a great idea. It was supposed to be that everything was recorded live at the Kazoo Club. I think we did it over two, maybe three nights. I can't remember. What I do remember is that I got ridiculously drunk. Which is something I don't usually do – I've never been a huge drinker, but for some reason I got fucking hugely drunk and I was playing second guitar on The Blisters at the time, and I absolutely fucked the entire recording. If you ever get a chance to listen to that record, in the background of The Blisters song you hear this really bizarre out-of-tune drone going on. That was me. That was why I wasn't in The Blisters anymore. That's not true actually, I was in The Blisters after that; Alex and I had an argument about fuck knows what, but it ended up with him throwing a Snickers bar at me and me not talking to him for months. So that's how I left The Blisters.

Graham Kemp (guitar/vocals, Urusei Yatsura): That Kazoo Club compilation was put out by Alex Kapranos. He had chosen the name Glass Records, as the 13th Note was on Glassford Street. I think it was actually me that said, 'Wait there's already a Glass Records that The Pastels had put singles out on', and he said oops and added a 'Y' on the end, so it's 'GLASSY' Records if you're going to be picky. There was a recording studio across the lane next to the Blane Valley and those guys ran some cables over into the bar and recorded a couple of nights in 1993 of all the regulars at the Kazoo Club. Our tune 'Guitars Are Boring' was chosen as the opening track, which was quite a compliment, and led to us having considerable trouble shifting our portion of the albums. I actually sold the last two I had on Bandcamp in 2023. Anyway, it was a massive thrill to hear ourselves on vinyl, and I have fond memories of going into BBC Scotland to be interviewed by John Peel about the fanzine [*Kitten Frenzy*] in 1994. I gave him a copy of the record and he just cued up our song and played it, unheard, there and then. It could only have been more perfect if it had been at the wrong speed.

From that Peel Show:

John Peel (Radio DJ): And you've very kindly brought me a record. Do you want to talk about that and tell me what this is? I've not had time to listen to it at all but what's the record about?

Jennifer (*Kitten Frenzy Fanzine*): It's from the Kazoo Club, which is a thing organised at 13th Note for new bands in Glassford Street. Basically it's a free night that has four or five bands playing and a few of the bands got together and put this record out to celebrate the first birthday of the club – which was last year as they are just having their second birthday this year.

Graham Kemp (guitar/vocals, Urusei Yatsura): It's pronounced Usurei Yatsura. It's named after a Japanese TV cartoon. I think the translation means 'those annoying stupid people from the stars'.

John Peel (Radio DJ): Well, thanks so much for. . . oh, of course, you're in the band as well? I thought that was a familiar face. Okay, excellent. . . have we discussed booking the band for a session yet?

Graham Kemp (guitar/vocals, Urusei Yatsura): No, but we'll be glad to do one.

John Peel (Radio DJ): Good, well thanks very much and thank you for telling us about Kitten Frenzy as well.

Elaine Lawrie (bass, Urusei Yatsura): It was mind-blowing to see your own record for the first time; for us I think that would have been the Kazoo Club album. It was like something you never thought you could achieve, that happened to other people, but there it was. Your own record. But I also felt the same about all the ephemera of being a live band – flyers, posters, fanzines, set lists, t-shirts, badges – I loved all of it, and was thrilled to see our name and artwork wherever it appeared.

RM Hubbert (Hubby) (guitarist/vocals, Me, Hubby & Thom): The Kazoo Club album has some great stuff on it. I'm hugely embarrassed by the Me, Hubby & Thom song on it, it was shit. More importantly, I was going through a phase of. . . I think I was copying Sandy from Poison Sisters, where when he talked on stage he'd adopt this odd transatlantic American accent, which really suited the Poison Sisters. But for some reason I started doing it and it just makes me cringe every time I hear it. That version of Me, Hubby & Thom wasn't a particularly great version. We went through quite a lot of bass players, so I think Glen from The Blisters was playing bass there. And the songs had quite complicated bass stuff, in the same way that El Hombre ended up having. The last iteration of Me, Hubby & Thom had Stevie Jones playing bass, who was the bass player in El Hombre. So it was that kind of angular, Beefhearty-type stuff. And I was very drunk and it's just a bit shit, so that was generally a bad experience. There is some great stuff on there though – The Savilles are on there, aren't they? I'd forgotten that.

The collection was a huge deal for the Glasgow scene. Although some of the bands were disappointed with their own contributions, the infrastructure that put it together turned out to be significant for kickstarting local labels.

The Subliminal Girls

The scene surrounding the GMC, the Kazoo Club and the 13th Note was now buzzing as new bands joined those who had formed earlier. Once such band was The Subliminal Girls.

Graham Gavin (Subliminal Girls): Subliminal Girls formed sometime in the same year that Glasgow's pumping chest was being adorned with the big shiny European City of Culture medallion. Myself and (a pre-Lung Leg) Annie Spandex had transported the contents of our Barras record stall and taken over Saturday nights at the downstairs lounge of the now-flattened Rooftops nightclub on Sauchiehall Street. Playing tunes of a noisier and often post-punk nature, we quickly shed, in their droves, a plethora of disgruntled indie kids who'd turned up expecting to hear what Tam Coyle had been playing at his long-running institutional Kes Club evening. The kids with their curtain haircuts and baggy Madchester attire quickly made their way for the exit. . . this made way for a lank-haired rag-tag contingent.

One such member of this entourage was John McKeown. John, talking at a million miles an hour, enthusiastically introduced himself with a spiel extolling the virtuous charms of Winona Ryder in the (just-viewed) film *Heathers*. As well as this, there was a lot of talk about Sonic Youth and The Fall: two bands that would easily have lifted butts from the tired velour seating onto the corner dance floor. Within months John and I became firm friends. Having previously played in bands that never amounted to anything, John suggested getting a trio together with him on guitar, his fellow Blantyre school friend Kev Hutcheson on cymbal-free drums and me on bass. My only problem was I'd never played bass before, but I quickly took to it and now consider it the instrument where my strengths lie. Borrowing Kev's bin-bagged Grant's jazz copy, we rapidly built up a setlist in a dump of a rehearsal space in Paisley (where, once, an amp we were going through alarmingly burst into flames!). We often unceremoniously lifted chunks of sounds from the bands we were aping. Sonically, we never ventured much further than those SST trios of the Minutemen/fIREHOSE that we so loved. However, elements of Dog Faced Hermans and some New York no-wave could sometimes be found in there too, although never a match for the actual source material that we were amateurishly copying.

Our route-one approach to lifting from others was also reflected in the company we were keeping in our Glaswegian music circles. Bands such as Stretchheads and dawson were spearheading an alternative to the offerings being heard from the jangly *C86* brigade of Glasgow. They acted as an antidote to those bands that are generally regarded to define the sound of the *NME's* era-defining compilation. There was always another side to this roster: bands that took Beefheart over The Byrds for inspiration (such as The Schrubs, Bogshed and bIG*fLAME) were all in the mix too. Aside from Stretchheads and dawson, Subliminal Girls were also inspired by similarly influenced Glasgow-located bands that added to the milieu such as Badgewearer and Whirling Pig Dervish, both of which had numerous releases on Jer Reid's Gruff Wit label.

Although our music could often be recognised and sidled along with those others, a major difference from that contemporaneous scene that separated us was in our lyrics. Heavy subjects such as globalisation, corruption and wars in far-flung countries such as Nicaragua were being swapped for literary, art and filmic references. Often this source material would be delivered through a narrative that adopted a high dosage of absurdity and comical bluster – they were always entertaining, if a little surreal. In retrospect, John's lyrics with Subliminal Girls were laying the early foundations for what evolved with The Yummy Fur later on.

Our nine-track, twelve-minute-long recording of our setlist (which we recorded at Tower Studios with Richie Dempsey), titled *The President's Grass is Missing*, became one of those tapes that made its way onto the airwaves. These were sold in Missing Records on Oswald Street as well as the grimy back room of Bath Street's 23rd Record Precinct. Jiffy bags with stamped-addressed envelopes also made their way through my parents' letter box. This always caused a worrying and bemused wrinkle to appear on my mum's forehead as she read the top line of the address and wondered what the hell I got up to at weekends as a member of this Subliminal Girls troupe.

Around the turn of 1992 there had been much talk of us progressing from a tape release to that of a personally funded 45 on vinyl. Leading up to this, I was increasingly becoming frustrated with my George Harrison role as an enabler to John's conveyor belt of tunes in the band. As my dexterity on the bass was increasing, so too were my ideas for new songs. Often these ideas were met with lacklustre enthusiasm and didn't move any further on from a brief play-about in the rehearsal room. As my frustration grew I decided it was time to give Kev his bin bag and bass back and start something afresh. Ironically, this new adventure with guitarist Dep Downie in the band Lugworm came about from an introduction from John McKeown. Knowing I was looking to get something new off the ground, John unselfishly introduced the two of us. . . It turned out Dep had been keeping those velour cushions of Rooftops Nightclub warm too.

The Yummy Fur

The Scottish indie scene in the eighties had been characterised by a UK-wide sense of sound and fashion, often with Scottish bands pioneering, or at the very least punching well above their weight. However, in the nineties, Scotland's indie scene was met with indifference from London. Glasgow in particular was very far removed from Britpop, which was about to emerge. For nearly ten years, Glasgow took a 'don't-give-a-fuck-what-London-thinks' attitude. One band at the forefront of this was The Yummy Fur.

The Yummy Fur had been formed by John McKeown in the early nineties and eventually became one of the most significant and influential Glasgow bands of that decade, still producing great music to this day. The band also became a breeding ground for talent and many of those who passed through its ranks went on to find success in their own right. They played many of their early gigs via the GMC and at the Kazoo Club.

The Yummy Fur

John McKeown (guitar/vocals, The Yummy Fur): I loved The Pastels and all that – they're all great – but I was never that interested in strumming chords and singing a melody. The hierarchy was still there but it changed for us. Some people still come up to you and say, 'How do you get a gig?' And it's like, honest to God, you get a gig because you're good. If you're struggling to get a gig, I'm suspicious about why you're struggling to get a gig. And that goes right back to '92 – everybody seemed to arrive with a band. I don't really remember any of these bands forming at the time. Everybody turned up at the club. And everybody seemed to have a band. A few people would play where you're like, 'Oh that's shite but they're nice guys'. So Alex would give them another gig. But generally, it was pretty obvious who was interesting. Alex's band The Karelia, The Poison Sisters. . . Pink Kross, Lung Leg, us obviously, Urusei, Trout obviously. And the only bands from Edinburgh that would come through would be The Male Nurse and. . . there's nothing else that was that interesting. But that's a lot of bands! It's probably a lot to do with being very serious about your music. And so you just want to see the good stuff or something new. Because it's quite eclectic. But basically, if you were good and you turned up at the 13th Note you would get another gig and another gig and another gig. But if you turned up and you were shite, and just strummy, strummy, sixties or something, it was like, 'Go and take it to the Cathouse mate'. The only thing that would probably get you a slagging was if you didn't sound original, or at least only do that one thing.

By 1994 The Yummy Fur's line-up had evolved to include Lawrence Worthington, Marc Baines and Brian MacDougall.

Brian MacDougall (guitar, The Yummy Fur): The Yummy Fur were a three-piece band to begin with. John McKeown, Mark

Leighton and Jamie McMorrow on drums. I understand that John and Jamie had a big fight about something or other. . . exit Jamie. Lawrence joined the band as drummer.

Lawrence Worthington (drums, The Yummy Fur): I had an old drum kit in my flat and played in bands at school so I joined and played on a couple of early records. But I was not from the same musical tribe at all – I had a New York Dolls poster, know what I mean? But everyone loved The Fall and the Fire Engines and David Bowie and dancing and sitting up all night laughing.

John McKeown (guitar/vocals, The Yummy Fur): In the eighties I was into everything. The Velvet Underground and Television, The Butthole Surfers, Sonic Youth, and the Minutemen, but I think by the time we started The Yummy Fur, American influences were really *verboten*. Not into it. Didn't like bands that sang in American accents and played hackneyed rock riffs. Basically every single thing that we didn't like is all the things that I specifically made sure that we did years later. The Yummy Fur was like the indie Taliban, our musical dress code. . . and when we were done with it [later, in the band, the 1990s] me and Michael (McGaughrin) said, let's do all the things The Yummy Fur told us not to do. At the time we were very anti-American. Very against Pavement. I don't mind them but I found it was more strumming. Just stop strumming your guitars guys! You're doing my bop in. This guy on the left is strumming his guitar and the guy on the right is strumming his guitar but higher up. So we've got a lot of strumming going on here. Fuck sake! Bill and Ben strummers. So we just played angular things. The only thing we would take influence from America would be The Contortions but we were more into The Fall and Fire Engines.

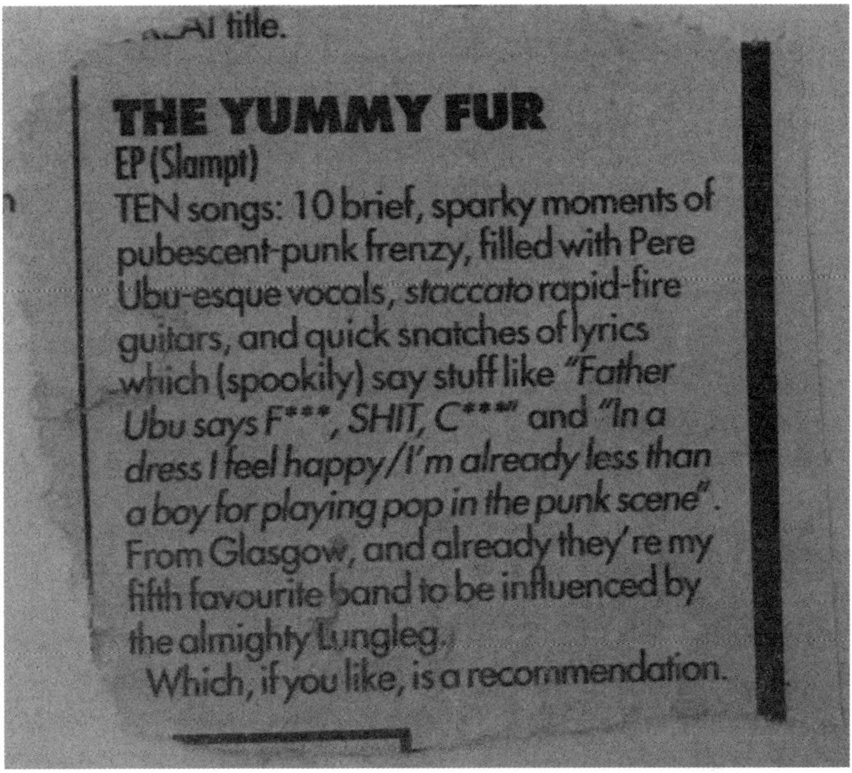

title.

THE YUMMY FUR

EP (Slampt)

TEN songs: 10 brief, sparky moments of pubescent-punk frenzy, filled with Pere Ubu-esque vocals, _staccato_ rapid-fire guitars, and quick snatches of lyrics which (spookily) say stuff like "_Father Ubu says F***, SHIT, C***_" and "_In a dress I feel happy/I'm already less than a boy for playing pop in the punk scene_". From Glasgow, and already they're my fifth favourite band to be influenced by the almighty Lungleg.

Which, if you like, is a recommendation.

Melody Maker review

In 1994 The Yummy Fur released their first single, the enigmatically titled 'Music By Walt Disney But Played By Yuri Gagarin Thus A Political Record' for the Newcastle label, Slampt. It was an important move, not only for The Yummy Fur but also for many of the bands and labels that followed.

Pete Dale (Slampt Records): The name 'Slampt Underground Organisation' was spontaneously hatched by my girlfriend at the time, Rachel Holborow, when we were in Italy in summer 1992. We were really into Beat Happening, K Records and the whole scene around Olympia, Washington and I think we hoped we could kindle a pop-punk Underground scene in Newcastle-upon-Tyne that might be comparable in some measure to the Olympia scene. We therefore put out a double fanzine package (*Slampt 1*) in early autumn 1992, with one of the fanzines having been written by me and the other by Rachel. Next, we did the Avocado Baby's *A Million and Nine* cassette (*Slampt 2*), also that autumn. The cassette caught on, eventually selling 350 copies. We put out a handful more tapes and then started doing vinyl singles from late 1993 or maybe early 1994. Perhaps inevitably, this led to vinyl albums and eventually (big sell-out alert) CDs. We said we wouldn't but in those days demand for CDs outstripped the demand for vinyl so we gave in. But we always liked cassettes best, because you could do a small run and still break even. Slampt put out 60 releases (mostly music but some fanzines and some ephemera of various kinds, such as gigs with catalogue numbers) between 1992 and 2000 and then we decided that we had done what we intended to do and a whole lot more besides so we stopped. We did get The Yummy Fur down to Newcastle to play a gig or two in 1994 and on one of the trips we got them in the First Avenue studio (eight-track reel-to-reel, £50 per ten-hour day) to record the EP in one day including laying down the basic tracks live, overdubbing the vox and mixing – all within ten hours.

John McKeown (guitar/vocals, The Yummy Fur): The EP's title was just straight out bizarre, strange Nouvelle Vague. We had another version of that title, spray-painted on a Greggs wall on Byres Road, we wrote 'Le Pastie de la Bourgeoisie. . . F&E', and Stuart from Belle and Sebastian saw that, and before Belle and Sebastian, that's what they were called at first: Le Pastie de la

Bourgeoisie. But he didn't know that we did it. That 7-inch – we did it in a studio called First Avenue in Newcastle. None of us had ever been a studio before. I knew that I didn't want it to sound cavernous and reverb-y, we didn't use any effects pedals on stage ever. It was very clean; very dry. No reverb. So we just knew we wanted it to go like that. In retrospect, they amped it up a little bit. What you think has no reverb probably has got a little reverb on it, just sitting there. And distortion – a wee bit just to pick things out. We were so extreme! 'No, none of this, none of this!' So it came in very dry. Probably more dry like whoa – this doesn't sound like the Fire Engines.

Music By Walt Disney But Played By Yuri Gagarin EP

John McKeown (guitar/vocals, The Yummy Fur): I remember we were on our way to a gig in Edinburgh to play with the Country Teasers, and it was pissing it down. And there was a car ahead of us. And I was like, that car is going awfully slow. And then realised at the last minute that the car wasn't going anywhere. It was sitting in the middle of the motorway, in the middle of nowhere, and it had already crashed. It was one of those moments where I was like, oh, we're actually going to hit that car. Like, that's definitely gonna happen in the next three seconds or something. I was in the front with Marc. And I was thinking, I wonder what this is going to feel like. Is it gonna be really sore? Is it going to be death? Anyway, bam! We hit this car. We stop, the other car went flying down the motorway. Our car was concertinaed. But we're all okay. Because we were bracing for it. Because we had that extra – what felt like a half an hour to get ready for it. We somehow got home and sat up all night making the sleeve separations for the record. You had to do the black, and then the colour separations and all that. We sent them away to get ready as they were going to come out in a couple of weeks and they sent them back. They were saying these colour separations are the work of mad men, what was up with you? We said we were in a car crash that night. And they went – 'Ah!'

Pete Dale (Slampt Records): I remember being amazed because they wanted two colours printed on white paper and they sent the two colours as separate sheets meaning that the chances of aligning the colours were small: in the end, it didn't look bad but it was more ambitious than most of the Slampt releases, all of which had been one colour on coloured paper. I took the two master sheets to a printer we used in Newcastle and he managed to make it work pretty good.

The Yummy Fur weren't just in demand with Slampt; London label, Guided Missile, already huge fans of Badgewearer, was eager to release something by them too.

Paul Kearney (Guided Missile Records): I bought a tape by The Yummy Fur in 1994 from a distro after someone said to me 'You'll really like this band!' I did. They were brilliant. Reminded me of all the bands I'd grown up listening to. Most notably The Fall, Nightingales and the Fire Engines. The lyrics were clever and funny. I instantly offered to put out a record by them and they accepted.

We talked about which songs to put on the single. They were all dead short. It was hard to leave any out as they were all great. I suggested if we have the 7-inch at 33rpm speed we could probably fit about seven or eight minutes per side. They were up for it. We went on to release several more singles and a couple of terrific albums, John Peel sessions, a tour of America. It was a great time.

The Slampt and Guided Missile connections were also important for another milestone band on the new Glasgow scene: Lung Leg.

Lung Leg

Jane McKeown was a huge fan of music as a teenager and loved The Velvet Underground, The Fall and Fire Engines. Ann Lafferty (Annie Spandex) had been involved with the Glasgow Music Collective for a number of years and had already played with We Are The Men. Amanda Doorbar had recently arrived in Glasgow from Newcastle. They were completely individual in their songwriting, focus and ideology.

Jane McKeown (vocals/bass, Lung Leg): Well obviously for me I have to put a disclaimer – as a younger sibling, where do you

Lung Leg

think I heard anything? I heard it in my bedroom, my ears were shoved against the speaker. I heard everything via my big brother, John McKeown, because he was two years older than me, so everything just got brought into the house but then from the age of about 15 we were just going to gigs together and then you just start to meet people.

Annie Spandex (guitar, Lung Leg): Snagglepuss – we came out of the Music Collective, I guess. One of the guys in our Music Collective band was Allan (McNaughton). When he left Snagglepuss we thought let's regroup. I'd been in a girl band, We Are The Men and it was completely different. So we just tried to get all girls and that was Lung Leg. . . and Lung Leg formed from the ashes of Snagglepuss.

Jane McKeown (vocals/bass, Lung Leg): Our introduction to music was – before the 13th Note, before the Kazoo Club, which Alex Kapranos put on – the Glasgow Music Collective that used to put gigs on. One night, two of my friends were walking up to the art school. . . and they said to me: we started a band. And I was about 17. And so I just said, I'm joining, and they were asking, what are you going to play? and I said I don't know but I'm joining the band. So they said, 'Okay, you can be in the band'. I'm in a band now. . . I can't actually play an instrument so I decided, because of seeing Kim Gordon and Kim Deal playing bass in the Barrowlands, and thought, that looks doable I thought I could play guitar but it was too busy, but the bass looked doable. I just started playing on the top string of my brother's guitar, in a band called Snagglepuss. My first singing voice was just a primal scream. I just screamed because – apart from singing hymns in Catholic school – I didn't know what my voice was so I just started screaming, literally, and then I went and bought a bass from the Barras. And that's how I started.

Jade Green (Amanda Doorbar) (drums, Lung Leg): I hadn't been playing drums long when I moved up to Glasgow but I had joined a band in Edinburgh. Didn't really know anyone in Glasgow but Marc Baines came to see us and asked if I'd play with him and John McKeown and we became Cotton Gum. It was a catalyst for getting to know some great people in Glasgow including Jane, who was starting Lung Leg and asked me if I'd play drums with them.

Jane McKeown (vocals/bass, Lung Leg): I always felt like I didn't fit in because I wasn't Scottish punk, like crusty, I was like glamour punk. I like New York punk. That's more my thing – Debbie Harry. And then luckily, when Lung Leg formed the Kazoo Club formed. So we were playing round the 13th Note – I mean, that's a major venue for all of us. We also got involved on the crest of the wave of Riot Grrrl too, which. . . we didn't form because of Riot Grrrl, we were there already. But when Riot Grrrl came to town, we were Riot Grrrl, so there's different layers for females. So that became something we were part of, too. We were musicians who we were all pals, the same as New York's CBGBs and things like that: it's just a bunch of people who are skint. If one of your pals was playing a gig that night, you could get in for free and you could get a drink from the rider because we had no money. So if The Yummy Fur played it meant I could go out that night and get a couple of beers and get in free. And vice versa.

Jade Green (Amanda Doorbar) (drums, Lung Leg): Most of our very early gigs were around Glasgow: first gig was at Nice N Sleazy with The Yummy Fur followed by a few more at the 13th Note and King Tut's, usually with friends' bands. It was exciting to share the stage with other girl bands such as Hello Skinny, Pink Kross and Sally Skull. Although the music was important, it wasn't just about the songs, it was more than that: the visuals, the passion and most of all it was just a group of girls enjoying what we did and having fun.

Jane McKeown (vocals/bass, Lung Leg): We used to go on tour about twice a year, generally us and The Yummy Fur in the back of a transit van. I mean, it's health and safety – mattress in the back of the transit van, placed so that they could fall completely on your head if you crashed, killing about five people from 18 different bands in Glasgow. And we'd just hop in there and we'd go, sleeping on everyone's floors, and go and play Leicester, Brighton, Manchester, London. And we used to do that about twice a year and then luckily, within about six months of Lung Leg forming, we started getting offers to make records.

At about the same time as the Yummy Fur debut, Lung Leg also released their debut, on Piao! Records.

Pete Dale (Slampt Records): Before Slampt, Rachel very briefly had a band called Tadpole with Amanda Doorbar (who lived in Newcastle at the time, which was spring 1992). Amanda moved to Glasgow at some point and in 1994 Rachel went up to visit her. She found out that Amanda had joined an all-female group called Lung Leg but Rachel also hung out with people from The Yummy Fur while in Glasgow, returning home with a demo-tape jam-packed with amazing songs. If I recall rightly, we wrote to both bands asking them to record singles for us but Lung Leg preferred to record with Piao! (Even though we asked first, but they said they preferred a London label – which stuck in the craw as we were really into the idea that Newcastle was cooler than London – but never mind. Awesome people them Lungleggers.)

Lawrence Worthington (drums, The Yummy Fur; later Country Teasers): I heard about Lung Leg from Marc Baines or Tom. We'd seen all those scabby wee punks around but it was still tribal – Jane called me the 'stupid Peter Tork-looking guy' and we laughed at their terrible hair dye jobs. It looked like they'd get one bag and all use it. But I went to a New Year's Eve party at their flat off Byres Road and it was very good fun. Jane said, 'Oh it's you. John says you're not actually that much of a wanker.' We have been besties ever since so I went to the first Lung Leg gig at Nice N Sleazy and I was totally smitten. I always loved The Raincoats and Kleenex and The Slits and here was my version. They [Slampt] wanted Lung Leg as it was a very post- and pro- Riot Grrrl label. I loved those trips to Newcastle. The [Yummy Fur] Yuri Gagarin recording was there, I think it was cheap because there was a group of mature men who would come in and record classic rock covers on Saturdays but would get too drunk by lunch to do anything. So the guy would call Slampt and they'd get a deal.

Jane McKeown (vocals/bass, Lung Leg): Well, our first release was on a label called Piao! Records based down in London. To be honest, I think I was so entrenched in the lifestyle. We all were so entrenched, we were living all-or-nothing lives. It was all about doing that, and nothing else mattered. So when we started getting offers to make a 7-inch, I was just so young I was like, yeah, yeah, no problem. It's probably the way kids are now because it's so easy to do. But I do remember when the 7-inch finally arrived, that was special. That was something completely tangible that you're like, holy fuck this actually is a special feeling. That and for the first time hearing yourself getting played on the radio.

Jade Green (Amanda Doorbar) (drums, Lung Leg): I'm not sure how the connection with Chris and Loretta from Paio! started. Rhodri Marsden asked us to play in London with the Keatons and maybe he just saw us at a gig or heard us somewhere but he liked what we were doing enough to put out a record. The recording was great fun although I think the sound engineer realised quite quickly that I was never going to be bossed by a metronome so he just let me do my own thing, hence the various shifts in tempo on our songs. Seeing and hearing our record for the first time for me was very emotional.

Annie Spandex (guitar, Lung Leg): We recorded nearly everything that was on our demo because a lot of the songs were only a minute or so long. So we picked the seven best songs and went to Toe Rag in London, which had all the old amps and everything. The band the Keatons came with us and helped us with all the technical stuff because we'd never been in a studio. It was just really exciting. You're in London recording a record. We made a Super 8, we played some gigs, made some films and then went back home to wait for the actual single to come. And we all helped design the sleeve and come up with the titles because a lot of the songs didn't have titles as well. Just really exciting. We never thought we'd get a single out. So that was it, we're done, we can retire quite happily now. We've got our first single: seven songs, 7-inch. It was magic.

The Negative Delinquent Autopsy EP

Jade Green (Amanda Doorbar) (drums, Lung Leg): When we recorded our first single we didn't know what to call it so just put our favourite words into a hat and 'negative delinquent autopsy' was the result.

The single was sent to the arbitrator of taste, John Peel, in the hope of a coveted play. For many, the thrill of a Peel Session was the ultimate accolade.

Annie Spandex (guitar, Lung Leg): You knew the single had gone to [John Peel], wondering if he would play anything. And he played three tracks and we were just like, 'Oh, my God.' And then he said 'get in touch'. We phoned up and said, 'We're getting in touch' and he just invited us for the Peel Session. And that's it, nothing else matters, you've made it.

Jane McKeown (vocals/bass, Lung Leg): The first time we ever got played on the radio, I can't remember; but the first time we ever did the John Peel Session, that's what I remember. I was in Blantyre at the time at my mum's. And we had the radio on in the living room and listened to it with my mum. And you're just waiting with bated breath, and I think he might have played the first song and didn't say anything. And you're devastated because you don't care about the music at that point, you just want him to say something like, say my name! And then I think he said something like, 'Oh, if I lived to a thousand I'd never tire of hearing that band'. And I was like, okay. Sadly he didn't. But that was exceptional. And that is very special because obviously you're either in that club or you're not anymore, nobody else is going to get that experience. He was a big deal for everyone. That was before there was a million radio shows and podcasts and it was like that or nothing.

Annie Spandex (guitar, Lung Leg): It's just really exciting. I remember doing the Peel Sessions, you got a recording and a cassette and you'd all listen to it on the train coming back. Before it's been broadcast, like 'this is amazing'. Just, wow.

CHAPTER SEVEN

A Modern Independent Glasgow

Urusei Yatsura start their own label, Modern Independent Records

In late 1994, Urusei Yatsura did a Peel Session and used the payment to form their own label, Modern Independent Records. The aim was to bring their own – and their friends' – music to the world, essentially taking their Kitten Frenzy *fanzine one step further. The first 7-inch release was a split single with Urusei Yatsura on one side and The Blisters on the other. The band were able to draw on their experience of putting together* The Kazoo Collection*, and The Yummy Fur and Lung Leg's experiences with Slampt and Guided Missile, including using the same pressing plant. Modern Independent Records was hugely influential for other Glasgow labels and, in a nod to Scritti Politti,* Kitten Frenzy *included instructions on how to make a record.*

Graham Kemp (guitar/vocals, Urusei Yatsura): I had sent John Peel a three-track cassette of songs from the live recording the compilation track was taken from and he told me later he had it in his car for ages and would listen to it on his journey into the BBC to do his show. We met him in '94 when he was in Glasgow for Sound City, and I went in to be interviewed on his show, which he was doing from the old BBC studios on Queen Margaret Drive. Alex had invited him and [John] Walters to the 13th Note the night before and he caught our last two songs. He asked us then to do a session and we had to admit we had no gear of our own and no way to get to London as we were all broke. He arranged for us to do it in CaVa Studios with Stewart Cruikshank the day after we recorded the tunes for the 'ALL HAIL' record in Maryhill at The Practice Pad. They came out a lot better, maybe because Stewart and Tony Doogan were really good, or maybe the random amps we managed to borrow were less broken. Who can say? We did 'It Is', 'Thread', 'Road Song', 'Teen Dream' and 'Taster'. The night of transmission we were all listening at my flat again. It was quite odd and exhilarating to hear ourselves on the radio, like we were a proper band or something. I had been listening to Peel for ages and never seriously considered any band I was in would ever be played on the show. We were all delighted, and the songs were the best we had ever managed to record up to then. We used the money to put out a split single with The Blisters, and previous plays on Peel had got us an offer to put out the 'ALL HAIL' record. We started getting offers and being taken more seriously in our hometown, so that exposure helped immeasurably.

Elaine Lawrie (bass, Urusei Yatsura): For me the biggest thrill was when we recorded our first Peel Session with Stuart Cruickshank at CaVa Studios. Because we always played very loud on-stage and at rehearsals, we couldn't hear ourselves a lot of the time. We kind of imagined what we sounded like and hoped for the best. When I heard 'Road Song' played loud, for the first time I felt like we were a band that I would be excited to see or buy records from.

The Blisters/Urusei Yatsura split 7-inch

Graham Kemp (guitar/vocals, Urusei Yatsura): We did the Modern Independent label. We chose that name to put out The Blisters/Urusei split single the Peel Session fees paid for. We ended up doing singles for Pink Kross and Eska, and Domino Rally, which was Fergus's brother Magnus with us backing him up. (That single was part of his final show at art school. We went over for the degree show and set up in front of his paintings, but we didn't play. It was more of an installation.)

We found a pressing plant in the Czech Republic which was affordable. We'd do wrap-around covers on the Drumchapel Youth Centre's poorly supervised Gestetner machine and put them in plastic bags, classic indie style. *Kitten Frenzy* would organise launch nights in the 13th Note and Nice N Sleazy, which would set an entrance fee, which paid for the pressing. We'd give out a single to everyone who came and managed to make our money back pretty handily. We had distribution with SRD and managed to sell runs of 500 singles. We pretty much just wanted to spread the word about bands we liked, so there was no thought of making it a business. Just pure enthusiasm. There's a comic strip 'how to' that we had on the back of the fanzine that showed how we did it.

Kitten Frenzy fanzine

Fergus Lawrie (guitar/vocals, Urusei Yatsura): Momentum started to build, people were putting out fanzines and you started to see posters and flyers all around town. We got our friends involved and started reviewing shows and interviewing the other 13th Note bands and touring groups. It was our first chance to get backstage and up close to gigging professional musicians. There were a lot of established indie labels from the eighties but grunge and Britpop were creating a signing frenzy and major labels were encroaching into their territory as well which meant there were a lot of tremendous bands touring during that period. One of my first interviews was with Sebadoh and I didn't have a clue what I was doing but Lou Barlow was fantastic and basically interviewed himself! My activist friend Gehan turned us on to a free copying machine at Drumchapel community centre. It was a clunky old Gestetner that would jam every few sheets until you set it up just right. We printed all the copies of our fanzine *Kitten Frenzy* on it, and I rode the bus out there several times with other bands to introduce them to it.

The success of The Blisters/Urusei single led to an expansion of the scene outside the confines of the 13th Note. The attention led to Ché Records releasing Urusei Yatsura's single 'Siamese' in 1995.

Fergus Lawrie (guitar/vocals, Urusei Yatsura): We started to get support slots and put on our own shows at venues like Nice N Sleazy and book other bands from beyond the 13th Note scene like The Delgados and Spare Snare, who would reciprocate. Spare Snare brought us up to Dundee for a show and we all got drunk together afterwards and crashed at Jan's house. ac acoustics were fantastically kind and gave us our first support show at King Tut's Wah Wah Hut. Outside of the band I had a bunch of drinking buddies and some small-time dealers I was friends with so I could always find someone to get drunk or wasted with pretty much every day.

'Siamese' was our hymn to the Kazoo Club really. 'Form a gang, a lo-fi band!' The first time we played it was at a gig at Sleazy's that Alex had booked that turned out to be the same night as the first T in the Park so everyone was out of town! The only people in the audience were Kazoo Club bands! It became our signature song and we would always end our sets with it in a massive noise freakout. There is footage of it being played at the Highbury Garage which gives a sense of the total chaos and energy of our shows. We crammed as many Kazoo Club bands into the words as we could and I think we managed to name check at least Pink Kross, Eska, Lung Leg, The Yummy Fur, The Blisters and Poison Sisters, and rip off a Trout lyric for good measure! Our songwriting was improving and we were growing in confidence. 'Siamese' was the first of a bunch of songs I wrote that included 'Plastic Ashtray' and 'Kewpies like Watermelon' that would all go on to be singles off the first album that got good radio play and helped establish the band and became a core part of our set.

Graham Kemp (guitar/vocals, Urusei Yatsura): Ché came up to see us play at the Cathouse based on hearing us on Peel and a mad letter and tape I sent them as one of six record companies I would consider working with. We were all big fans of the 18th Dye album recorded with Steve Albini, and Ché had put that out, so we thought they were cool. We liked them. They got us into a small studio under some railway arches in Leytonstone with a guy called Charlie Mackintosh and I think we recorded six songs. We were only initially going to do one single. Ché were very open to things like colour vinyl, which was a bit uncool at the time but we really loved it. Everything now is colour vinyl so it's hard to believe, but it was viewed as being substandard and maybe un-serious back then. I think they put out 500 copies (which was viewed as a really limited run in 1995) and quickly sold them, so did a couple more re-presses in different colours. I remember walking home with my copy in a carrier bag and stopping at Charing Cross because I had to look at it again. I was very pleased with it as an object and because we had the best song we had at the time on it. One of my many major malfunctions is being totally uninterested in the numbers side of things. I remember the initial quantity, I remember there being two represses, but I never thought to ask (and this continued throughout our so-called career) how many copies we sold. Of anything. I just cared whether we could do another one.

Elaine Lawrie (bass, Urusei Yatsura): We were used to playing to our friends; suddenly there were people we had never met packing the place. We were getting given boxes full of letters and presents from fans, even from Japan, America and Europe. But everyone seemed to have the same sensibility as us, so it was more like we had found our audience and they had found us. Our gigs became celebrations of everything we loved. Disjointed fuzzy pop. Fanzines, vinyl, cartoons, manga and pop-culture. If I hadn't been in the band I would have come to see us, and would have loved it.

Fergus Lawrie (guitar/vocals, Urusei Yatsura): Ché had hooked up with Seymour Stein at Sire Records and were shopping for bands. He had made a lot of money in the eighties licensing British bands for the US market. The idea was – instead of licensing – to develop a stable of bands in the UK, where it was easier to break bands, and get them into the press and then sell them to US anglophiles. A sister label called Primary was to be set up in New York to handle the imports. But Ché weren't suits: Nick and Vinita were real indie fans who knew all the bands and had been putting out fanzines and records in London since their teens. They were the same age and dressed the same as us. I'm not sure if it was a demo we sent or they heard us on Peel but they got in touch and came to a couple of shows and we trusted them straight away: they could offer us a wage and US releases and tours. We were concerned about selling out, as Ché was just a front for Sire really, but we knew the band wasn't sustainable for much longer as things stood – we were all on the dole except Elaine and we had reached the limits of our local scene and needed another step up. We had total respect for The Delgados and what they were doing with Chemikal Underground but we knew we didn't have the right dynamic or business sense to follow that route.

Before the Modern Independent label went into hibernation, they released two further 7-inches, the 'Abomination' EP by Pink Kross, and 'Trucking & Paving' by Eska.

Colin Kearney (guitar/vocals, Eska): Urusei Yatsura were big boosters for Eska from early on, which was very exciting as they were a band who'd released actual, honest-to-God records and were on the rise. I think the first interview we ever did was with Graham, and maybe Fergus, from Urusei Yatsura for the *Kitten Frenzy* fanzine, and I'm forever grateful for their sensitive editing of my puerile drivellings. They proposed a 7-inch release, so we went to The Practice Pad in Maryhill and banged out 'Trucking & Paving', 'False Start' (the one and only Kenny Macleod composition in the Eska catalogue, and it probably clocks in at the sub ten-second mark!) and 'These Are The Dry Years'. Our friend Mark designed the artwork, inspired by one of the many lies we trotted out about the meaning/origin of our band name, in this case that it was an acronym for Eagles Sometimes Kill Antelopes (other fibs included other acronyms, such as Esoteric Secret Knowledge Association, and apocryphal yarns about spontaneous chants at football matches – we talked a LOT of shit during interviews). The Modern Independent trick of printing the covers on A4 coloured card, which when wrapped around the 7-inch left a semicircle of the record on display at the back, is still a stroke of genius in my opinion.

The Delgados and Chemikal Underground

One of the most successful Scottish independent labels, perhaps even one of the most successful independent labels of all time, was born from this scene: Chemikal Underground. It's difficult to put into perspective the vast success of the label. Others fade in comparison. Fast Product and Postcard Records both ran for two years, with only 12 releases each; and Factory was in existence for about 15 years, with 2–300 releases. Chemikal lasted 30 years, with more than 250 releases, many in a period where the music industry was at its lowest point. It can't be overstated how successful this label was and is – in terms of resilience, in terms of it being run by a working band and most importantly, in terms of it releasing some of the most significant musical releases of the last 30 years. And it was all accomplished by a group of friends from the outskirts of Glasgow and Dumfries.

Emma Pollock (guitar/vocals, The Delgados; Chemikal Underground): I grew up in Castle Douglas, a rural community and I was completely green. I had absolutely no real knowledge of what was out there because my record shop was Woolworths. I didn't even know about record stores in the way that you could get if you went into Dumfries because when I went into Dumfries as a teenager, I was shopping for clothes. And I adored music. Music was in my house from the moment I was born. My mum was a huge pop fan, she was a massive Kate Bush fan. She introduced me to an awful lot of fantastic music.

Paul Savage (drums, The Delgados; Chemikal Underground): In Motherwell, where myself, Alun and Stewart went to school at Dalziel, a few other friends formed this band (Bubblegum) and it grew a little bit and became a six-piece. It was lots of people strumming guitars. Stewart playing guitar, Alun playing guitar. Me playing guitar. And a guy called Bruce playing guitar.

Had The Yummy Fur's John McKeown known, he would have been horrified at this amount of strumming.

Paul Savage (drums, The Delgados; Chemikal Underground): Everyone sang except for me, and there was a bass player and a drummer. It was early nineties, '92 from that point where it was really influenced by Teenage Fanclub. We were incredibly influenced by Teenage Fanclub. I was learning how to be a sound engineer through a guy called Ted Blakeway who recorded *A*

Catholic Education. Ted was teaching at the SAE, the School of Audio Engineering.

Stewart Henderson (bass, The Delgados; Chemikal Underground): I wouldn't give Bubblegum, as an entity, an ounce more respect – which is very little, I have to say. And that's in no way meant to be a dig at anybody that was involved in Bubblegum; Christ, I was in it. But it was next to nothing. We achieved nothing as that band, nothing at all. It just happened to be the kind of failed or failing band that most musicians find themselves in before they arrive at the band they do anything with.

Emma Pollock (guitar/vocals, The Delgados; Chemikal Underground): When I got to university, I met Paul, eventually – took me years. But you see, Paul and I [Paul Savage: husband, drummer in The Delgados, producer], were both studying physics, except he didn't really go in until the afternoon because he was a lazy sod. And so we got together in my third year at university. And when I met Paul, that was a music education like no other. . . And so I kind of got involved; I was invited to become a member of a band.

Paul Savage (drums, The Delgados; Chemikal Underground): I had dropped out of my course in physics. And I had been doing my year course at the SAE to be a sound engineer. That's what I hoped I would be. And so in that year, Bubblegum got Emma in to sing backing vocals. She guested on a song by Bubblegum, and we were shocked to find out that some of the guys in the band didn't really want to continue.

Stewart Henderson (bass, The Delgados; Chemikal Underground): Some of the guys in the band decided that it wasn't working and they wanted to split, and that was fine, I didn't give a shit. I wasn't really that fussed about it either way if I'm being honest. But Paul had phoned me up one night and said, 'Alun and I have been talking and we're going to start another band.' Emma, who was Paul's girlfriend at uni, was going to be in it. But we've not got a drummer and we don't have a bass player. Incidentally – I was friends with Alun in primary school but Paul and I were kind of inseparable through high school; pretty much joined at the hip, really really good friends.

Paul had phoned me up and said, 'Look, I'm going to learn how to play the drums, will you learn how to play the bass?' I would have to get a bass guitar. I was shit at the guitar anyway. I really was, I never practised on an instrument. So I'd not got a bass. And Emma worked at GR Management and knew the guys from [the band] Texas. Paul said that Emma said that Johnny [McElhone]'s going to give us a loan of a bass guitar for a while. Right. Okay. It was just one of these things. You always have to be careful about going back and bolting on a kind of mythology that maybe wasn't there at the time. But I know that when the four of us went to the studio and started rehearsing, it definitely sounded different immediately. From the very, very first time. Obviously it's going to sound different because you've got a guy playing the drums that can't play the drums and a bass player that's never played the bass before. So it's always going to sound different. But I think the thing about it was it sounded kind of good, I suppose. For want of a better word. There was definitely something different about it. And that was how we started. I think we probably had that first rehearsal around October '93.

Emma Pollock (guitar/vocals, The Delgados; Chemikal Underground): The Delgados were formed – pretty quickly. We were very, very opinionated. Of course we were. We had huge ambition. We knew that things were possible, all you had to do is be organised and at the time, all we really did from a financial point of view was each put something like £200 pounds in, and suddenly we were able to make our first single. We were able to make. . . I can't remember. . . it would have been under a pound at the time to actually have a 7-inch made. And so we all put in £200. We recorded the very first single – two songs. Paul was training to be a sound engineer at the time. We had access to a studio in Hamilton that we then bought, which is a bit, 'you did what?' Yeah, we bought it. We got a loan from Paul's dad, and we bought a recording studio. So we were very, very lucky that way. But I guess what I'm really meaning to say is: we knew what we wanted, and we just had to work out how to do it.

Chemikal Underground was born. Its first release was 'Monica Webster' by the label's own band, The Delgados.

Stewart Henderson (bass, The Delgados; Chemikal Underground): I think that there's a few key decisions in there right at the beginning, that we thought long and hard about and I think ultimately got right. First of all, the brand of the label was important. The name of the label was important and how we projected the brand was going to be really key. We didn't want to be, as proud as we were of being Scottish, it certainly wasn't a tub-thumping thing. We didn't want, as pleased as we were to be in Glasgow and doing our thing in that city, we didn't want it to be a Glasgow record label. We wanted it to be a big record label that happened to be based in Glasgow, but it wasn't a defining thing. We set out for that not to be the case. The first thing we did with the label was get the distribution deal. It was straight off the bat. And again, these are things maybe in black and white that can read wrongly. But we weren't interested in 500 singles under the bed. We were like no, fuck that, fuck it, we're not doing that. Because no. If we're going to start the label, then the whole thing is about distribution. It's about getting everything out and basically trying to get what records we do choose to put out, out as efficiently and as professionally and as effectively as possible. . . and that was what we set out to do early doors. There were a couple of distribution companies that we approached, and we ended up settling with Southern SRD.

Emma Pollock (guitar/vocals, The Delgados; Chemikal Underground): We were so inexperienced. And very principled. We had a distribution deal. That was one of the most important things, right? So when you get a thousand pieces of vinyl made, you're not about to drive them around Glasgow in the boot of the car, which I know is how some of the early record companies started. Where they would literally deliver records to the local shops. But we always knew that we needed national distribution. And so we had got in touch with SRD at the time, a guy called Harry – who was nicknamed 'Harry the bastard'. He got in touch and really liked 'Monica Webster'/'Brand New Car' and so he said, 'Yeah I'd like to put this out, I think this is good.' So we went and got all the records made.

Paul Savage (drums, The Delgados; Chemikal Underground): The label was run, initially, from our top floor flat in Cartside Street in the Southside. So we get the 7-inches delivered. We're top floor in this tenement and this delivery driver phones up.

He says I've got a delivery for you. Great okay, we're top floor. And he's like, you're kidding. These boxes are heavy. It's a thousand 7-inches and we run down and we're helping him up. And I think he was quite pissed off, but we did help. So we got these thousand 7-inches into the flat and I remember opening that up and that feeling of 'it's made'. It's made real. It's incredible. It's a brilliant thing and I'll never forget it.

Emma Pollock (guitar/vocals, The Delgados; Underground): And then we got in touch with Harry again. We said, 'Harry, we've got all the records made.' He said, 'What? I don't remember you guys. I have no idea what you're talking about.' So we sent him a cassette again and he listens to it and says, 'Oh yeah, yeah, I do. I do like it.' It's like, for Christ's sake! Anyway. That was a close call for a little bit there. And Harry did indeed come through and we put it out on SRD. And it did well. I mean, it made Single of the Week in *Melody Maker*.

Stewart Henderson (bass, The Delgados; Chemikal Underground): We didn't start up Chemikal Underground to put out Delgados stuff. We did put out our stuff because it made sense and it seemed the more responsible thing to guinea pig our music as opposed to fucking up someone else's. So The Delgados was the first single that was out on Chemikal Underground, well of course it would be. Because if we were going to make a fucking rickets of it, then we would rather do it with ours than with other bands.

Emma Pollock (guitar/vocals, The Delgados; Chemikal Underground): I remember distinctly that this idea of starting a record label was a double ambition in that it was not just a calling card. It was not just a 'Look, we've put out our own single and we can show you that people want it' because it pretty much sold out. We did a thousand copies and it pretty much sold out in the UK. It was always with the ambition that we knew that there was a scene.

Vesuvius Records

Brian MacDougall from The Yummy Fur, Pat Crook from Melody Dog and Marc Baines set up Vesuvius Records to represent many of the scene's uncompromising bands. Vesuvius was an entirely different entity to its peers, producing lavish cover-art, beautiful pieces of work in themselves. The label documented much of the scene's output and, like all labels in the new scene, it was done out of love and altruism.

Pat Crook (Melody Dog; Vesuvius Records): We lived in Otago Street at that point, Katrina (Mitchell, of Melody Dog and later The Pastels) and I. But then, completely separate to that, me and Brian (MacDougall) had this other group of friends and other stuff going on. . .

This other group of friends included The Yummy Fur, Sally Skull and Lung Leg among others.

Brian MacDougall (guitar, The Yummy Fur; Vesuvius Records): As I understand it we had found ourselves bang in the middle of this scene that was coalescing, where bands were forming and London and the music industry were far off and completely irrelevant. Fanzines were starting everywhere and every single person we knew had been energised to do something creative. If you could form a band you could get a gig; if you had a typewriter and Letraset you could knock out a fanzine and hopefully interview your heroes.

Marc Baines (artist, Jad Fair; Vesuvius Records): The zine activity was frantic. I was contributing covers to Lung Leg guitarist Mo Mo's *Bittersweet*, Sally Skull's Saskia produced *Heavy Flow*, Hello Skinny's Lucy McKenzie produced *Violet*, Brian did *Stinky Snax* and there was one final issue of *Hairy Hi-Fi*. . . Pat, Brian and I became friends with people locally making zines and forming bands that started playing at the old 13th Note club. The Yummy Fur and Lung Leg from Glasgow, Sally Skull and Starstruck from Edinburgh. At one of the Jad Fair shows I'd played in Edinburgh, I'd been impressed by the support band's drummer [Amanda Doorbar], if not the band themselves, and asked her if she'd be interested in a new band I was starting with John from The Yummy Fur. The band, Cotton Gum, was very short lived but it introduced Amanda to Lung Leg and cemented their early line-up.

Jane McKeown (bass/vocals, Lung Leg): Pat and Brian ended up sharing a flat with Amanda and Jade Green, who was Lung Leg's first drummer, And Brian was in Yummy Fur. We were just all round their flat. They were the long-serving couples, a bit like mum and dad, you know. We'd all just be round their flat. So I think Pat saw Lung Leg and Yummy Fur and thought maybe this is something quite special and interesting. It's the same as Postcard. You have someone that wants to put the records out and you have the bands – it's an alchemy.

Pat Crook (Melody Dog; Vesuvius Records): I was just really like, 'We should be putting these records out.' It's really great stuff and nobody's paying any attention to it. So I got some money together to be able to do that. I think it was £1000 or something. And then me, Brian and Marc were the triumvirate of people that were involved in that. Always hopeless at PR and always hopeless at any marketing whatsoever. And having to deal with London was pretty awful as well. We were all not extroverts at all. It was just like, 'Oh God, do we have to?' But you did kind of have to.

Brian MacDougall (guitar, The Yummy Fur; Vesuvius Records): I think Pat got some money together and we got hold of a fax machine from *Exchange & Mart*. That was the extent of the business plan.

Marc Baines (artist, Jad Fair; Vesuvius Records): Lung Leg had a couple of singles on the Piao! label that I'd help Jane Egypt design the covers for, but Pat, Brian and I started hatching plans to start up a label to put out records by all these new Glasgow and Edinburgh bands that we loved watching every week at the 13th Note. When Pat got some money through a business start-up scheme we set about putting the *In Spelunca* compilation together.

Annie Spandex (guitar, Lung Leg): Vesuvius was a start for everybody. That was the first record for loads of us, even though it was a compilation.

Pat Crook (Melody Dog; Vesuvius Records): We worked with Southern Record Distribution in London. I can't say they were amazing, but they were okay. Mostly just through mail order. . . we started with *In Spelunca*, the 10-inch, and then the money just generated itself. We made some profit actually, on *Spooky*, the compilation CD. That was probably the biggest money-maker. But we never had contracts with anyone, it was always just money to pay for the next one.

Annie Spandex (guitar, Lung Leg): That's my best pals basically – Marc, Brian and Pat. . . Marc was in Cotton Gum, and Brian was in a band as well. And they just thought let's put out a 10-inch. We recorded it in a flat just off Great Western Road. It wasn't a proper recording studio. It was all done in his house. . . From that they decided to try and continue releasing. It was totally self-funded and they were just putting out bands that they really liked. And it just so happened a lot of them were from Glasgow.

Pat Crook (Melody Dog; Vesuvius Records): Marc had a lot to do with that in terms of. . . just loving music to bits.

In Spelunca, *Vesuvius Records' debut release, was a lavish 10-inch compilation in a beautifully designed sleeve, characteristic of future releases. It was a highlight of the period, attracting many like-minded folk, following the philosophy set by Craig Tannock and also creating one-off collaborations.*

In Spelunca album cover

Marc Baines (artist, Jad Fair; Vesuvius Records): An impromptu studio was set up in Alec Prentiss's Bank Street flat and most of the recordings were done there. With zero mixing experience I somehow got it into my head that I could mix the Cotton Gum track and set about pretty much destroying the recording. I was dissatisfied with my guitar tone and added a heap of distortion, burying the much finer guitar playing of John McKeown in the process. It sounded fine and clear on headphones but in the clear light of day and over an ordinary hi-fi it was clearly an act of vandalism that spelled the end of the band.

Pat Crook (Melody Dog; Vesuvius Records): It was amazing. I loved everything about being friends and coming together and making a thing. That's always my favourite thing anyway. And showcasing as well – Marc's artwork for *In Spelunca,* I just absolutely loved it. Like nothing else. And then doing a 10-inch, which is totally stupid in terms of finance; everything's stupid financially that we ever did. But we were just like, that's what we want to do so can we afford it? I think it was the Czech Republic we got it pressed in. That was where everything got pressed at that time as well, again for cheapness, and it wasn't bad quality either. That was how we could afford it, you know. It was 500 we did, I don't know if we ever did any more – just that 500. But it was enough to generate the money for the next one.

Poison Sisters

Another of the early Kazoo Club bands was the Poison Sisters, including Sandy Black, who would become a crucial element of the scene as it progressed. Typical of the scene, the band was entirely different to anyone else.

Sandy Black (vocals/guitar/keyboards, Poison Sisters): The Poison Sisters were formed in the West Highland village of Tighnabruaich in Argyll in 1989 by me and my brother Peter Black and the purchase of a Casio RZ-1 drum machine, which was christened 'Honey B'. The name was partly inspired by The Pointer Sisters and the fact that any name involving the word 'brothers' sounded like a folk band, which, coming from where we did, was really not on. There were also songs that were written from a female character's point of view, so, it just seemed to fit at the time, but appeared to confuse just about everybody else from that point onward. Musically, at that time, we were probably inspired by The Ramones, The Cramps, The Velvet Underground and The Jesus and Mary Chain, among a whole host of others of that ilk.

Sandy had a fortuitous meeting in Glasgow with RM Hubbert (Hubby) and Gordy (The Stanleys), which had an equally fortuitous influence on each of them, the wider scene and the birth of another new Glasgow label, Flotsam & Jetsam Records.

Sandy Black (vocals/guitar/keyboards, Poison Sisters): I met them both [Hubby and Gordy] through the Kazoo Club at the 13th Note on Glassford Street, which was run by Alex Kapranos and his band The Blisters (who later changed their name to The Karelia). Gordy was in The Stanleys (who later changed their name to Tonic) and Hubby was in The Blisters and Me, Hubby & Thom (and in Glue a bit later on). We were all playing pretty regularly at the Kazoo Club and became friends through that.

By this point, I'd already put out the Poison Sisters' 'Chicane' EP on Class Records and I think Eska had asked the Poison Sisters to do a split 7-inch with them. Gordon's band Tonic were also planning on putting something out and possibly Hubby was thinking about it as well. Somehow, the three of us ended up having a conversation about it at the top of the stairs in the 13th Note. I think Gordy suggested we should start a label to put out these up-and-coming records. Hubby and I said, 'Aye, that sounds like a great idea!' And we took it from there. Pete and Rachel from Slampt Records in Newcastle had told Urusei Yatsura about how to get a 7-inch single pressed (comparatively) cheaply at a pressing plant in the Czech Republic. Urusei then printed the step-by-step instructions of how to do this on the back of their *Kitten Frenzy* fanzine for everyone to read and follow.

They then proved it was possible by releasing their split 7-inch with The Blisters on Modern Independent Records. I'd read this and used it to press and release the 'Chicane' EP.

We then subsequently used the same method to press and release all the 7-inch vinyl for Flotsam & Jetsam.

Various other people read or heard about it and either started up labels or released their own records using the same method. This is a classic example of how bands and labels help each other to get things done.

Flotsam & Jetsam Records

The 13th Note compilation had highlighted the astounding breadth and variety of talent that had emerged in Glasgow. Urusei

Yatsura's label, Modern Independent had reinvigorated a country steeped in independent record history. Now, Gordy Davidson from The Stanleys (and Tonic), Sandy Black from Poison Sisters and RM Hubbert put together Flotsam & Jetsam (F&J) Records, one of the most quixotic and criminally unrecognised labels to represent the diversity of Glasgow's blossoming music scene.

Gordy Davidson (The Stanleys; F&J Records): We'd found out that getting a record made wasn't just something that other people did. By then, the Kazoo had fully incorporated bands like The Yummy Fur and Lung Leg, and that whole popkid scene, and they had something of a head start on us 'cause they'd been backed by a north-east England bedroom record label called Slampt, and a Glasgow one called Vesuvius and I think in turn had come to the attention of Guided Missile in London, so there were 7-inch singles in existence from bands we knew, with national distribution, albeit at a small scale. This was quite enough to make the rest of us feel like runners-up in the grand race to superstardom, you know? So Sandy, Hubby and I, after probably quite a lot of late-night chats in the 13th Note, resolved to start a record label that would release stuff from our own bands, but also stuff from some of the other Kazoo bands who were even less organised than us. We weren't at all bashful about admitting that we were doing this 'cause no-one else wanted us. Flotsam & Jetsam Records. F&J.

Sandy Black (vocals/guitar/keyboards, Poison Sisters; F&J Records): We weren't really a normal record label. We quickly realised that a lot of the bands that we were seeing every week at the 13th Note/Sleazy's/etc. were going in and making recordings of their songs, but were just using them for demo tapes in order to get gigs. We then went to some of these bands and said, 'Why don't you put those recordings out on a 7-inch single instead? You pay for the pressing, we'll organise it for you and get you distribution and you'll make the money back by selling the records either by distro or at gigs.' Our only payment was 50 singles from each pressing to sell at my merch stall/mail order, which helped to pay for all the running around/postage/setting up of launch gigs etc.

Essentially, we helped bands to put out their own records, but gave them distribution and a label to do it on. (Although we did pay for one or two pressings later on.) The reason we were called Flotsam & Jetsam was because we were putting out the bands who the other labels in Glasgow didn't want to deal with for some reason or another. We had no qualms about whether a band fitted the 'label style' – if it wasn't too offensive to any of the three of us, then it was in.

RM Hubbert (Hubby) (F&J Records): We were very different from those other labels because I'd had this idea of starting a record label that ran on the same principles as the Kazoo Club. There was Gramofonové Závody, where if you were okay not getting a test pressing and not checking the artwork you could get 500 singles into the country for about £300. Urusei started doing it, Chemikal started; once we did the Kazoo Club album and once we saw Urusei doing it we realised, fuck I didn't realise we were allowed to do this. It was something that grown-ups did. It wasn't something that we were allowed to do! All of a sudden we were allowed to do it. I'd had this idea that, in the same way the Kazoo Club would let anyone come and play as long as they weren't dicks, I thought it'd be really good to offer a service to any band that wanted to release a record but didn't know how to. So that's what F&J was. That's why the output is so varied and weird. It was myself, Gordy and Sandy from Poison Sisters. We had three very distinct roles. Gordon was the grown-up; he was older than us and he knew how to deal with imports.

Gordy Davidson (The Stanleys; F&J Records): The rough theory was that each band would find its own cash to front a pressing, and SRD (Southern Record Distribution), the distro company that made a habit of handling wee labels, would tout our wares round the hundreds of independent record shops on their books, and that money would come back straight to the band to cover their outlay. If it ended up making more money than the pressing cost, we'd call that profit, and maybe build up enough to start doing proper fully funded releases with bands that we liked.

The favoured batch size turned out to be 500 x 7-inch singles – and at least to start with, a GZ pressing with a fairly plain sleeve wasn't costing much more than £500, if you ignored all our running about and incidentals. SRD paid something like £1.02 per 7-inch successfully sold, so stuff sent to them, again in theory, at least washed its own face. Meanwhile, whatever band was involved would hope to sell 100 of their shiny new singles at a local launch night gig, probably for a huge £2, and Sandy would take a wee portion, just a couple of boxes of 20 perhaps, to sell through mail order, again at more than SRD paid, but not hugely. So, overall, no-one should lose money, and maybe some good records would land on the turntables of the impressionable youth. That was the theory anyway. The reality was a good deal more chaotic.

RM Hubbert (Hubby) (F&J Records): The basic deal was, we'd release a record by anyone if they gave us the masters. We would get the record manufactured and distributed. That was the ethos behind F&J. It was never supposed to be a proper record label. It was supposed to help people like us who hadn't quite clicked they could do it themselves. We did the grunt work for a lot of bands so that they could release records and we thought it was kind of a cool thing to do.

Gordy Davidson (The Stanleys; F&J Records): I think the Stanleys EP was the first release. . . catalogue number SHaG001. . . Sandy, Hubby and Gordy 001. But The Stanleys were having an identity crisis, 'cause Gerry had spotted a band down south with the same name, and 'cause they were in Yorkshire or something, the assumption was that they were a couple of hundred miles closer to getting signed than we were, so we rebranded as Tonic, which wasn't a name any of us were particularly happy with, nor did it mean much to our legion of fans, but we were pretty stupid and knee-jerky back then, and maybe convinced ourselves a fresh start was better than clinging to the several years of goodwill we'd built up locally.

So, anyway, Tonic, as we now were, had been convinced by some wee amateur manager we'd picked up to spunk a huge amount of money on recording four killer tracks for our debut, with all sorts of fancy-dan overdubs, cellos (hello Cora), trombones (hi Simon), guest vocalists (no memory of who it was, but we'd already done a much better demo of the same song, 'Siren Sings', with a girl called Joy who I'm still in touch with, and whose daughter is now doing really well in the music biz).

All we had managed to do, to borrow a phrase from mid eighties Madness, was produce a highly polished turd. If The Stanleys had any appeal, it was in our rough, scratchy energy, but the live band got forgotten when we shuffled into the studio, and we didn't know enough about recording to verbalise that to either the engineer or each other. I think Shane (Connolly, drums) at the time spotted it, and suggested we scrap the lot, but he had a lot less money tied up in that recording than I did, so I resisted, hoping that the release would somehow find people to love it. So – muddled recording, unfamiliar name, and like a punch-drunk boxer we were like, 'Let's press this as a 10-incher, that'll be cool'. Fucking idiots. Ten-inch singles don't fit in the 7-inch singles trays, and they disappear in the 12-inch racks. It's cool for a rockabilly repressing perhaps, or if you're already famous, but as a 'Hello world, here we are' we'd have made more friends tying each of those things to a helium balloon and letting them go in George Square. So F&J Records' first release died like a sheep in a ditch. Luckily there was plenty more lined up on F&J's fledgling production line. Next was a single by Eska.

Sandy Black (vocals/guitar/keyboards, Poison Sisters; F&J Records): We had become pals with Eska through the Kazoo Club/13th Note and they suggested doing a split 7-inch together as they'd just been in and recorded a couple of songs. I think they had also recorded the songs for the 'Trucking & Paving' 7-inch for Modern Independent by then as well, but I'm not sure. I think that came out first. We had already recorded 'Unclean', so we put that on it and I recorded 'Lo-Fi Girlfriend' in twenty minutes at my flat on the four-track and stuck that on it as well. It then became the second F&J release after the

Tonic 10-inch, as had already been decided at the previous 'let's set up a label' discussion.

Colin Keanrey (guitar/vocals, Eska): The split on F&J was the result of Sandy from Poison Sisters proposing it, I think? People that were at gigs all the time seemed to like us, and maybe intuited that we couldn't organise a tombola in a church hall, so F&J led us by the hand so we could release some music. I'm a bit hazy on the details – I seem to remember scene stalwarts like Rat and Gordon from The Amphetameanies being involved with the label, and they were keen to help document all the fun bands that were playing at the time, like Pink Kross, El Hombre etc. My main memory is that we kinda messed up the recording of 'Aristotle', which was a noisy live favourite, so we had another pass at it the following year and released it as an uncredited song on our first release on Love Train, 'III Spike'. I don't know how much better the second take on it was, to be honest, but it'd take a cabinet of booze for me to go back and do an A/B on them!

Sandy Black (vocals/guitar/keyboards, Poison Sisters; F&J Records): Seeing a band for the first time who weren't all that good, but then they appeared back a few weeks later and they'd got a bit better, then they appeared back again a few weeks later after that and they were now starting to sound great and by the fourth time, they were fully formed and now superb, was a complete joy. All because the band had somewhere regular to play that encouraged them to do whatever they wanted. Alex Kapranos has mentioned this as well before – it really was wonderful to see these bands transforming before our very eyes and ears in such a comparatively short period of time.

Pink Kross

Pink Kross, who had been on the scene from the earliest 13th Note days, were another of the bands to appear on Urusei's Modern Independent Records, with subsequent releases on F&J.

Jane Chalmers (Jane Strain) (vocals/bass, Pink Kross): I wasn't in the original line-up. The original line-up was Jude Boyd on guitar and vocals, her sister Vic Boyd on drums and vocals and Geraldine Kane on bass – Geraldine, is very sadly no longer with us and died in December 2008. Jude, Vic and Geraldine met Redd Kross at the Reading Festival 1993 and Pink Kross performed in the middle of a Redd Kross gig, at the Cathouse, in Glasgow, later that year. So Redd Kross stopped playing and introduced Pink Kross and they came on and played, in the middle of Redd Kross's set! There continued to be a long friendship between the bands.

I was a Pink Kross fan. I'd first seen them play in the 13th Note and thought they were amazing. I thought they were an American or English band and couldn't believe they were based in Glasgow. I played guitar but had never met the right people to be in a band with. . . I got chatting to Jude at a festival in Queens Park in 1995 and she suggested I join to play second guitar. I was chuffed to bits, as being a fan and then getting to join a band you really love is pretty damn good! Geraldine left to have her wee baby, so I moved over to bass duties.

The vision for the band came from the original members who were influenced by the garage punk bands that came out of America in the 1960s like The Sonics; but there was the influence of bands like The Cramps, The Ramones and The Lunachicks too. . . all American bands. I loved these bands too, so that's why I was drawn to what they were doing.

Pink Kross's first two releases were the 'Punk or Die' EP on their own Bouvier Records in 1994 (predating Modern Independent, Flotsam & Jetsam and Chemikal) and the hugely influential US label, Gasatanka Records, home to Redd Kross. Pink Kross's 'Abomination' EP was the final release on Modern Independent in 1995.

Jane Chalmers (Jane Strain) (vocals/bass, Pink Kross): The 'Abomination' EP came about when Graham Kemp from Urusei Yatsura asked us if we would record a single on his label. We had done a few gigs around Glasgow with Urusei Yatsura, who we loved, so we were really chuffed when Graham said he wanted to put a single out. It has two songs re-recorded from our very first demo tape on it ('Velocababy' and 'Hot Trash'). Stevie Mooncat from local band The Zoo recorded our very first demo on a Tascam four-track and really helped establish our primeval drum sound. I think it was at this point we decided we didn't really need cymbals as he managed to get the drums sounding so huge. We later did a UK tour with Urusei and Number One Cup from Chicago and had a fantastic time, the best fun ever. The 'Abomination' EP was recorded at Apollo studios underneath the Merchant City Music Shop by Jim Brady (aka Rick Flick). If Pink Kross has an honorary member, it is Jim. He was a huge encouragement to us and did all our early studio recordings. He was one of the few people that knew how to record our drums!

The band also recorded another EP and split single for Flotsam & Jetsam.

Jane Chalmers (Jane Strain) (vocals/bass, Pink Kross): We recorded in The Practice Pad, which was a recording studio in Maryhill, Glasgow. Our pal 'Hubby' (RM Hubbert), recorded us. He was part of the record label Flotsam & Jetsam, who released the EP in association with Bouvier Records, Pink Kross's label.

Flotsam & Jetsam was run by Hubby, Gordy Davidson (The Amphetameanies) and Sandy Black (Poison Sisters). . . hence the release numbers being 'SHaG', being short for Sandy, Hubby and Gordon. It was the first ever recording I was involved with, so the excitement for me probably outweighed any aspirations. It just felt good to be recording with a band that you loved being in.

Gordy Davidson (F&J Records): Pink Kross were three girls playing a stripped-down punk thing, while kinda looking like the Shirelles or the Vandellas. Vic the singer was also on drums, and she was almost always on a big tribal toms beat, while her sister Jude thrashed guitar and Jane thrashed bass, with some shouty backing vox. Much more Riot Grrrl than Ramones. Vic sung low and growly, and the overall effect on stage was these 90-second bursts of anger, then they'd be really quiet and self-effacing between songs, then back on the furiously fast fury again. Their 'Active Dalmatian' EP was the first thing that F&J funded itself, at least the first thing that wasn't for one of our own bands. We thought it was pretty good, but it wasn't the first thing Pink Kross had put out, as other labels had released stuff for them, so it didn't have the impact of a debut, and the girls themselves seemed a bit equivocal about it at the time.

Most of the releases we'd done up to 'Active Dalmatian' had

come back from GZ in plain sleeve, or thin plastic covers, and the bands had sleeves printed locally, and just folded and inserted them into the plastic dust cover. For our Pink Kross release, which Sandy, Hubby and I felt was a move up from what we'd released so far, at least in terms of its potential to get a bit of attention and sell lots of copies, we shelled out for a printed sleeve from the plant... but that meant preparing and sending our own printing masters on film. What was this? 1995 perhaps? 1996? The internet wasn't really a thing, and nor was emailing designs as PDFs. So Jane had provided a tiger stripe design in red and black (which we hadn't dared question, although as far as we knew, Dalmatians had spots), and I'd took it to a print place which had produced a film master, which we'd sent to the Czech Republic with the mastered DAT tape and a note of the desired CMYK colours. In a hilarious mix up of language and specification inexperience, the sleeve that came back from the pressing plant was not red and black, but pink and white. From the colours of the anarchist flag to the colours of Barbie's beach outfit. It wasn't a good start.

'The Active Dalmation' EP

Jane Chalmers (Jane Strain) (vocals/bass, Pink Kross): The live shows were always a great mix of nerves, excitement, sequins, animal print and usually alcohol for 'Dutch courage'! The main thing was always the music and enjoying playing, even if we were nervous. I think we got faster and faster as we played through the set. . . I think that was usually my fault. . . I sped us up. . . nerves, I reckon!

We occasionally encountered sexism. . . most memorably from a dodgy sound-engineer, down south somewhere, thankfully can't remember where. The memories are more of people being enthusiastic. It was nice when girls (and guys) came up to you after the gig and you'd made them think about going and starting their own band. . . We never really officially ended. . . we did a one-off gig years after our 'last' gig. It was after Geraldine died, as it felt right to commemorate her – our friend Gary O'Connor who ran a label called Bubblegum Records had asked us to play his club, he was a friend and a Pink Kross fan. We played because it was Gary's club and because of Geraldine.

CHAPTER EIGHT

A New Edinburgh

The Male Nurse and Country Teasers

After the demise of The Shop Assistants, Rote Kapelle and Jesse Garon, Edinburgh never really regained the vibrancy it had enjoyed in the late 1970s and early 1980s. The Edinburgh Musician's Collective was certainly influential in Scotland but despite having venues like the Cas Rock and The Wee Red Bar, the city lacked a Craig Tannock or an Alex Kapranos. Perhaps it was that absence that dented Edinburgh's nineties music scene.

However, there was Tom Worthington's wonderful Bosque Records, there was Sally Skull and there were two interconnected bands: The Male Nurse and Country Teasers.

The Male Nurse

Keith Farquar (vocals, The Male Nurse): I'm a born and bred Leither. Went to Leith Academy Primary and Secondary. I left school before my 17th birthday. Stupidly took a job at Standard Life. Absolutely hated it. Wanted to leave after eighteen months. Worked another eighteen months so I'd be entitled to a full grant before packing all that job stuff in, to study sculpture at Edinburgh College of Art. This is the time when The Male Nurse formed. As with many working-class families at that time, no one in my family had been to uni so higher education hadn't seemed like an option. It all had to get a bit desperate before it became possible. It should be noted that Ben's entire interview for the book was conducted via email which has a very specific formatting and storytelling style.

Ben Wallers (vocals, Country Teasers; guitar, The Male Nurse): I failed to get into Cambridge because I was too thick so I went to Edinburgh because I'd read in the *NME* that Mark E. Smith lived there. I looked up all the M. Smiths in the Yellow Pages and cycled to one of the addresses before I realised that I was late for my tutorial on boring American literature. I am from Berkhamsted, Hertfordshire and I wanted to get as far away as I could – that's the third reason I put Edinburgh next on the list of university choices and the second reason is it came next alphabetically after 'Cambridge'. But once I was there I took to it like a duck under a bridge, I loved the place and never left willingly. . .

Felicity Macreath (friend of Ben Wallers): I first met Ben in Edinburgh, when I was in my third year at university. He was going out with some girl that was a friend of a friend, came 'round to my flat, and we became best friends. I think the flat I lived in was on South Clerk Street. Anyway, it was easier to escape the noise of a shared flat (and libraries filled with screaming Yahs) and go and do our homework in various old men's bars nearby. Traditional pubs on South Clerk Street and Nicolson Street, sometimes ones in the town like The Waverley. They were quiet in the afternoons, just old boys watching the racing, and they always had a separate bar area, or nook, for the ladies, so we could get some work done for the price of a few pints (the landlady always providing free rolls at lunchtime). This was our student life and some of my favourite memories of Wallers. Ben was hilarious, creative, great company and super smart. We initially bonded over a love of The Fall (my claim-to-fame is that Mark E. Smith came to a club I used to run in

Glasgow, when I was 17. He was very sweet to a tongue-tied fan and bought me a pint and some B&H fags. I remember him dancing up a storm to 'Mickey's Monkey'!).

Ben Wallers (vocals, Country Teasers; guitar, The Male Nurse): My best friend was Felicity Macreath, who rescued me from the Living Death of studying English at university and freed me into the world of old men's pubs where the music of the sixties and seventies played softly in the background. . . Other musicians, you say. . . hmmm. . . The Male Nurse group, and its extended family Country Teasers, tended to mistrust and be mistrusted by outside arties like other bands and musicians. Yes we sounded a bit like The Yummy Fur but anyone from Glasgow was strictly looked down upon from the great heights of Edinburgh. The thing about people from Glasgow was they smelled, because there were no showers over there. Oops, I didn't mean 'arties', that was a Freudian slip, I meant PARTIES.

Keith Farquar (vocals, The Male Nurse): Ben Wallers was studying English literature at Edinburgh and had a crush on Felicity Macreath who was at the Edinburgh College of Art [ECA] and was friends with The Male Nurse. I think Alan Crichton brought Ben to a Male Nurse gig and we hit it off immediately. Ben began moving in our circles. Ben is the most original and idiosyncratic of artists. Country Teasers and The Rebel have had significant influence on so many bands that have come after.

Felicity Macreath (friend of Ben Wallers): At this point, Ben was a solo musician. My friend Steve Mason (later of the Beta Band) would come through to Edinburgh to attend scooter events and to DJ, so we would go out to clubs and to open-mic nights.

Ben came onstage as The Sensational Alan Davidson. My wee sister described him as 'your friend who wears the dead man's clothes' and he wore the same clothes on the stage as well as in real life. He loped onto the stage, scuffed brogue-like shoes, battered hat, rings on his fingers, massive specs, but his polite, softly spoken accent was gone; in its place was a deep American growl. He was Harry Dean Stanton, Lee Hazlewood, a better-looking David Lynch! The most shocking thing was the music: it was country. It was so different to anything anyone else was doing. We bumped into The Male Nurse in the street. I knew various members through their siblings, clubs and pubs, and ECA. Ben had The Male Nurse painted on his nails, which they found funny.

Keith Farquar (vocals, The Male Nurse): I was in a band called Lucid with close Leith Academy friends (Craig Gibson and Spencer Smith), which evolved into The Male Nurse. Alan Crichton joined and then Ben Wallers came to some early shows and later joined too.

I'm not a musician, so I was the singer. In those days, and among us, there was a real night culture at the ECA. In my final year, I'd come in about midday and would often still be in the studio until well after midnight. There were a few of us across painting and sculpture who formed a peer group and Male Nurse members were often around too: sitting until all hours in the studios, drinking cheap bottles of wine, chatting, plotting, causing trouble. There would often only be us and one janitor in the building so it felt empowering. We played the Revel the year of my graduation.

As far as influences go – there is no doubt that The Fall were a huge influence on our early songs. Ben, Alan and myself were all into The Fall. My first love as a teenager had been The Smiths. Later we got into krautrock, Can, Faust, Cluster etc. I loved PIL's Metal Box. There are major progressions in The Male Nurse sound, between the early, faster, Fall-like stuff (the first Peel Session) and the slower, more melodious, and sometimes extremely heavy stuff (the second Peel Session and album).

Davy Henderson (guitar/vocals, Fire Engines): I was invited to attend their first recording session at the studios behind Easter Road stadium. I remember it was early afternoon and the gear was set up in the live room ready to go. . . I was introduced to a sophisticated gang of young men who were The Male Nurse (I'd met Keith previously). After a few minutes I suggested they go in and do a take, just initially to see how it was sounding, so they did and then we listened back. To me it sounded like the greatest English psychedelic album ever made, *Dragnet* by The Fall. . . not in a derivative way, in a great way, like The Supremes sounding like Motown. I felt I didn't really have anything to contribute, they had their sound. I didn't want to interfere, there was no point, so I left after about seventeen minutes.

Ben Wallers (vocals, Country Teasers; guitar, The Male Nurse): Felicity took me to the pubs and her boyfriend was George Miller who used to be in the. . . was it the Ventures? No, but a similar surf-type band based on the themes of Flash Gordon, not the movie with oh, whatsisname, the Swedish actor, he plays the painter in *Hannah & her Sisters* who gets very angry when Michael Caine's client, a rock star (played I think by the second criminal in *Home Alone,* i.e. not little Joe Pesci but the other one; BUT DON'T QUOTE ME ON THAT!) Yes, so Gordon. George was the frontman – and I don't think he'd mind me using the word *Obersturmführer* – of a band called The Kaisers who executed an immaculate completely waterproof identikit copy of 1963 Beat music but with their own songs, which George wrote or sometimes co-wrote, and their own style. He was a graphic artist by trade and made great sleeves and posters for the group, the whole thing was watertight. . . no – I think 'airtight' is the word I was looking for. Anyway, he sought escape from this self-imposed jail and asked me if he could play drums behind me, having come with Felicity to [a] very high-up open-mic night.

George Miller (drums, Country Teasers; also The Kaisers): I would hesitate to take credit for being involved in starting the Country Teasers unless saying to someone, 'Hey, you really should start a band' counts. I'd heard Ben Wallers' 'the Rebel' stuff and thought it was brilliant although I was so wrapped up in my own thing at the time, I don't think I fully appreciated what he was doing. I just loved the sound of it and I thought the lyrics were sharp and funny. I don't think that's a bad appraisal, but there's more to it than that. Ben's an artist and probably doesn't need a guitar or even music, but I'm glad that's how he chooses to do his thing. Anyway, I said to him, 'You should start a band – I'll play drums' and he did, and he let me play drums, or whatever made a percussive noise. I wasn't with them long, but I'm proud to have been involved.

Ben Wallers (vocals, Country Teasers; guitar, The Male Nurse): George wanted to play drums so I thought, well we can't just be a duo like Peters & Lee, I'll hafta I'll have to get a third person, and I was completely in love with Jon Spencer at the time – weren't we all, right girls? – so I thought two guitars was okay and I asked my flatmate Simon Stephens who was trying desperately to survive as a playwright working in James Thin's bookshop. up there on Princes Street... or was it the street behind? Soon Alan Crichton was sleeping on the floor of my bedroom so he joined as lead guitarist, which meant Simon could move over to the bass and at last the mistake was rectified: you actually *can't* have a band without a bass guitar. By this point I had fallen in love with The Male Nurse you see, they were the best band in town, probably the best thing going on in Britain, I wouldn't be surprised. But you'll hafta google that. Felicity and I went to see them a lot and I painted 'M A L E N U R S E' on my fingernails with her pink and custard nail varnish. I think we had played one concert as the three-piece though, at a pub in the 'pubic triangle', I can't remember its name but it was very nice upstairs, but I remember Alan being in the tiny audience, and my friend Lucy described him as 'the incomparable Crichton' although I might have got the adjective wrong, I know it's 'admirable' in pop culture isn't it. But she didn't say that. He was wearing his sports jacket. Anyway when he joined we were a band and off we went, not quite alongside The Male Nurse but close behind them, and holding hands affectionately. I had been Keith Farquhar's replacement singer for a little while when he went to Baltimore on an art school exchange trip. I can't remember whether that was before Country Teasers or after. . . I mean during. . . oh what a mess! But When we moved to London, Alan, Eck and I were in both groups; and then Lawrence was in both groups for a period, when Eck went AWOL.

Lawrence Worthington (drums, The Male Nurse): Before moving to Glasgow I went more to gigs in Edinburgh because of my brother and I would see Alan Crichton at a lot of those. Every city had a Baby Gillespie and he was that in Edinburgh for a bit, perfect curtains of hair. He and I really got along; a lot of folk struggled with his sense of humour but I thought he was the funniest fucker I'd ever met. We always talked about getting a band together but we were both lazy and he was disappointed when I moved to Glasgow. He hated Glasgow: his theory was that Glasgow is nice and supportive so you get dozens of okay bands that all go to see each other. In Edinburgh everyone is dismissive and no-one comes to see you so you have to believe in yourself despite the evidence. One really great band now and then, instead of dozens of okay ones. That was his theory. I heard from Tom that he was playing in a band that was like 'Johnny Cash playing Pussy Galore'.

Ben Wallers (vocals, Country Teasers; guitar, The Male Nurse): Alan Crichton. . . [and I] ended up living in the same flat in Stockbridge with Felicity and Eck but that wasn't really very good fun. He was very good at picking riffs. We wrote some songs together, a bit like Lennon & McCartney, although I can never really spell his surname right unless I actually go and look at a CD. Actually, 'Pipes of Peace', that's a record I'm looking forward to hearing again on my new record player. We played a gig at the horribly named Cas Rock Café. I think George got it together, and the guy who put on the gigs said I should send a demo to Crypt Records, so I did, and they released 'Anytime Cowboy'. Yes, it was very exciting although like everything in life except childbirth it was a bit disappointing. The red was a bit off, the fonts, etc., you're never satisfied.

Paul Kearney (Guided Missile Records): I'm grateful to John from The Yummy Fur for introducing me to Country Teasers. I went along to see them and instantly fell for them. Ben the singer was intriguing, such a mixture of things; a posh boy from Eton or Harrow or one of those schools. (I remember once having a conversation with him about who the most famous person who ever visited your school was. Mine was Tessa Sanderson and his was the Queen.) He looked like William Burroughs, played a guitar that sounded like crisps, made country riffs sound like The Fall, and the lyrics. . . just weird, genius, satirical, extreme, piss-taking, hilarious, conversational and at times just pure cabaret. No two gigs were ever the same and so I went to all the ones in London and a few up the road too.

Keith Farquar (vocals, The Male Nurse): The playground that was Edinburgh in the nineties – ditto with Glasgow's west end at the same time. Many mental characters. Many great times. The Leithers and the Weegies. The Glasgow west end scene around The Yummy Fur and Lung Leg was glorious. So many great people. We visited, caused trouble, crashed on floors and got the bus back.

Paul Kearney released records by both Country Teasers and The Male Nurse on his Guided Missile label.

Paul Kearney (Guided Missile Records): Shortly after I became friends with Country Teasers, their guitarist Alan Crichton told me that Country Teasers was Ben's band but he'd asked Alan to join. In return, Alan had asked Ben to join his band The Male Nurse. Did I want to hear them? It's one of the stupidest questions anyone's ever asked me. Yes, of course. At the time The Male

Nurse had not released anything and I don't remember exactly what song I heard by them that made me instantly invite them to be on Guided Missile. I had a lot of funny times with those lads. We're banned from Brighton pier for doing poppers on the waltzers when we were down there doing a little indie festival. (Melting Vinyl? Was that it?). Their song 'My Own Private Patrick Swayze' remains one of the best and daftest songs ever made.

The Male Nurse, *Patrick Swayze* 7-inch

Keith Farquar (vocals, The Male Nurse): The Male Nurse sent an early demo to Food Records with 'Swayze', and also a cover version of the *Are You Being Served* theme tune on it (yes, we covered that). A week later, Alan Crichton received a very strange phone call reply from Food saying how shit the demo was. (Now, why would a record company actually phone back a band they thought were shit?) Anyway, next thing Blur released the song

'Parklife', which has quite a resemblance to 'Swayze' – same driving rhythm and spoken lyrics. Not only that, but Elastica released 'Connection', which has an uncanny resemblance to the *Are You Being Served* theme. We may never know if this demo laid down the foundations for Britpop. (I think it did.)

Ben Wallers (vocals, Country Teasers; guitar, The Male Nurse): I don't recall playing the single with the band. . . I don't even remember giving them copies, I hope i did; can't remember! I did! But it wasn't like, 'Ooooh the single's here, gather round, let's play it!' Also, I don't recall much 'kinship' going on. The Male Nurse and Country Teasers felt of ourselves as Edinburgh bands: not Scottish. We didn't really like Scotland per se, nor her bands. Guided Missile was a thing that happened when we all made the same mistake of going down to London. That label was great, and released all of us – Glasgow and Edinburgh bands alike. So that was what connected us. When I met Lung Leg I fell in love with all four of them instantly of course. And I listened to my Yummy Fur EP, 'Kodak Nancy Europe' a lot. Indeed I liked all of my Yummy Fur records; I thought 'The Canadian Flag' was great. But the very idea of bands helping each other and being friendly was anathema to me. The idea of a band for me was like a gang: we will ignore you, alienate you along with your audience and 90 per cent of ours, and the only time we'll meet you will be to beat you up and steal your equipment, that type of thing. We never/rarely owned our own equipment so we always had to borrow. In this respect I was the Paul McCartney, being polite to the other bands, venues, sound guys etc. I found this very stressful and exhausting; I worried about gigs non-stop, right up until we were actually there. Using people who had cars, all that shit. Yuck! Nightmare. Borrowing, borrowing, borrowing. Deeper and deeper underground like Jamiroquai's soundtrack to the *Watership Down* remake.

Bosque move to Glasgow

By the mid nineties, Edinburgh was beginning to feel closed off. Venues were disappearing, and people were being priced out of the city centre. Tom Worthington and Mark Gibbons decided to move to Glasgow, which by contrast was full of rehearsal spaces, venues, and other musicians operating on the same DIY wavelength.

Tom Worthington (Hee Haw, Starstruck, Bosque Records): You put more in than you got back. By '95 I was spending two or three nights a week in Glasgow and it was obvious that's where everything was happening. So we chucked Edinburgh – stability, jobs, the lot – and moved.

The move west changed everything. Starstruck found new players, and Bosque evolved from a name on a Hee Haw sleeve into a working label that released small runs of records by Glasgow and Edinburgh artists. The city's energy gave Tom new ideas, and Bosque became a link between the two scenes.

Tom Worthington (Hee Haw, Starstruck, Bosque Records): The one thing that worked was the music, and that wasn't dependent on Edinburgh. Our rhythm section were already west. We folded our duo, Starstruck, into a full band and got on with it.

Glasgow's DIY community encouraged recording anywhere and however you could. There was little money but plenty of drive.

Tom Worthington (Hee Haw, Starstruck, Bosque Records): No one had money, studios or deals; you had to do it yourself. Mark brought incredible musicality and attitude. We were recording ourselves, distributing ourselves, screwing up and learning – like tracking the first Yummy Fur LP before we realised the Dolby switch on the quarter-inch. We laughed and carried on.

Tom's political interests also fed into the label's approach. For him, making art wasn't separate from the world around it.

Tom Worthington (Hee Haw, Starstruck, Bosque Records): I wasn't interested in art as something to hide behind. If there was an anti-Poll Tax meeting, or Bosnia on the news, that came into the room with the guitars and tape machines. Glasgow was more working-class than Edinburgh – people were known by where they were from – and it shaped the music.

Bosque Records started releasing other people's work around 1994–95. Early releases from Dominic Waxing Lyrical and Trout marked the beginning of a short but active period for the label.

Tom Worthington (Hee Haw, Starstruck, Bosque Records): We started properly releasing other people such as around Dominic Waxing Lyrical and Trout as we left Edinburgh for Glasgow. There was room. I never had money, but enough to keep another record underway. Seeing two catalogue numbers side by side in a fanzine – that felt like a real thing.

The label remained small: Mark was spending much of his time playing music for other bands and Tom never found the requirements he needed to grow it beyond a cottage operation. He had short discussions with bigger labels, but nothing came of them.

Tom Worthington (Hee Haw, Starstruck, Bosque Records): To scale it you needed organisation. I wasn't a natural bureaucrat and never found the right sidekick. Mark was off recording loads of other people. I fished for a bigger label to graft onto – a little money to play with – and I thought I'd found it twice, including with Creation, but it didn't work out.

While some Glasgow bands began to move towards commercial success, Bosque and its circle remained defiantly underground. Tom looked back on the contrast with some humour.

Tom Worthington (Hee Haw, Starstruck, Bosque Records): We played Fat Sam's in Dundee with The Delgados when London labels came up. They were together, had a plan, sounded great. I was faffing about what to wear and thought I was Prince on a multi-level stage. They got signed; we got a story. Fair play.

Despite those differences, there was no resentment. The Glasgow scene of the mid nineties was busy, communal, and largely self-sufficient.

Tom Worthington (Hee Haw, Starstruck, Bosque Records): We had everything we needed locally. Every night someone was making something great. You went to London and came back relieved to be home. It was chaotic, ridiculous, often unhealthy, with plenty of casualties – but amazing.

Bosque's most ambitious moment came with a pair of multimedia gigs that Tom organised in Glasgow, combining music, art and film.

Tom Worthington (Hee Haw, Starstruck, Bosque Records): If you want a parable, try our two nights at De Val's, a former porn cinema. I wanted multimedia: films, bands, performance. We premiered Richard Kern shorts and put Gilded Lil, Dominic Waxing Lyrical and Trout on one bill; then The Male Nurse and a deranged Sheffield stripper. Grotty, joyous, plural – with a fanzine to go with it.

CHAPTER NINE

DIY Looking Out

West Lothian: Z28s

Simon Alexie Grant (drums, Z28s): [We were] garage pop-punk noise merchants from Wild West Lothian. We formed Z28s in the late eighties/early nineties. One review said [we were] like The Ramones meets The Clash on speed. We were a four-piece but had gone through a few different participants: Lee the passing Chinese waiter on vocals, Batch on bass and Doctor Douglas Deviant on rhythm guitar. The final settled line up was Rockin' Rick Buzzin' on guitar, Skid Mark Tyme on vocals, Strange Stringer on bass and Spacequeen on drums (me). We didn't take ourselves that seriously and would rip through a set back-to-back with no breaks, just bang bang bang. We played gigs almost on a weekly basis in the Cas Rock in Edinburgh and also The Venue, Bannerman's and Liquid Rooms. Further afield we had gigs in Glasgow: Nice N Sleazy, Cathouse and 13th Note to name a few. We supported bands like Jane County and the Electric Chairs, UK Subs, 999, Man or Astro-man?, Nashville Pussy and New Bomb Turks to name a few.

The scene in Edinburgh was rocking although Glasgow gigs always seemed to be more fun and boisterous, and it was a huge part of my younger years. Influenced by bands like the Ramones, The Clash, Iggy and Sub Pop bands, although I was a proper indie kid. Gigs were always high-octane, full-on chaos. Rockin' Rick Buzzin' used to have a fanzine called *Running Wild*, which was all about Americana and the American car scene in Scotland, hence the name Z28s. Ricky used to be in constant contact with Marky Ramone, who would get the fanzine. We were all born in the wrong country – should have been stateside, we would have still been rockin'. It was constant gigging, sometimes three or four times a week but so much fun and we didn't get home until the sun came up on numerous occasions.

Dundee: Spare Snare

Despite a plethora of local characters such as 'Mad Robert', 'Wee Alfie from Lochee' and 'Fast Eddie', Dundee was not known for maverick bands. In the 1980s, the city's emerging independent music scene had lagged behind the thriving worlds of Glasgow and Edinburgh. Yet in the early 1990s a band emerged that would become one of Scotland's most enduring underground acts – Spare Snare.

Jan Burnett (vocals/guitar/synthesizer, Spare Snare): There was nothing happening in Dundee at that time, and I mean nothing. I was playing about with a four-track cassette recorder, very cheap guitars and synths. There was no money, but I was determined to release a 7-inch single. Before Spare Snare, I'd released a one-sided thing on my own label under the name The White Leather Club – a track called 'Shandy on the Rocks'. *Melody Maker* reviewed it and said 'Rebuild Hadrian's Wall'. I was pleased with that. Nobody really got that it was my take on what Bill Drummond was doing at the time. But without that single, Spare Snare might never have happened – it opened doors to US releases, tours, and a deal with Deceptive Publishing. It all joins up.

Jan Burnett's first single as Spare Snare, 'Super Slinky/As a Matter of Fact,' appeared in late 1992. The release, through his own Chute label, sparked unexpected attention abroad.

Jan Burnett (vocals/guitar/synthesizer, Spare Snare): After releasing the first 7-inch, a US label in Minneapolis picked it up. They asked if the band could come over, but there was no band – just me. So I spoke to a few friends who could play, and they were in. Our live debut was at the Coffee Bar in Dundee Art College. After a handful of gigs, we flew to America and played six more. At the last show, at CMJ in New York, Steve Lamacq and Tony Smith from Deceptive Records saw us and offered us a publishing deal.

Dundee was hardly known for its independent scene. But a small network of musicians and venues – the West Port Bar, Bar Chevrolet and the Art College – were a nucleus for new ideas.

Barry Gibson (drums/various, Spare Snare): There were quite a lot of bands in Dundee in the early nineties and a couple of venues that put them on, with the West Port Bar probably the most significant. The bands were diverse, but the most recognised locally were still influenced by the blue-eyed soul and big pop sound that Glasgow was known for. That wasn't what we were doing. There was a small punk scene too, with bands like Broccoli, who we'd sometimes play with.

Alan Cormack (guitar/various, Spare Snare): By the late eighties I was going to the Dance Factory nights at Fat Sam's, seeing Half Man Half Biscuit, The Soup Dragons and The Wedding Present – those nights were a big influence. I got to know Barry from gigging, and Jan was the DJ at the venues we played. By the time we joined Spare Snare, a wee scene was developing with like-minded bands like Gerils, Broccoli, Muppet Mule and Hate Foundation. Those were great times.

What began as a solo recording project soon became a full band. Spare Snare's lo-fi approach, swapping instruments and embracing imperfection, reflected the American Underground acts they admired.

Jan Burnett (vocals/guitar/synthesizer, Spare Snare): Influence-wise, I've always been a synth duo guy – OMD, Soft Cell, Blancmange, Pet Shop Boys. But because of OMD, I discovered The Velvet Underground and early Factory Records. It all connects. Later it was more guitars, but always about the tune, or the lack of one.

Barry Gibson (drums/various, Spare Snare): Jan had been doing DIY recordings and one live show with Graeme Anderson before forming a band to play his songs. Alan and I had been playing together and were assimilated as the rhythm section, though early on we'd often swap instruments, like Sebadoh used to.

Alan Cormack (guitar/various, Spare Snare): Jan became the regular DJ in the pub where I worked. He gave me a copy of the first single and said he was putting a band together to play some gigs in the US. I loved the single – it sounded like Pavement!

There was a definite Sebadoh, Pavement, Guided by Voices, Archers of Loaf influence back then.

Spare Snare's Chute label became one of the earliest examples of Scotland's next generation of DIY imprints, predating the likes of Chemikal Underground.

Jan Burnett (vocals/guitar/synthesizer, Spare Snare): It might sound like I had a plan, but I didn't. I just knew what I wanted. Our single and album came out before The Delgados or Urusei Yatsura. It was lovely to hold the first single, though it was hard work painting sleeves and re-pressing copies for K Records. Calvin from K wanted to sell it, but I never heard back, so I sold them through myself. Rough Trade took five, then called for more. There's no big secret to running a label – record, press, promote, repeat. I always believed owning your catalogue was everything. Now everyone says it, but back then people laughed.

Spare Snare also later worked with Ché and Deceptive, though their DIY principles remained intact.

Jan Burnett (vocals/guitar/synthesizer, Spare Snare): Nick at Ché saw us a few times. It was all handshake deals. They had a Warner connection but didn't like to talk about it. We were on their first split-single series. Ultimately, catalogue is everything. I've no patience for artists who moan about not owning their music. We kept our rights, even when Deceptive's publishing deal with EMI came up – I insisted on a ten-year term instead of twenty-five. Maybe it meant less push from them, but I'm glad we own it all now.

Barry Gibson (drums/various, Spare Snare): Most of the labels we worked with were small DIY outfits doing things hand to mouth. Deceptive was the biggest, but they had their hands full with Elastica. There was never a big multi-album deal – just short-term arrangements that suited everyone.

Spare Snare's independence resonated with John Peel, who gave them radio sessions and a Reading Festival slot. Yet Dundee's distance from the central belt often meant fewer eyes on them.

Jan Burnett (vocals/guitar/synthesizer, Spare Snare): Peel definitely saw that we were doing something different. He called a couple of times for our first sessions and later invited us to play live at Reading on his stage. It was great having all those BBC tracks released together – you can hear us grow. As for Glasgow bands getting more attention? Only if they were shit. It's easier for London A&R to get a train to Glasgow than to come to Dundee for one band.

Barry Gibson (drums/various, Spare Snare): Dundee's always been overlooked. Most of the Dundee musicians who made it big had to leave — Ricky Ross, Billy Mackenzie. There was never the infrastructure Glasgow had. But the Glasgow bands we did meet – The Ranters, The Delgados, Urusei – were welcoming, and we made good friends.

Alan Cormack (guitar/various, Spare Snare): The *NME* called it 'The New Scottish Underground' – us, The Delgados, Urusei Yatsura, bis, Ganger, Long Fin Killie. We played great gigs together and built real friendships.

As many of their contemporaries wound down in the late 1990s, Spare Snare continued, powered by persistence and a need to create.

Jan Burnett (vocals/guitar/synthesizer, Spare Snare): It's partly stubbornness, but mostly that I can't not do it. Things slow or speed up, but it's constant. Bandcamp has been brilliant for us – owning and selling direct feels right. The late nineties were bleaker with the publishing deal gone, but we kept going. Perseverance, pure and simple. Don't let the fuckers get you down.

Barry Gibson (drums/various, Spare Snare): Some might say we were too dumb to stop. But without a big label, we didn't have that pressure. We could take breaks and experiment. When Paul moved to London, the three of us messed about recording ideas that became *Animals and Me*. Nothing was off limits – some great stuff came from that freedom.

Alan Cormack (guitar/various, Spare Snare): I've great memories of touring with The Delgados in '96, playing T in the Park, Reading Festival, the US tours, the Peel Sessions. Kudos to Jan for making it all happen.

Three decades on, Spare Snare remain a testament to self-belief, stubbornness, and the enduring spirit of DIY Scottish music.

CHAPTER TEN

Slight Return: ac acoustics

ac acoustics had already released a debut album, Able Treasury, *on Elemental Records in 1994, and two acclaimed singles 'Sweatlodge' and 'Hand Passes Plenty'. As they had been established earlier, ac acoustics were slightly on the fringes of the 13th Note scene but they were very much a part of the Glasgow scene. Their early success meant they could offer support to many of the upcoming bands, especially Urusei. After a short hiatus when guitarist Roger Ward became ill, they reassembled with a new line-up.*

Caz Riley (bass, ac acoustics): There was no split. Roger [Ward] started becoming increasingly ill, unable to play guitar, write, tour or even function in daily life. I remember and have photos of the first Reading Festival we did, Roger could hardly walk. But he played a blinder and after the gig he collapsed, totally spent all the energy he had. Turns out he had multiple sclerosis, took the doctors ten fuckin' years to diagnose him.

Paul Campion (vocals, ac acoustics): There had been an interesting band around for a while called Big Burd. We had seen them quite a bit and they were enthusiastic fans of the band. Colin Hardie, who went on to have a very successful career in band management, and Mark Raine, an obviously really special guitarist. We asked Mark if he wanted to join the band. He did. He could play every one of our songs already. Couple of rehearsals, warm-up last minute gig to a lot of hostile locals at a pub in Helensburgh and on stage at T in the Park a couple of days later being recorded live to be broadcast on Radio 1. We were familiar with this but it was new to Mark. He was absolutely fearless and faultless. We were the first band to play a note at the first T in the Park. More accurately, Mark was.

Mark Raine (guitar, ac acoustics): ac acoustics were one my favourite bands. I loved the 'Hand Passes Plenty' EP and must've been one of the first to buy *Able Treasury* on the day of release. I think I actually started to follow them before they were signed and couldn't believe they were an unsigned band. So being asked to join, albeit only initially for a short period until Roger got over his illness, was unbelievable, but also very nerve-wracking. Caz phoned me, and it was when you only had house phones. So I was in my living room in Cumbernauld at my mum and dad's house. My dad was watching football and my mum was reading, and Caz is on the phone asking if I'll stand in for Roger in one of my favorite bands, at three gigs, two warm-ups and then T in the Park! He then read out a set list I had to learn for the first rehearsal in three days.

Caz Riley (bass, ac acoustics): We thought Roger's illness was just a temporary thing and had other gigs lined up. T in the Park being the next one. We knew Mark from Big Burd, he was a cool guy and played really well, was a fan of the band and knew the songs, so after a bit of discussion it was decided to see if he would stand in and cover Roger till he was better.

Mark Raine (guitar, ac acoustics): I was very nervous in the first rehearsal. Although I kind of knew them a bit, Paul and Caz could be a bit intimidating, not intentionally, more through my perception of them at the time, but especially now I was entering into their territory to replace their fantastic guitarist, and friend. And I had Roger up there as one of the most creative guitarists I'd seen so it was also daunting trying to follow him, who had a completely different virtuoso style of playing that I didn't really have – I was shiteing it.

The rehearsals went okay. I found the band to be very professional and focused, the equipment and studio to be better and everything was overall up a level from what I was used to. We played a tiny warm-up gig in Largs and another one, maybe in Paisley, and then T in the Park! We were actually first on the line-up on the second stage, which I think means we actually opened TITP, but the gates hadn't been opened by the time we started. So we played the first song, at the first TITP, to absolutely nobody. By the time we finished the second song, there were 5000 people in the tent and the gig was fantastic. And that was supposed to be that. Roger was supposed to get better and I was supposed to go back to Big Burd. But for a number of reasons that didn't happen and I was asked to join ac acoustics full time. I was able to finish my course at university and then move 'full time' to rehearse three times a week for six hours and go on tours etc.

Paul Campion (vocals, ac acoustics): Playing songs is one thing, but writing them is another. Mark just seamlessly fitted in. We always pretty much wrote by jamming. Someone would have a bit of a guitar part, bit of a bass line or a bit of a drum part and we would just develop these for hour after hour and put finished arrangements together. We would record them in rehearsals on two tracks of a four-track. I would develop vocal parts by singing gibberish (some would say the final outcome was also gibberish) and then work at home on the other two tracks on the cassette. This was the way we always did it and Mark was just a natural new part. The music was just an evolution again. He shared our laser-focused absolute confidence in the quality of what we did and how we did it.

Mark Raine (guitar, ac acoustics): We had to write new songs, and this is where some problems started. I became very insecure about how anything I wrote would be good enough for this band, so I was reluctant to share any ideas I had, instead trying to jam along with something someone else started. But I wasn't very good at that, certainly not as good as Roger was. Roger was also integral to the songwriting process, more often than not initiating the jams with riffs or chord progressions he had come up with. So not only was I not contributing great creative 'virtuoso' guitar parts to the ideas others were bringing, I wasn't bringing any ideas of my own. And it became quite noticeable. There were conversations about bringing Roger back into the band, keeping me as well as I had a more melodic/pop slant on things, but getting Roger back as the chemistry wasn't quite working. But it was this conversation that jolted me into action as I thought it was now at a point where there was nothing to lose. I'd been coming up with lots of ideas and riffs but just not sharing them with the band: it was now or never. So the first one I shared was the riff that eventually became 'Stunt Girl'. Dave picked up the punk-pop vibes straightaway and Caz and Paul followed quickly afterwards. That gave me the confidence to share the rest of the ideas I had and we started on a slightly different way of working than the band had previously – we never looked back from that point onwards.

Paul Campion (vocals, ac acoustics): Placebo released their first album at the same time. It was properly promoted by Hut. Full-page adverts in every magazine and music paper. Massive posters, when these things weren't treated like vandalism in the way they are today, in every town and city across the country. We got a few posters at Ladbroke Grove and adverts the size of a fag packet in the arse end of publications where people were selling off second-hand instruments. It was absolute madness. Brian [Molko] wore our 'Stunt Girl' t-shirt when Placebo deservedly appeared for the first time on *Top of the Pops* with 'Nancy Boy'. Both bands had become the best of friends. Lu Hunt, who worked at our management company, came up with the idea. She thought it would be make a brilliant skinny t-shirt. She was right. It continues to feature in Placebo's merchandise, which is continuing testament to Lu. Lu was the one person at our management company who genuinely had absolute faith in us. She supported us. She fought for us. I want to thank her and pay tribute to her. She died at a young age from breast cancer and we all miss her terribly.

CHAPTER ELEVEN

Beginnings

bis and Belle and Sebastian

bis seem to have been unfairly overlooked as part of Glasgow's music story. Perhaps this is the inevitable public perception of the dreaded one-hit-wonder, which is unfair to the band. bis have always been an integral part of Glasgow's musical scene and very much respected by their peers. bis are a magnificent band. They were probably the only band since The Undertones able to convey youthful pop-punk energy in the same way. They were full of exuberance and wit, and encapsulated everything that being young is about. Their huge back-catalogue is worthy of discovery. A completely unique band.

Steven Clark (Sci-Fi Steve) (bis): Myself and John, being brothers, had been writing and recording demos from the tender ages of 13 and 11 around the start of the nineties. We actually used to rehearse in Tower Studios every Saturday morning and quite often The Pastels would be in after us. Amanda (MacKinnon) was at school with us and was one of the only other people into alternative music so it was a no-brainer to get her involved and our sound slowly moved away from the

Madchester and classic indie style to the somewhat idiosyncratic beast we became infamous as. We started gigging as a three-piece in 1994 but 1995 was really our year zero. Our influences were all over the place and we stole little bits from such a wide variety of bands that we became something unique. The obvious influences would be Devo, The B-52's, Blur and Huggy Bear and there's loads of XTC bits too. The less obvious but massive influences range from The Beastie Boys (we were massive fans before working with them, 'Kandy Pop' is essentially a Beasties riff sped-up), there's big bits of New Order and even Duran Duran all over *Social Dancing* and our core inspirations of late eighties/early nineties 'indie/dance' (for want of a much better term) and Riot Grrrl are never far from the surface. Locally, it's fair to say The Yummy Fur and Lung Leg opened our ears to a lot of the late seventies Rough Trade Records, wiry post-punk bands, The Raincoats and Kleenex especially. There's also a Japanese band called The Plastics that we inadvertently ripped off massively, Paul Cox from Too Pure Records gave us a tape of them sometime in 1995 in London and we stuck it on for the drive home. Hilariously close!

Amanda MacKinnon (Manda-Rin) (vocals, keyboards bis): I was a big alternative/indie music fan in the early nineties but found it easier to listen to records than learn to play an instrument. I couldn't play anything, I just mucked about and played synth by ear a teeny bit. I'd seen posters for Steven and John's band, Black Iron Skyline, around our school and local neighbourhood and went to see them with my best friend whenever I could as Steven was 'the hot guy from the year above'. When I started going out with Steven it was almost like an indie dream to be dating the singer of a band I liked. Alternative music wasn't something many kids at school liked so it was amazing having two people I could go record shopping with and attempt to get into over-18s gigs with. I was then invited to take over on synth in their band, which stretched their mini line-up from two to three people they abbreviated. They made an acronym of the band's name, and that's where it all began for me.

Steven Clark (Sci-Fi Steve) (bis): Initially when Amanda joined, it was just myself, and John on vocals. There's a famous moment from the basement of the original 13th Note when we debuted 'Kill Your Boyfriend', people who were sitting up the back, half paying attention, suddenly all stood up and were stunned to see the previously quiet Amanda turn into the all-screaming Manda-Rin. There was a great community of other bands, musically disparate but like-minded.

Amanda Mackinnon (Manda-Rin) (bis): I love that memory! I've always been quite a bashful and shy person so it certainly took me a lot of courage to not only get on a stage (normally hiding to the side) but to shout into a mic. It was so scary when all eyes turned to me! I don't think there was a gig after that where I didn't sing/shout so it's crazy how things developed.

Steven Clark (Sci-Fi Steve) (bis): Like lots of other bands, Alex Kapranos gave us our first real shows. Urusei Yatsura were massively supportive and helped with fanzine production too. We played with Lung Leg, The Yummy Fur and Pink Kross loads too. We were the oddballs with our drum machine and synths but the scene was genuinely supportive as far as I can remember.

Amanda Mackinnon (Manda-Rin) (bis): The aforementioned 'cool' bands are certainly large influences but I suppose I didn't really know much about Devo or XTC until we were actually compared to them and could then discover their early stuff. I'd always been a fan of eighties music like Madonna, the Go-Go's and the Bangles – all strong female singers. When I then heard Riot Grrrl bands like Bikini Kill and Bratmobile it changed my world and gave me an oomph and desire to go for it. When I heard bands like Sleater-Kinney and Bikini Kill talking about their influences like X-Ray Spex and the Slits it gave me a mission for my next outing to the record shops. It was unbelievable to discover bands like this existed and were around the year I was born. Poly Styrene from X-Ray Spex is a unique and powerful lady who is probably responsible for half the bands I like.

bis released their first offering, not on a Glasgow label – or even a London one – but a label from Spain.

Steven Clark (Sci-Fi Steve) (bis): Jesus from Acuarela Records was holidaying in Edinburgh and picked up our fanzine in Avalanche Records, saw we were playing a show in the 13th Note in Glasgow and came through. I can't remember which show it was but I think it was fairly poorly attended though that failed to put him off opening discussions about making a record. I think we had finished the recordings by early 1995 and sent them to Spain before patiently waiting for our lovingly created five-song gatefold 7-inch to arrive back. In the pre-internet days, we somehow slightly lost touch with Jesus and by summer 1995 had given up on the record coming out. Which was fine, as only two of the five songs were still in our set by then and the recordings were basic even by our standards! So essentially the 'Disco

Nation' EP was meant to be our debut single but the Spanish EP arrived about two weeks before it. I don't know exactly how many copies Acuarela sold in the wake of our post-'Kandy Pop' fame but we certainly never saw a penny!

The Spanish EP was named 'Transmissions on the Teen-C Tip!'. The band would be indelibly identified with the term 'Teen-C' in their early years.

Steven Clark (Sci-Fi Steve) (bis): The Teen-C thing was kind of meant as a joke. It's really just a play on the Scottish word 'teensy' which at some point I'd misheard as 'Teen-C' and thought it sounded like a good name for an imaginary punk scene. The first TLC album was called *Ooooooohhh. . . On the TLC Tip* so we played on that for the EP title. As always with bis, it started as a joke and we've had to explain it away ever since! I think the *Melody Make*r tried to turn Teen-C into a genre, not a bad journey for a stupid wee pun.

Belle and Sebastian

Belle and Sebastian, one of the most recognised Scottish independent bands in the world today, had their beginnings in illness and unemployment. Unlike many of their contemporaries, they weren't part of the initial Kazoo Club scene. They did things in their own way from the start. The driving force and vision of the band is Stuart Murdoch who had, much like in the spirit of the classic 'indie' superstars, been dreaming of his perfect band long before its reality. This was especially profound for Stuart who had been suffering from a debilitating illness.

'Le Pastie de la Bourgeoisie'

Stuart Murdoch (vocals, Belle and Sebastian): I was sick with ME. So I was still in a complete wilderness. I couldn't really get anybody to play music with me, for love nor money.

I'd spent the whole summer trying to put on a club night called Le Pastie de la Bourgeoisie, which was graffiti that I saw on the wall of Greggs on Byres Road. I found out afterwards that The Yummy Fur crew had written 'le pastie de la bourgeoisie' to describe Greggs.

I did have at that point a little three-piece band. I booked the Queen Margeret Student Union for a date in August and the idea was that we were going to run this club night and then my new band, who were called 'Le Pastie de la. . .', were gonna play in the middle.

Lawrence Worthington (drums, The Yummy Fur): [I] did eat a fuck ton of Greggs.

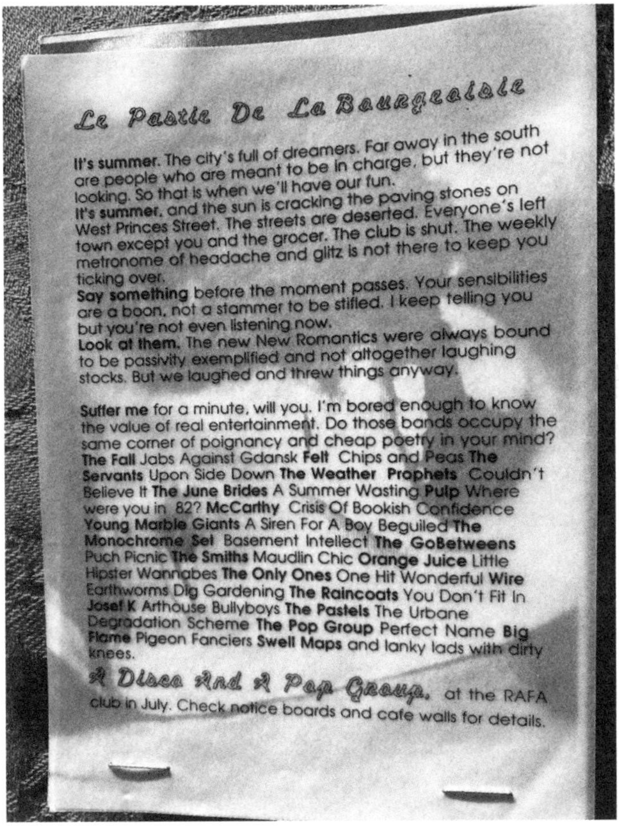

'Le Pastie de la Bourgeoisie' flyer

Stuart Murdoch (vocals, Belle and Sebastian): It was a disaster. My so-called band was just me and two other guys, and the drummer decided not to do the gig the night before – so we didn't in fact get to play. And that was the end of that. So the club night just became me playing records. And nobody showed up. It was the middle of summer and the students were all away.

It was a huge, big Queen Margaret Union room. And I remember thinking fuck's sake, another disaster. I was on the periphery of every scene going.

I remember being at the School of Art – the Divine Club at the art school was a great hub at that point for ideas and hanging out and people. And at that point from the early nineties until '94, people were always looking back. They were so in love with The Faces, The Small Faces. I mean I love that stuff – The Kinks; the whole 'sixties-ness'. I remember mentioning to somebody that I was trying to form a band and they were like, 'Why would you do that?' It was seen as such an obsequious thing to try, why would you do that? You know, the great tunes are out, why would you form a band? There was real negativity. That kind of Glasgow negativity. There was a lot of that.

Things soon changed for Stuart after he was enrolled on Beatbox, a scheme for unemployed musicians run by Glasgow Council.

Stuart Murdoch (vocals, Belle and Sebastian): I just started the music business course called Beatbox, which at that point I had found to be useless. . . I'd been on the sick register for years. After having come down with ME at the end of the eighties. And I think it was my doctor – he was trying to make some progress. I'd just been signing on sick, so he was like, okay, why don't you try this? I think they were trying to encourage people that had been on the sick list for a long time to get off. And this was a way that they could get me off the unemployment register. I remember being a little bit upset with the doctor that he was trying to force me back towards gainful employment.

Stuart Murdoch wasn't the only future member of Belle and Sebastian to be enrolled on Beatbox in an attempt to get them off the unemployed register.

Stuart David (bass, Belle and Sebastian): There were no windows in the concrete walls, just a single metal door at the top of a short flight of stairs. As I pushed the heavy door open and stumbled inside, I felt as if I was entering a strange subterranean labyrinth, or an underground bunker built to withstand a nuclear blast. I'd pretty much decided halfway through my first day that I wouldn't go back to Beatbox again. From what I could tell, the course was a total shambles. Just scores of unemployed musicians sitting around in a dark, airless labyrinth, doing nothing. No one seemed to be in charge. There was a music computer room with five or six Atari STs, which mostly seemed to be for playing computer golf on. There was a songwriting room with a digital piano and about 40 empty chairs in it. And then there was the recording studio, which comprised a live room where the temperature was five or six degrees below zero, and a control room whose door was firmly locked.

Stuart Murdoch (vocals, Belle and Sebastian): It was just ridiculous. I remember a guy with a long ponytail playing slap bass at us for an hour or so. In the first lesson, a guy with a long ponytail. I was thinking this is torture! What is he trying to do? Is he trying to teach us? Is he just showing off? And I don't mean to be too mean to people that were trying to do something. There were these random Glasgow musicians, and they would do their thing and they would maybe wait for you to copy them or do something. So I didn't last. I started not going in. And the one great thing that Beatbox had bestowed on me was a bus pass. And that changed a lot for me. The easiest thing in the world was to sit on the bus and not go into Beatbox and go to Easterhouse or Castlemilk instead. And suddenly I was seeing parts of the city that I'd never been to before. And suddenly the city became this lovely, bigger place for me. That really was a great boon.

Stuart David (bass, Belle and Sebastian): Time dragged [at Beatbox]. All day, nothing happened. No one played any music, no one even picked up an instrument and held it just to pose. There didn't seem to be any musical instruments anywhere in the whole building, except for a drum kit with no hi-hats and no cymbals in a corner of the freezing-cold live room.

Stuart Murdoch's days spent riding around on Glasgow buses were reflective and inspirational for him. The debilitating illness of his early youth had taken a huge toll on him and his aspirations, but now songwriting was about to enter his world.

Stuart Murdoch (vocals, Belle and Sebastian): I'd been knocking around Glasgow, sitting on buses, sitting in cafés, not enough energy to sustain a relationship or start things with anybody, but enough empathy to be able to write a song about a woman who just walked out of a newspaper shop, just the look on her face. So that was my own secret world. I wouldn't be a songwriter if it wasn't for ME. I only started writing songs when all the rest of my life fell away, when there was nothing left but me sitting in my parents' room, not well enough to do anything. That's why fortunately I started playing the piano and felt a need to express myself. And that was the moment when I realised that I could form a song, I never looked back – that was it. That was my consolation. It was everything. It became so important to me, and a way of expressing how I was feeling but also became the bread and butter of my existence. It was something to prove that I was alive. It was like a secret. It was like it was my own secret. It goes hand in hand with spirituality, because it seemed at exactly the same moment, that's when I started thinking about the existence of things other than everyday life. Like you know, God and spirituality and those sorts of ideas – it was happening at exactly the same time. So that was a secret.

So those two secrets went hand in hand. And to an extent, a lot of my songs were obviously me recording my experiences for God. Also for an imaginary audience, as well. People that I used to see around, people that I imagined, I would write songs for them. I would write songs to them, I would write songs about them. I went back to Beatbox, like a dog with its tail between its legs. And I went in there and thought, fuck it. Fuck everyone, I'm going to do it myself.

Stuart Murdoch's return to Beatbox differed profoundly from his previous exposure. His developing skills as a songwriter now allowed him to view their limited facilities as an opportunity to advance.

Stuart Murdoch (vocals, Belle and Sebastian): Beatbox had primitive computers. They had music computers, which was an area that I wasn't really interested in but I thought to myself, well, I don't have to listen to the guy who's playing the slap bass. . . It gave me a determination and I started going in every day. I learned programming on Cubase, which was on the Atari machines that they had, and it became addictive. Suddenly, I was in there all day, every day as much as I could manage, learning the things. It was fascinating to me that you could actually programme everything, drums and bass – and move chunks of music. You could see chunks of music being moved around and you could duplicate them to make the song longer. That was a big step; that was important and actually some of the music that I made on the Atari machines, eventually, a year and a half later, was going to become Belle and Sebastian music.

Stuart David (bass, Belle and Sebastian): For years, he [Stuart Murdoch] had been putting posters up in music shops and cafés, looking for potential bandmates. Sometimes his posters were cryptic, sometimes just a list of bands he liked. I don't think he'd ever had any replies – he had a clear idea of the people he'd like to find, but so far no one had come forward. Finding those people, though, had become his constant aim.

It was a concept I hadn't really come across before. Most people around Glasgow threw their bands together with whoever was closest to hand, and there were already quite a few people at Beatbox who were willing to be in Stuart's band. But he had an ideal vision in mind and he didn't want to compromise it.

Stuart Murdoch (vocals, Belle and Sebastian): Suddenly I became part of the furniture and realised that Beatbox actually had a good vibe. It wasn't the structure, it wasn't the teachers, it wasn't the schedule – it was just the people that happened to go in there, it was all the musical loose change of Glasgow. And we were just a funny bunch and Stuart [David] was one of them. And also they were completely unseen. Like, my scene or the one I was on the periphery of was the art school scene where everybody was cool, you know, and dressed completely 1969

Mod, Carnaby Street, all that stuff. Nobody was like that in Beatbox, it was a mad fucking mix of people. I mean there were people where the only reason they were in there was because they did karaoke in old Glasgow pubs on the high street – but it felt like they'd carry on this pub life. There'd be large-breasted women doing karaoke, carrying on the weekend into Beatbox and chatting as if they were sitting in a little pub, but they were just sitting with cups of tea. And they were happy, they were just misplaced. This was a way for them to carry on their preferred lifestyle but still keep their dole money.

Stuart David (bass, Belle and Sebastian): Stuart's songwriting became insanely prolific around this time too. He was often writing three new songs a day, and an unreasonable percentage of them were good songs. He said that the songs often started out as jokes, and then developed into something real. That seemed to perplex him, even made him sad. But he continued to think up the jokes, and the jokes continued to turn into songs and sometimes he was writing them too fast for me to learn before he'd discarded them again. I'd go to watch him doing a solo acoustic spot at The Halt Bar, or supporting other songwriters, and he'd do songs I'd never heard before and would never hear again. There was one called 'Adidas', which was simply a list of all the things Adidas had been claimed to be an acronym for when we were at school; another about jazz boys and jazz girls which made me stop in wonder. Many more. But most of them were never finished.

Stuart Murdoch (vocals, Belle and Sebastian): It was a rare mix of folk [at Beatbox], and Stuart [David] was enigmatic. There were a lot of enigmas there. But he was enigmatic. He sort of wore these leather trousers that were stitched at the side, and almost like a puffy pirate shirt and a waistcoat. The way I was looking, I wasn't cool. But that didn't matter, you know? He had his thing. My feeling about Stuart was I got this hint that he had had another life, that he had tried to be a musician; that he'd already gone through this whole process of going down to London, really trying to be in the business and pursuing a music career. And he'd ended up, years later, back at his mum and dad's in Balloch, Alexandria. And I realised that he was a little bit like me – that he'd ended up with Beatbox but it was a way for him to get out of his mum's house. And he was just going to stay, he was giving it a go, he was just gonna stay there until something happened. So he was definitely part of the fabric of the Beatbox experience.

Stuart David (bass, Belle and Sebastian): One afternoon, standing outside the metal door at Beatbox, underneath the flyover that led up into the business park, Stuart asked me if I'd be the bass player in his band, if he could ever get one together. I said I'd help him put his band together, help him to get it going, but that I had my own band and my own thing to be doing.

'I'd really like you to be in my band,' he said. 'I'll help you put it together,' I repeated.

Stuart Murdoch (vocals, Belle and Sebastian): The good thing was that Stuart decided to play the bass. He was a guitarist but he said he would play the bass on my records because there wasn't really a bass player around, which was great because he played a super simple rhythmic bass part – just pinning it down. A proper bass player would be tempted to come in and play all over it. So that was great, that he just pinned that down. I had real simple guitar skills at that time. And he brought his drummer in, Dave McGowan – who wasn't on Beatbox – who was in a band called Raglan Street Rattle. And Dave was great. So that was the basic rhythm section.

Stuart David (bass, Belle and Sebastian): 'I think the secret to finishing a song,' he said to me one evening, 'is knowing what the song's about before you start.' That seemed to be a revelation for him, and his songs really started to take shape after that. He got a batch together that he decided he would record in the Beatbox studio if his day ever came around.

The day did come around – but it wasn't yet Belle and Sebastian. The loosely put-together group were temporarily named Rhode Island for the session.

Stuart Murdoch (vocals, Belle and Sebastian): The very first time in the studio that I managed to corral a bunch of people together, we recorded the actual song 'Belle and Sebastian', which I'd just written.

Stuart David (bass, Belle and Sebastian): Stuart was firmly in charge, with a clear vision of exactly how he wanted the sounds and the arrangement to be. We'd only rehearsed the rhythm section beforehand, just the three of us – David, Stuart and me. It was a case of creating the record in the studio, with Stuart's ideas struggling against what was possible with the available equipment, and it continually pushed Steve's (the engineer) knowledge to the limits.

Stuart Murdoch (vocals, Belle and Sebastian): I was producing the session, even though I didn't know that's what it was called.

I was running the session, and he (Steve) was great. He was just trying to get the nice sounds, he was making funny jokes, you know, it was just a relaxed demo session. But it was a big deal to me to have the studio for a day. And we got a lot done.

Stuart David (bass, Belle and Sebastian): We recorded four songs – 'Dog on Wheels', 'String Bean Jean', 'The State I'm In', and 'Belle and Sebastian'. Stuart built up arrangements track by track, making full use of the other musicians on the course, bringing them in one at a time to overdub their parts and then disappear again.

The unconventional approach Stuart took to the recordings began right at the start, when he decided to lay down his acoustic guitar parts on tape first, along with a scratch vocal, and work upwards from there. There were no click tracks, no percussion instruments, and the tempo of his guitar wandered around unconstrained, following the wonky metronome in his head. When David [McGowan] turned up at the studio, that part of the session was already complete, and David had to play the drums in time with the guitar, taking the strumming as his guide, speeding up and slowing down in little increments as he went.

Steve was baffled by the approach initially, and he struggled gamely to reorganise the set-up to try and make it work, going against all the rudimentary techniques and procedures he'd learned so far. David wasn't too keen on the situation either. As far as he was concerned, the drummer sets the timing; everyone else follows the beat the drummer is keeping. But Stuart's conviction was that his own vocal performance of the song should set the pace, and that it should be a fluid thing.

It's a common approach in folk music, particularly in unaccompanied ballad singing, but it met with some resistance among musicians used to playing pop and rock, where the beat holds primary importance.

The songs didn't see the light of day for a few more years, eventually being released as 'The Dog on Wheels' EP. For now, the demos were sent to local radio. The band intended to do things very differently from day one.

Stuart Murdoch (vocals, Belle and Sebastian): That first EP that eventually came out was all pre-Belle and Sebastian proper. Belle and Sebastian started the first day of 1996.

CHAPTER TWELVE

DIY Production Superstar

El Hombre Trajeado

Hubby, still part of the Kazoo Club and producer of a vast majority of Glasgow's DIY scene, continued to further his own recording and performing career with El Hombre Trajeado.

RM Hubbert (Hubby) (vocals/guitar, El Hombre Trajeado): Me, Hubby & Thom got very quiet for a while. I joined an existing band called Glue, that's how I got into Glasgow Music Collective. Glue had already released an album and were touring Europe a lot, so I spent a couple of years with Glue doing that. I was still involved in the Kazoo Club and everything else, but we would go off and tour Europe a couple of times a year and be playing these DIY squat venues and things like that. It really opened my eyes to that scene, which was very influential to me.

Those are venues that I still play, like the OCCII in Amsterdam, because the bizarre thing is that the squat venues in Europe were generally much better run than the commercial venues in the UK. They had better sound systems, they had better promotional stuff, they had a better scene around them. There was one I remember really clearly in Paris called the 105 Squat where the squatters ingratiated themselves to the locals by offering free childcare during the day. The bigger squats would have childcare for local communities, they'd have cinemas and theatres. There was one in Berlin, a really famous one that's still there. As well as providing housing for people there'd be photography labs and things like that. They would teach you how to do stuff and it was really fucking inspiring. I came back from doing all that stuff. Glue finished up with a very bad tour. Angus (McPhee), the original member that had left the band, and I had a huge falling out. A lot of it down to my general bad mental health but also just a shitty tour. We didn't want to do that anymore. It put me off touring so badly that El Hombre never actually toured outside the UK because of it.

When I got back I wanted to start a new band. I got in touch with the old drummer from Glue, who had quit previously. Stef Sinclair, an amazing drummer. We got on really well. Stevie Jones, who had been the last bass player of Me, Hubby & Thom. Brought him in, and we called it El Hombre Trajeado, which was possibly the worst choice for a band name you could ever imagine. Not only is it in the wrong language, it's actually grammatically incorrect. It's supposed to be a Spanish translation of 'the man in the suit', so it would be a tongue-in-cheek thing because we were so deep in the DIY scene that I would never form a band called The Man In The Suit. We got a drunk Spanish friend to translate it, and she translated it wrong.

Like members of Belle and Sebastian, Hubby used Beatbox too.

RM Hubbert (Hubby) (vocals/guitar, El Hombre Trajeado): The original three-piece recordings – we recorded loads of stuff at Beatbox but it never got released – it was very spiky. Very angular, of that Minutemen, Big Flame, Glasgow punk school. In fact, I distinctly remember after our first gig talking to John from The Yummy Fur. . . it was really angular but the main thing with El Hombre, and it was kind of true with Me, Hubby & Thom as well, was always that we wanted to swap the normal sonic focus of a band. It was a traditional set-up, a three-piece set-up, and then when Ben (Jones) joined it was keyboards as well. But normally in that type of band where the focus would be on the voice and guitars, we wanted to pull the reverse of that and have the focus on the bass and the drums instead. So all of the songs were kind of written around that; if there are vocals in there there's normally just one or two spoken lines. The guitar became more minimal as the band went on. . . we'd all started getting really into Warp Records, stuff like The Black Dog and Aphex Twin. We really liked the idea of trying to structure music in that way but with a traditional line-up. That was the basic idea. That's what people generally know as El Hombre. Very early on it was minute-long songs with 400 time signature changes. It was super complex, Glasgow DIY math-rock. Very much of the dawson school. And John [from The Yummy Fur] in his usual fucking cutting way said to me, 'Hubby you know what, I would have fucking loved that five years ago.' I still remember that cunt saying that. That was twenty-five years ago.

The fact that Hubby had his own label, F&J, was incredibly helpful, allowing El Hombre to release their own material. It quickly showcased the band's clear talent and led to an association with John Peel and Guided Missile.

RM Hubbert (Hubby) (vocals/guitar, El Hombre Trajeado): Guided Missile were doing Country Teasers and Donkey. Donkey were a great band. They were doing a lot of cool stuff. We put out the first El Hombre single, 'Moon Unit Manual', on F&J, and John Peel picked up on it really quickly and was very supportive of it. I think we did our first Peel Session really soon after releasing it. Again, we had no fucking idea what we were doing. We didn't know how the industry worked, so we just ignored it. The reason we got our first Peel Session was because John Peel had played the single, said he liked it, but he played it once so I wrote him a letter basically saying, thanks so much for playing the record, by the way we're going to be in London on this day playing a show with The Yummy Fur, can we do a session while we're here? His producer phoned back a few days later and said yeah. But it was just pure ignorance as to how the industry works, because that's really not how it works. It's just not the way that's supposed to work. It was bravado and I thought, well he played the single, why wouldn't he want us to do a session? A John Peel Session's a huge thing. It's still a huge source of pride for me now, that we got to do those.

We did a couple of singles on F&J, the other being a split single with The Karelia. They both sold well. They both got bigged up in *NME* and *Melody Maker* and got decent reviews. We started getting gig reviews and things like that. I can't remember how I actually met Paul Kearney, who ran Guided Missile Records. I think he was just up in Glasgow a lot because The Yummy Fur were there. I think he came up whenever some of the London bands or Liverpool bands were playing. I must have met him that way, and I think he asked us to do an album first. I remember really clearly we were out at 13th Note at a gig or something and he just asked me when we were drunk if we'd like to do an album. I was like, aye, that'd be awesome.

That was it, he gave us £1000 to go and make a record, and we went and made *Skipafone*, which was amazing.

Paul Kearney (Guided Missile Records): Hubby is a Glasgow legend. Such an incredibly talented guitarist and songwriter; just a good guy with a heart of gold. El Hombre Trajeado were the nicest lads you could ever hope to meet and when I got the demo for the album the first day, I played it in my car. I actually crashed it and wrote it off. That's pretty good now I think about it but at the time it was an inconvenience.

RM Hubbert (Hubby) (vocals/guitar, El Hombre Trajeado): I was really keen to go and record with a guy called Jamie Watson at Chamber Studio. He had done the Long Fin Killie and Ganger records and I loved the production on those records. He'd also recorded The Vaselines' first album and Dog Faced Hermans, who we loved. We wanted to go through and record with him and he was really into El Hombre, so it worked out well. It was the first time any of us were in a proper recording studio. Actually, that's not true. It was the second time. The first proper recording studio we were ever in was Maida Vale when we did our Peel Session, which is quite a jump. Chamber Studio was a brilliant studio, Jamie's a joy to work with. I think every record we made was a very stressful experience. That first album I remember Stevie and Ben were fighting loads on it. You never remember why. Fuck knows.

There's a very short, interesting story on how we actually ended up as a four-piece, directly related to the John Peel sessions. When we released the first single, 'Moon Unit Manual', it was backed with a song called 'Logo', which Stevie had put some keyboards on. But we didn't have a keyboard player. When we got offered the Peel session we found out that you got paid per person in the band. Each member got something like £120, so as a way to make more money out of it we pretended we were a four-piece, with a keyboard player. We got Stevie's brother Ben, who we'd originally met through Thom. Ben went down and did that first session and played three notes on it or something. Then we decided it actually worked quite well and it'd be good to have that as a permanent thing.

CHAPTER THIRTEEN

Glasgow Infiltrates the Mainstream

bis on *Top of the Pops* and Chemikal Underground

The Britpop era and the re-emergence of 'indie' music had many notable cultural highlights. The most obvious were the battle between Blur and Oasis for the Number 1 spot, and Jarvis Cocker mooning Michael Jackson at the Brit Awards. Another was bis appearing on Top of the Pops, *performing 'Kandy Pop' from their 'The Secret Vampire Soundtrack' EP released on Chemikal Underground. It was a huge moment for Glasgow's new indie scene.*

Stewart Henderson (bass, The Delgados; Chemikal Underground): People will quite rightly talk about Chemikal Underground in terms of Arab Strap and Mogwai, and just how important those acts and how seminal those albums were for the label and how crucial they are to what Chemikal is and what it became. But it's all bis – the whole fucking thing happened because of bis.

Steven Clark (Sci-Fi Steve) (bis) I don't think I knew anything about The Delgados until their 'Monica Webster' 7-inch appeared at my job in Missing Records. It was pretty unusual at that time for a local band to get a vinyl release, there weren't really any labels left and decamping to London was the done thing if you wanted your band to be a 'serious' thing. Not only did the design aesthetic, with the cut-out hole on the back etc, appeal – it just so happened that the songs contained within were amazing. I think we must have either sent or handed them our latest demo and we were totally thrilled to be asked to release it as a single on Chemikal.

'Disco Nation 45', the second release for both bis and Chemikal Underground, resulted in further positive exposure for band and label, most especially with the music press.

Stewart Henderson (bass, The Delgados; Chemikal Underground): CHEM02 was the 'Disco Nation' 7-inch.

Steven Clark (Sci-Fi Steve) (bis): There was only a minor buzz about us at that time. I think we'd maybe played in London once, so they (Chemikal Underground) really did take a bit of a gamble on us. To be fair, 'Disco Nation' is a really strong record. I'd redo my vocals for sure, but it sounds great for something that cost almost nothing to make.

Amanda MacKinnon (Manda-Rin) (bis): We'd grown up buying the *NME* and *Melody Maker*, and also listening to John Peel on the radio. For us to now be included in there was surreal and quite overwhelming. I've always thought of bands in the media to be so out of reach and like superstars I suppose, so to then see our ordinary wee faces on the same page in a magazine was mental, never mind my far-from-perfect voice on the radio after Kylie.

Steven Clark (Sci-Fi Steve) (bis): I think when we got our first *NME* review, it felt massive. The review made it sound like a record I would run out and buy myself, something along the lines of 'Equal parts Devo, Blur and Huggy Bear'. From there, our shows in London were getting busier and the bigger record companies and publishers started sniffing around. We played at the very first Camden Crawl, in a scout hall, and it was dangerously full and sweaty. That was the first night I can remember thinking that we had actual fans – there was a tangible euphoria in the room. Live reviews at the time would say, 'Next big thing', 'Every song could be a single' etc. It felt we were going somewhere but we still had jobs or school and there wasn't really a sense of what madness lay just around the corner.

Emma Pollock (guitar/vocals, The Delgados; Chemikal Underground): You've got that first release of theirs, 'Disco Nation 45' in August '95. And between then and the release of the 'Secret Vampire' EP, there was this industry rush. Massive interest. By the time we'd announced, or by the time we'd decided we were putting out, the third EP, we're putting out 7-inch and CD, the quantities have been upped.

Richie Dempsey (engineer/co-manager, bis): We recorded at MCM Studios in Hamilton, which became the first CHEM19 studio. Paul Savage was with me. I love Paul. I had started co-managing the band with my friend and then business partner, John Williamson. Things were starting to explode for bis at the time.

Paul Savage (drums, The Delgados; Chemikal Underground): bis were really on an upward trajectory, really quite impressive. Harry at SRD helped us understand what was going on because we'd just done a thousand 7-inches before, but he was saying that for this bis CD, I think you might need 3000. We were like, okay, right. I don't know if we can afford that. I'm not sure. And he said, I think you'll sell them. And you can do a thousand 7-inches or two thousand 7-inches or whatever you want. But I think you'll sell them. Okay, right. We need to find a way of getting that money. We were trying to work out how we were going to do that and bis were going up and up and up, to the point that two weeks or three weeks before the single, or the week before the single. . . we performed on *Top of the Pops.*

Stewart Henderson (bass, The Delgados; Chemikal Underground): It was just one of those crazy stories. The label was being essentially run out of Paul and Emma's kitchen in the Southside. I don't know if we even had a computer. I think we had a fax machine. But the kind of story that floats around about the 'Kandy Pop' thing is true insofar as we had a few hundred pounds in the bank. We used the money from 'Monica Webster' to put out the 'Disco Nation' EP, we had a few hundred pounds in the bank, and then we got a call saying that Chris Cowley was going to put bis on *Top of the Pops.* And that we were going to need 35,000 units of the CD single. And that's one of those moments isn't it? A total crossroads where you're kind of like, okay, this is going to go one of two ways.

Emma Pollock (guitar/vocals, The Delgados; Chemikal Underground): We knew that we weren't going to have enough money to press. So our distributor had to front some of the money – most of the money! Because I think that single the 'Secret Vampire Soundtrack' EP, which 'Kandy Pop' featured on, sold 30,000. I think 'Secret Vampire' EP sold about 30,000. So we had to have that money fronted by a distributor because they knew it was going to fly. But the funny thing was, there was no album ready to go. There was nothing to really capitalise. Press and radio started coming on board and offering their services for free. On the proviso that the band continued to work with them when there was an album.

Stewart Henderson (bass, The Delgados; Chemikal Underground): Either this is going to happen or it's not going to happen. And one of the big lessons, really big salutary lessons that we learned then, was that the music industry absolutely fucking loves a certainty. It loves a winner. Everybody does! But especially in the music industry. So all these people, whether it was manufacturing companies, whether it was radio pluggers, press promotions people: fucking tripping over themselves to give us their services and their products for fuck-all. Because they knew that it was going to sell, they knew that bis were going to be on *Top of the Pops*, they knew that the single was gonna fly. And it was this minor televisual phenomenon. *Top of the Pops* was going through one of several death rattles by this point and they were trying to play around with the format, trying to find something to energise it. And it fell to this unsigned band from Glasgow – why don't we give them a crack at stardom kind of thing, we'll put on these young kids, because Jesus they were like 16 or 17.

Amanda MacKinnon (Manda-Rin) (bis): 'Kandy Pop' got B-listed on Radio 1, quite a jump from just the occasional play on John Peel or the Evening Session like most small bands got.

Steven Clark (Sci-Fi Steve) (bis): By this time, we were on the verge of signing a publishing deal which would give us enough money to pack in the jobs and do the band full-time. We also had a booking agent. I can vividly remember sitting in Chemikal's studio in Hamilton getting the phone call asking if we wanted to do a month-long joint headline tour with the Super Furry Animals. It definitely felt bigger but again, there wasn't really a sense that it was about to go nuts. It's ['Kandy Pop'] an odd-sounding record and it still astonishes me that Radio 1 started playing it during the day but I think that's when we started to escalate. The press picked up from there too but the big moment came on a chunky mobile phone in our little awful van somewhere on a motorway on the Super Furries tour. The record wasn't even out and all we really had were a few Radio 1 plays but for some reason *Top of the Pops* had called and wanted us on. It may subsequently become our millstone, but there was simply no way we could have said no.

On the day of the performance, the media storm became even greater.

Emma Pollock (guitar/vocals, The Delgados; Chemikal Underground): bis being on *Top of the Pops* was bonkers.

Steven Clark (Sci-Fi Steve) (bis): While the leap from playing to fifty people sat on the floor of some dingy venue in Derby to being on the actual telly was a fairly quantum one, we had developed a core belief in ourselves so I don't think we were actually all that phased. I dare say we simply expected to be on *Top of the Pops* many more times but obviously the music industry and the general public had other plans for us!

Richie Dempsey (engineer/co-manager, bis): We were out with Super Furry Animals for a month and we got a call from our publisher informing us that we would have to miss our gig in Buckley next week as we were 'chosen to go on *TOTP*. Oh, and did we have an instrumental version of "Kandy Pop"?' Did we fuck. Didn't see any reason we'd ever need one. Anyway, I called Paul and asked him if he had any spare studio time. He had one hour on a Saturday morning between 8 a.m. and 9 a.m.. So I went in there for an hour and mixed an instrumental version for *Top of the Pops*.

Amanda MacKinnon (Manda-Rin) (bis): It was crazy how many people saw that *TOTP* performance. I'll never forget walking into the studio in Glasgow after it and a builder up on scaffolding across the road shouting 'I just saw you on the telly!'

As Glasgow bands, friends, associates and members of the public eagerly watched, the band were introduced on Top of the Pops. *But they weren't billed as 'bis, on Glasgow's new independent label, Chemikal Underground'. Cruelly, they was instead presented as 'the first unsigned band to appear on* Top of the Pops*'.*

Steven Clark (Sci-Fi Steve) (bis): The first we knew about the 'unsigned band' thing was the day after filming when we watched the actual broadcast with some of the Super Furries in a hotel room. I don't think we thought much about it at the time but it's become a really irritating legacy. Certainly nobody asked us if that proclamation was either accurate or approved by us! I suspect a producer or press agent saw the opportunity to hype the situation and it hindered us as much as helped us I think. It absolutely made it seem as if Chemikal was our own label, which I know must have been frustrating for them. I've never really discussed it with any of them but looking back it probably soured our relationship a bit.

Emma Pollock (guitar/vocals, The Delgados; Chemikal Underground): On this single we absolutely were total upstarts, we refused a discount on the single. And we really pissed off the distributor and the retailers and so the single was actually much more expensive than everybody else's – than all the other singles. We just knew that we had a record that everybody wanted. And yet it was still being touted as being unsigned when the band hit *Top of the Pops*.

Amanda MacKinnon (Manda-Rin) (bis): Chemikal Underground thankfully had confidently pressed enough copies that the single made it to Number 25 in the charts, but that was all they'd pressed and who knows what could have happened if there was more available. Definitely our fault that people would go into a shop asking for 'Kandy Pop' and not leave with it, because it wasn't the title of the EP – 'Secret Vampire'] was.. Idiots [us].

Steven Clark (Sci-Fi Steve) (bis): I think we knew we were going to sign for a bigger label, we had world domination in mind and Chemikal was still being run out of Southside flats at the time so it was inevitable we'd move on but it did end on a flat note. Looking back now, we should have stayed a little longer. We took ages to make up our minds about who to sell our souls to and ended up releasing the follow-up single ourselves, which was a slight disaster. We were on the front cover of the *NME* but there was a delay in manufacturing, we weren't on the radio this time and we ended up stalling outside the Top 40. Ludicrous for a band on the cover of the *NME*. We didn't release the single ourselves to make money, we were pretty solvent by this point, so I regret losing the consistency of releases that being on Chemikal gave us. Arguably we should have released a debut album with them too, as by the time we eventually released an album a year later, none of the 1995 songs were on it.

'The 'Secret Vampire Soundtrack' EP (CHEM03) peaked at Number 25 in the UK charts and established bis and Chemikal Underground as a huge force from Glasgow. The band and label parted company but it had been an amazing achievement for both of them. bis had the attention of the press and major labels. While Chemikal may not have been name-checked on the show, they were certainly now on the music industry's radar.

Stewart Henderson (bass, The Delgados; Chemikal Underground): At the time with bis, all of these things happened and I think from an industry point of view that story about not discounting with HMV is an important one. Not so much for what it meant for us, but I think what it meant down south, down in London. I think we were the talk of the steamie a wee bit. I think there was a sense of 'that band who told HMV to fuck off'. And you know what it's like, the music industry is full of grannies. I think it helped to establish the idea that Chemikal Underground was this record label, it planted a seed.

Steven Clark (Sci-Fi Steve) (bis): I certainly am proud that we helped change Chemikal's fortunes but they have to take the credit for then signing epoch-defining bands as well as having one themselves. Easy to wonder what may have become of us had we hung about a bit longer.

Amanda MacKinnon (Manda-Rin) (bis): If they wanted to take another gamble and try an album with us now I'd certainly be up for it.

CHAPTER FOURTEEN

A Glasgow Explosion

V-Twin and Ganger

V-Twin

V-Twin's importance to the scene belies their small output and relatively late releases. Despite their meagre discography and the fact that they tried very hard not to be part of any scene, they were responsible for bringing many of their contemporaries together. It should be noted that singer Jason McPhail will probably hate being referred to as having any contemporaries. They also released some fantastic music. And they definitely did it their own way.

V-Twin formed in 1995 when Michael McGaughrin met Jason MacPhail at a record fair, both looking to complete a Bobby Gillespie mix-tape of influential sixties and seventies musicians. In a short space of time the band became one of the most lucrative potential signings of the scene, in part due to their ambivalent attitude.

Jason MacPhail (promoter; vocals, V-Twin): I was always trying to get myself ready to be in a band. I was obsessed with putting on Dan Penn, I was obsessed with Dan Penn as a kid. I must have had that Peter Guralnick book, *Sweet Soul Music*. Dan is described in it as the secret hero of the book. And you couldn't actually hear anything but there was just something about the mystique of Dan Penn, like, who the fuck is this guy? A white guy with a cowboy hat, but he's supposedly the world's greatest soul singer of any colour. I just told him to come to Glasgow. I got him a return ticket and a gig at the 13th Note. That's how I got to know Craig (Tannock). But I hadn't been in a band. I just wanted to be involved. The next year we put on Kim Fowley, and the next year we put on Alex Chilton, which made it really easy to do things. Once you've done things that suddenly, maybe it's not deserved but people take you a bit more seriously. Even if it's putting on somebody else's gig and not your own.

When I worked at the 13th Note I went out of my way to avoid every fucking band that was there. I was there all the time. I worked there all the time, but I never saw any of these bands because I made a point of not wanting to see them. They were down the stairs, so you're there but they were downstairs. Thirty years later, John McKeown is a friend but I had no interest in it. I never saw any of it. I made a point of working upstairs. You're in the thick of it; people come in and they order drinks, you get to know everybody. It wasn't a snooty thing, I just had no interest in it. Also they had no interest in me because I had no interest in them. They were in their own wee world, which is fine. It was very, very their own wee world, but maybe we were in our own wee world as well. It wasn't some kind of aesthetic. A lot of people listen to the music that they want to emulate.

Michael McGaughrin (drums, V-Twin): I was pretty much the same, I don't think I went to that many gigs. We'd go to the occasional thing but I was never part of that scene. I became friends with John later on at parties when we started up. I think I saw The Yummy Fur once, by accident when I was watching Dub Narcotic one night. I wasn't a big gig-goer. Occasionally, but I'm still not really.

Jason MacPhail (promoter; vocals, V-Twin): It's an ideology, people like indie music. I never liked indie music, I still don't like it. Whatever that means, I don't like it. Never did. Subscribing to that whole thing of Rough Trade like, 1976–82: I don't care. It's a great record label to work with, if you manage a band or are in a band.

Michael McGaughrin (drums, V-Twin): Jonathan Richman's on Rough Trade, there are exceptions.

Jason MacPhail (promoter; vocals, V-Twin): Record companies would come and see us. It was stupid. Stupidity. They'd come, and you're fucking around or whatever. I think probably the person with one of the biggest influences on V-Twin was Laurence Bell [Domino Records]. There was a stupid phase where I knew every time I went home from The Grosvenor, there would be three messages on my answering machine from a record company. Maybe it was a period of a week, or two weeks. It was like [mimics London accent], 'Hello this is Zach from Fontana', or whoever it was. I did the same thing every time, they'd phone up and say, oh somebody, or Mig from Nice N Sleazy's says you're really good. And I just went, we're not. [Laughs.] But I genuinely believed that. I was like, we're not.

Michael McGaughrin (drums, V-Twin): [V-Twin] was always Jason, me and Simon [Shaw]. We'd have a guitar player for a few months, and then it'd be someone else. We've probably had hundreds of people in the Twin.

We weren't good enough as a band at that point. We were at points, but it was a shambles most of the time.

Jason MacPhail (promoter; vocals, V-Twin): We were learning. In fairness to Domino, they weren't the powerhouse that they are now. However, in fairness to Laurence, he did something that nobody else would have done. You can turn around and go, we should have had more money or we should have got this or that, I don't know. I don't think it would be accurate or fair to say that. I think we got exactly the level of support that we merited. Now maybe there'd be more money to throw at it. But also with Alan McGee or Laurence, sometimes they don't sign bands, they sign people. I get it, they identify people who have the energy and who want to do things and they get in there early, they have conversations.

V-Twin 'Gifted' record, released by label Domino

Eventually, V-Twin made a small compromise and recorded and released a record, the splendid 'Gifted' on Domino, complete with the tantalisingly mysterious 'unknown' writing credit.

Michael McGaughrin (drums, V-Twin): It's a cover. It's not even called 'Gifted'. Because it was such a rare soul song, no one knew what it was called. A girlfriend I had at the time had this tape with all these old Northern Soul rarities on it. Probably a decade later we found out it's actually called 'I'm Tempted' by Sandy Hollis. We just knew it from this tape. It just sounded like 'I'm gifted' and when you actually later find out it's 'I'm tempted' you think, of course it's that. It's a cover but we couldn't credit anyone for it. We were just happy that we'd put out a record.

The band soon put out another single, 'Thank You, Baby', featuring Chris Geddes and Stevie Jackson from Belle and Sebastian, and a video directed by Stuart Murdoch. It was produced by Kid Loco, who had been asked by Domino to provide mix work for previous Domino-related bands from Glasgow and had developed a strong relationship with the city which remains today. (He recently worked with Louise Quinn, after earlier working with her band, Quinn, on their Gates of Light *collaborations.)*

Kid Loco (French DJ; artist): I remixed Mogwai and Quinn. And I got this offer to work on 'Thank You Baby' by V-Twin. When I listened to the track, I just loved it and didn't want to do a remix; my idea was more to achieve what the band started, so I guess it's producing. [Sometime-member] Chris Geddes was my man in the band, a great lunatic guy, nice, charming and so fun to hang with. The first time we met, he invited me to drink a bottle of red wine on top of a hill in Glasgow. I was wearing white trousers and when he opened the bottle, half of it went on these white trousers. Didn't have a change so I was looking like a stupid drunk clown the day after in the plane. Unforgettable.

Michael McGaughrin (drums, V-Twin): ['Thank You Baby'] is probably about ten different rip-offs.

Jason MacPhail (promoter; vocals, V-Twin): It's an amalgamation of ten different songs.

Michael McGaughrin (drums, V-Twin): Like most V-Twin songs. . . it's Bobbie Gentry.

Chris Geddes (keyboards, V-Twin and Belle and Sebastian): V-Twin is definitely almost like a kind of references band; in Belle and Sebastian, though there are references there, it's not so much part of the process of making the music. In Belle and Sebastian, the song was written and then we would sort what we felt was needed on the song and if you end up throwing in something that references something, then that's fine, but just don't tell the songwriter you're doing it. . . whereas with V-Twin often the process would start with deconstructing some old records and trying to work out what made it tick and then trying to reverse engineer. It was interesting, the V-Twin thing. I enjoyed it socially as well. Michael was a good friend at the time and great company. And then as Belle and Sebastian got a bit successful, I definitely felt like I had the sense that I owed my place in Belle and Sebastian to having been connected with the Twin initially. So I felt like I owed it to V-Twin to stick around and contribute what I could if there was an opportunity to keep doing so.

After a series of highly praised singles and a compilation they eventually released their album, The Blues is a Minefield, *a fantastically odd, wonderful, unique and varied release.*

Jason MacPhail (promoter; vocals, V-Twin): Domino would put the singles out and then eventually we were going to make an album. And [Lawrence Bell] agreed to do that. We tried to make a record that should have cost £100,000 but we did it for £10,000. A lot of it was learning how to do things that – I don't want to sound like Trevor Horn – we couldn't do, because the technology wasn't there. They're very modern, from the point of view that we were absolutely trying to make records that you could only just make, because the technology had literally just come out.

Michael McGaughrin (drums, V-Twin): I've not listened to the album in a while but I've always liked it. I don't really listen to music that I've made very often anyway, but I like it, I think it's pretty wild. I think all the songs are good on it, which doesn't usually happen. Or nearly all of them anyway. I think it's great.

Jason MacPhail (promoter; vocals, V-Twin): I don't know. I mean I really, really, really, really, really fucking love Teenage Fanclub. I was talking to Gerry [Love] the other night and I had a fanboy moment. . . Gerry said he really liked that record, that it was a really un-Glasgow record, he said it doesn't sound like anything else and it's great because of that. In a lot of ways that's about the best compliment you can get, if somebody says it doesn't sound like anything else. Maybe not, maybe it's shit and it doesn't sound like anybody else. [Laughs.] But it was Gerry, so I was really happy about that. The 18-year-old in me was happy. Gerry Love liked it and it's nothing like Teenage Fanclub, and that's fine. I think there's some crap in the record, but for the most part it doesn't sound like anything else. Also we were belligerent, it was difficult, it wasn't easy to make. I'll stand by the most of it. It wasn't successful but then again neither was *Sister Lovers.*

The Blues is a Minefield *came out at a time in the record industry when vinyl releases were almost unheard of, and even CDs were starting to come under threat. In many ways it was ahead of its time and perhaps if it had come out a few years later, as Franz Ferdinand were becoming huge (and the band behaved as a normal band) it likely would have received huge success. But it was not to be.*

Jason MacPhail (promoter; vocals, V-Twin): I don't know if they (Domino) acknowledged it. I don't think they were having an easy time as a record label; we weren't having an easy time. Nobody was having an easy time. We asked for it not to come out on vinyl. What a fucking stupid fucking thing to do. [Laughs.] The guy who was managing us was like, 'Nobody will buy it anyway, just get it pressed up on CD.' We were like, 'Fine, we don't care.' There was a lot of caring too much and a lot of not caring, at the same time. I'm glad it exists, I'm glad I did it – or we did it. Yeah. I don't really care about it. Then Andrew (Loog Oldham) turned up.

Andrew Loog Oldham, manager of the Rolling Stones during their greatest period, and originator of the legendary Immediate Records, did indeed turn up in Glasgow.

Jason MacPhail (promoter; vocals, V-Twin): I got finished copies of the CD [*The Blues Is A Minefield*]. I had [Loog Oldham's] email address because somebody else had his email address. I was cheeky and as I'd done before, I sent him an email. He was in Colombia and I said, can I send you this because we like the music you've made. He came back and said, it reminds me of soul music or Motown. He identified one or two songs as being particularly interesting. He asked what we were up to and I said we're going to Paris to do some press interviews for this record, and then we're doing a show in London. He said good luck with all that and I said, thanks very much and thank you for being kind and listening to the record and taking the time out to speak to us. Two weeks later we were playing in London and prior to going on stage he walked through the door in north London in Camden. I said, wow, you never said you were coming to London. He said, well, I wasn't, I was going to go to Argentina. Oh right. He says, yeah I was gonna go to Buenos Aires. All right. He said, but I thought let's go to London and see Jason and V-Twin. I was like, oh very good. [Laughs.] He said he'd like to make our next record, which was quite far out. Then we were on stage and I was like, this is wild. The show was a fucking disaster. I hit the keyboard player in the face with a plastic bottle, which wasn't my finest moment. It was kinda for fun but he didn't take it that way. Then Andrew came to Glasgow and we walked around for a week talking about stuff.

Andrew Loog Oldham (producer/ex-manager, Rolling Stones): My son, Maximillian, said to me near the very end of the last century, 'Why don't you make a record so I can see what it's all about and whether there's anything in it for me?' I went to Glasgow and found V-Twin. There are no accidents. I got a great education and you got V-Twin.

V-Twin with Andrew Oldham

Andrew produced an album by the band, which remains unreleased as yet. It would be a crime if it never saw the light of day as it is one of the finest albums from that period. Amazingly, they also have another unreleased record, produced by Alex Chilton.

Jason MacPhail later became the manager of John McKeown's 2000s band, the 1990s, featuring Michael McGaughrin and Dino Bardot, soon to join Franz Ferdinand and later, confusingly, a reformed The Yummy Fur. The last word on V-Twin's career, however, comes from Michael.

Michael McGaughrin (drums, V-Twin): I quite enjoyed sitting in a van with Jason driving, coming back from Dundee, full of speed and Jason vomiting in the front on the window and in the side mirror while driving on a motorway. That's the thing I'm gonna remember.

Ganger

Yet another band to emerge from the 13th Note scene (yes, there are a lot) was Ganger, an exemplar of the vast melting point of ideas and interpretations of music offered by the 13th Note and the Kazoo Club. Along with Mogwai, they were one of the few instrumental bands from the period. And they played very long songs.

Graham Gavin (bass/guitar, Ganger and Lugworm): I guess by the time the nineties came around in Glasgow there was more of a distance between older scenes and genres, which (in a way) would have given more ground for those bands to draw influence from. What got soaked up by a disparate array of groups was an extra decade of energy, ideas and sounds. Sounds that perhaps the *C86* brigade would have been aware of, but that were still relatively fresh for their ears to draw influence from. So, instead, they looked at the 1960s for inspiration. At the time, I didn't really feel there was any direct opposition to the swathes of those sixties-influenced guitar bands, but I guess the goal is there to produce something different from what went before you. A lot of those groups became the establishment and are still being lovingly written about by nostalgists today, as if it was the only sound that Glasgow had to offer. Bands such as The Mackenzies were also operating around that time, chaotically splurting out shards and bursts of Beefheart/Pop Group atonal funk licks. Bands such as The Mackenzies, although largely undocumented, probably have more in common and bear more influence with those bands at the sharper end of nineties Glasgow.

Ganger originated when Graham Gavin met ex-Fenn member, Stuart Henderson (not to be confused with Stewart Henderson from Chemikal Underground). Fenn's drummer was the legendary Richie Dempsey, of dawson, Stretchheads and recording engineer fame.

Stuart Henderson (bass, Asp, Fenn and Ganger): I knew Richie Dempsey from recording a demo while in the band Asp. That would have been mid-late '93 so I guess he felt my bass playing was up to scratch for them. They had all been in other bands that I wasn't really familiar with at the time. They were great live, there was a Swervedriver thing about their music and I knew Richie was a great drummer so was excited to join. After getting up to speed, the intent was to keep playing while writing new material to keep options open for another album release. I missed my uni graduation that year to play a few gigs around London with them. The new material didn't happen as quickly as we'd hoped though, affecting the momentum by late '94. We did do [a] split single with Beetroot and had a great night playing together at the 13th Note. Perhaps the writing was on the wall when Richie and I started working out King Crimson's 'Lark's Tongues in Aspic' (part 2, of course) during practices. It was a shame when Fenn split but I think everyone was ready to move on.

Graham Gavin (bass/guitar, Ganger and Lugworm): Ganger formed from a combination of factors. I was frustrated, playing short tunes in my other band, Lugworm. I was constantly trying to expand sections of our songs. This, however, was continually met with opposition from my fellow bandmates. Erstwhile Lugworm band member, Dep Downie, understanding my frustration, introduced me to bass player Stuart Henderson. Stuart was having similar thoughts to me of embracing seventies German music alongside other genres. Undercurrents of the post-rock genre were bubbling away at the time, it was there in the ether. Subconsciously, this probably fed into a braver belief system for us; encouraging us to think more freely about expanding the length of songs, maintaining the groove, playing with soundscapes and time signatures, and focusing on the thrilling power and energy that existed within the framework of the music. Although post-rock was around and perhaps twitching away at our collective ears, my personal influences were often less modern. Aside from the propulsive grooves of Stereolab and the rhythmical patterns of The Ex and Dog Faced Hermans, I was more fixated on bands such as Soft Machine, This Heat and the aforementioned German groups of the seventies. With hindsight, it is now easy to draw parallels with these groups and what was being produced by the nascent post-rock fraternity.

Stuart Henderson (bass, Asp, Fenn and Ganger): Dep Downie, who I knew from Missing Records, introduced me to Graham Gavin in the 13th Note; they'd already played together in Lugworm. Graham was wanting to start a band with krautrock influences, playing longer tunes. . . and have two bass players. A lot of the krautrock catalogue was being reissued around then and James [Young] and I had been listening to everything from Can, Neu, Faust, Kraftwerk and Popol Vuh to Amon Duul, Ash Ra Tempel and Magma (well, maybe that was just me). Graham didn't have to persuade me. Luckily, things clicked and we were soon sketching out our first few tracks. James joined us soon after along with Lucy McKenzie on clarinet and guitar. Early on, the line-up was fluid. Annie Spandex (Ann Lafferty) from Lung Leg played cello briefly. It was probably James who asked Steven Clark from bis to join shortly after that for keyboards and second drums. Martin Allen joined us a little later, replacing Steven on keyboards.

Steven Clark (Sci-Fi Steve) (bis): For some reason Ganger let me be the second drummer/synth player for the first EP and gigs.

Graham Gavin (bass/guitar, Ganger and Lugworm): Ideas were often bashed out by Stuart and I in his Maryhill flat in Glasgow. These were then presented to the others and fleshed out at a weekly practice meet-up. Fairly rapidly, we had an unashamed three-song, 30-minute setlist together. An early home for us to present our wares was the 13th Note on Glassford Street. Gigs were always busy as there was always a supportive network around us. This network was made up of friends from other bands as well as regular gig-goers who would frequently take the gamble of paying a humble entrance fee of 99p to witness the spectacle of what was on offer. The 13th Note was a key venue in the proliferation of nineties music in Glasgow. It not only served as a buoyant live venue with an in-house PA with a non-pay-to-play policy; it also served as a hangout for like-minded individuals to share ideas and listen to interesting music being played on club nights that would often be far removed from the associated indie guitar music from the stages of the venue's two floors. Turntable nights of jazz, dub, electronica and noise were all in the mix and would often find their way into the unfolding fabric of the bands that were emerging.

Stuart Henderson (bass, Asp, Fenn and Ganger): Graham [Gavin] and Lucy [McKenzie] were good friends with Pat Laureate, Brian MacDougall and Marc Bains at Vesuvius. 'Half Nelson' was to be my first record [with Ganger]. Vesuvius already had a few releases under their belt, which was reassuring, and they were all lovely people so we were excited about it. Brian also did the cover art, which turned out great, and sorted out our cover art style for the early releases. Richie recorded us at The Practice Pad in Maryhill where the full band normally practiced. I have snapshot memories of us playing and hanging out in the studio room. James and Richie no doubt made sure the drums were high in the mix and the rest is lost to me, as are many Ganger facts and experiences. Graham has a habit of reminding me about this or that event that I can't now recall. It was very cool to see the first stack of pressed vinyl; Vesuvius did a great job with that. As to how it was received, reactions were varied but it was good enough to get us noticed. . . mainly though, I think we timed it right. There was a proper buzz about the Glasgow music scene by then with the papers and labels showing an interest. We were decent live, krautrock was 'cool' again and we got lucky.

Graham Gavin (bass/guitar, Ganger and Lugworm): Domino became interested in us. We met up on a Sunday morning at the old Grosvenor Café in Ashton Lane sometime in 1996, paid for our own coffees and empire biscuits and individually signed a contract to release our further recordings on Lawrence's label. Money was always extremely limited, but the budget to record in higher-end studios, such as Chamber in Edinburgh with Jamie Watson became available, and our subsequent recordings offered a clear picture of how we really sounded as a band.

Over a year after our inception, the band's stability and line-up was continually changing. Martin Allen joined on keyboards, London-based improvisor Caroline Kraabel loosely joined on saxophone, Sci-Fi Steve left due to commitments with his other band bis, and around the turn of 1996/97 Lucy McKenzie handed in her notice. Around this time, I was becoming disgruntled and gave it until April 1997 whereupon I played my final gig at Dingwalls in London supporting Thrill Jockey's Trans Am. A review of that gig was printed in *Melody Maker*, which pretty much concurred with an audience member's disgruntled opinion of us when he vehemently hollered, 'Fuckin' Hawkwind'.

The earlier promise of all possibilities being explored were now increasingly becoming more marginalised. Like most bands, after a couple of years, a settled sound was becoming more apparent in our playing style. This was coupled with an emphasis on becoming more technically proficient, whereby our playing was now becoming less about feel and instinct and more replaced by laborious mental counts of unconventional time signatures and sequences. Double-math lessons had overtaken fun music lessons and it was now time for my departure. Promising Lawrence at Domino that we'd record our 'James Brown song', we reconvened after a few months and recorded a final 12-inch, titled 'With Tongue Twisting Words', on the same evening that Princess Diana died in Paris. This final release also served as a crossing-over point that introduced listeners to fresh members of Ganger that were now coming through the front door as opposed to the older members that preferred to use the door marked 'Exit' at the back. It was a thrill to be in a band that appeared to hit the ground running, be offered gigs regularly, to have interest from friends and labels who were willing to run the risk and release recordings of an unconventional instrumental band who sometimes had the audacity to pommel out a 20-minute monstrous groove. It's an easy thing to take for granted that your music will be published and find willing listeners, but really, in the grand scheme of things, most groups trudge their wares for a few years and largely disappear undocumented and go away ignored.

Highlights with Ganger include being requested by Stereolab to support them at The Wag Club in London where they played under the pseudonym of Soop. Similarly, we requested Birmingham's Broadcast play with us at a Christmas gig at The Piao Club in London, which they did. It was also flattering to be in a group that was given the remix treatment on numerous occasions, one of those remixes being done by Andy Weatherall. I'll also take away Lucy McKenzie's comically apt observation of Stuart Henderson and I brandishing our basses at each other, 'Going at it like a pair of grappling Godzillas'.

Stuart Henderson (bass, Asp, Fenn and Ganger): Glasgow might have been cool in the mid-nineties, but the outside interest moved on and we were all in our mid-to-late twenties by '98. Very few people were making money and the reality of that starts to bite. Also, and I'm generalising here, it wouldn't be unusual for bands to burn out musically in two-to-three years, never mind four. Writer's block plays its hand, something I've struggled with, or people move on as their interests change. It's a challenge to make a success of it and even the closest relationships can become strained. We were luckier than some to have a record deal but it comes with its own pressures. We were never paid a wage, having to hold down jobs between tours. We had to work for three months to save enough money to tour with Mogwai (thank you, Mogwai). Merge Records in North Carolina did everything they could to help us but it was a stretch financially for them as well (thank you, Merge). Making money from music today must be difficult but it wasn't easy back then either. There comes a point where you have to stop and figure out how the hell to move forward with the normalities of life.

CHAPTER FIFTEEN

Beta Bands and Sally Skulls

The Beta Band

We last encountered Steve Mason in Volume 1 (Postcards From Scotland), when he was part of Edinburgh's garage scene. By now, he had got together with John McLean, Gordon Anderson and Robin Jones to form one of the greatest bands from the period, The Beta Band.

Steve Mason (vocals, The Beta Band): It was towards the end of my time in Second Generation, around 1988/89, that I saw Happy Mondays and The Stone Roses and I realised that what I was doing was like, last century. So I had a bit of a rethink of the whole thing, left the band, started taking ecstasy and going to nightclubs and dancing to acid house and techno. . . I started going to clubs in Edinburgh, at The Venue and the Citrus Club and raves. I didn't know John McLean or Gordon (Anderson) at school but I bumped into those guys at those places. It was really through hanging out with John and a lot of his art friends from Edinburgh Art College that I sort of got into art and got into poetry and Burroughs. I didn't know anything about art. The environment I was in, the word 'art' never came up, the word 'poetry' never came up, the idea of writing down the way you feel about something was ludicrous to the environment I was in. I was a car mechanic. What I realised was this kind of pathetic macho environment that I was in was just a bunch of really scared, narrow-minded weaklings, and what was really brave, what was the most exciting thing, was what these artists were doing. And so I jumped ship pretty rapidly and quit being a car mechanic and just became a full-time layabout. . . there was no discussion at the time of making music. We were too busy being into the music that was being made. That period – 1992, '93, '94 – was such an exciting time to be going to clubs, and there was so much great music being made. *Screamadelica* [Primal Scream], the *Portishead* album, Massive Attack and Tricky. Then I moved to London and discovered jungle. I moved to London because a girl from Glasgow at that time went off to London to become a student nurse. I had already quit being a car mechanic and I followed her down to London. John came down to the Royal College of Art in London. And Robin followed him. And then a very long story short, I ended up living under their staircase beside their gas meter. And we formed The Beta Band.

The Beta Band went on to create three ground-breaking EPs. A genuinely original, innovative band.

Sally Skull

The garage scene in which Steve Mason had been involved continued to evolve in Edinburgh. Saskia Holding formed Sally Skull with Clare Scrivener, who had been in The Pterodactyls.

Sally Skull

Saskia Holding (vocals/bass, Sally Skull): Sally Skull came about in early 1994 when I got talking to Clare Scrivener at a Voodoo Queens gig in Edinburgh. We both loved the gig and felt inspired by the band. Clare had played rhythm guitar for Edinburgh garage band, The Pterodactyls. We did have a second guitarist, Jane, for a little while but she left due to college commitments when she couldn't commit to a 'tour' (I use the term lightly – it was quite a disorganised pre-internet visit) in France with Gila Monster in the early summer of 1994.

Clare and I asked Phil Bull if she would play drums because we knew her. She played in several other bands including Wee Free Kings and Gila Monster but didn't play drums in either of those bands! I was still playing guitar and singing in a band very much inspired by Riot Grrrl called Fudd, but I moved onto bass for Sally Skull. Fudd formed after a Huggie Bear and Bikini Kill gig at the Cathouse in Glasgow in March 1993. By May, Fudd were playing the 13th Note when it was in Glassford Street with some rudimentary songs.

I was influenced by bands like The Cramps, Sonic Youth, Hole, and Babes in Toyland. Quite American I guess, but also influenced by the attitude of bands around me such as Gila Monster and The Pastels. Clare came from a more sixties garage-influenced background and she introduced me to bands like The Brood and The Pandoras as well as introducing me to Lenny [Helsing] and The Thanes and that whole 'let's just do this' attitude that they brought to things.

Phil was multi-talented, playing lots of instruments, and she was also much more eclectic in her music tastes. She left the band sometime at the end of 1995 and then another friend, Katrina Dixon, joined us on drums. She played with Policecat and Hula Hula and brought in another set of influences.

In mid-1993, Tom Worthington and I started putting on all-ages gigs at (Richard) Demarco's Gallery in Edinburgh. We put on Fudd, Pink Kross and Hello Skinny (then Melody Dog), Lung Leg and Starstruck. Later, Brittle Hip, The Yummy Fur, The Mongers and Sally Skull. At some point Richard Demarco lost interest in us and we had to find another venue for these all-ages gigs. We tried St Stephens Church, Walpole Hall and put on a few gigs at the unemployed workers' centre in Broughton Street, but they just never had the same vibe as Demarcos.

I also organised quite a few gigs at The Cooler, which was downstairs at The Venue. I'd get Lung Leg, Hello Skinny and Pink Kross through from Glasgow and have all girl band nights. Just because I could! It was great having so many young women playing in bands at that time. Later, Sally Skull played at The Tap (that was a perfect venue) and the Cas Rock (another great loss) a fair bit. Calvin Burt who organised gigs at the Cas Rock was always very supportive of the band. Our reception was usually fine. Occasionally we'd get some heckling, but I think people were mostly bemused by our non-conformist songs and simple style of playing! We probably became 'easier' to watch and listen to/less challenging as time went on when we knew our instruments better and started writing more conventional verse-chorus-verse-chorus songs.

Sally Skull released the 'Tantivy Tracks' EP on Vesuvius in 1995, followed by 'Fractious' on Slampt in 1997.

CHAPTER SIXTEEN

Imperial Phase Part One

Belle and Sebastian record and release two albums in one year

Back sleeve of *Tigermilk*

The sheer driving force within the Belle and Sebastian project, then still called Rhode Island, is awe-inspiring. With Stuart Murdoch in the driving seat it became clear that in 1996 his dreams would become reality. Not since the days of the mid-sixties, when it was common practice, would many bands contemplate recording two albums in a single year. This is the account of how, in an unbelievably short period of time, Belle and Sebastian became a fully formed band and released two of the most beloved albums in the history of independent music: Tigermilk *and* If You're Feeling Sinister. *It was a remarkable series of events.*

Stuart David (bass, Belle and Sebastian): I don't know why it took me so long to find out that my flatmate Richard [Colburn] played drums. During weekdays, it was always just the two of us at breakfast. The same in the evenings too; we usually ate dinner together waiting for the rest of them to come home. In contrast to us, they all left very early in the morning and came back quite late at night; we were on music courses, and the hours were more relaxed than they were in the real world.

Richard Colburn introduced the band to one of the most important opportunities in their career: Stow College's Electric Honey label, which had been set up by Alan Rankine from The Associates. It was a way for students on Stow's music business course to identify promising, upcoming bands and give them the opportunity to release a single. The focus was on students (one of whom was Richard) being taken through the mechanisms of the music industry. As this was the early 1990s, Electric Honey released only CD singles.

Stuart David (bass, Belle and Sebastian): I knew Richard had practised with some of the top snooker players back in Perth before he'd come to study at Stow, and I knew that the students on his course had to release a single by a band they chose as part of their coursework. We'd had an announcement about that at Beatbox, and I was planning to submit my Raglin Street Rattle tape when the time came. I'd asked Richard to keep me up to date with when they were ready for submissions. But I didn't know he was a musician, only that he spent a lot of time in his room listening to the widest range of music I'd ever heard.

Then one morning, while we were sitting at the kitchen table, Richard said, 'You've got something to do with Rhode Island, haven't you? Are you in that band?' I told him it wasn't really a band yet – it was just Stuart [Murdoch], with me helping him out. He asked if I could get him a tape. One of the students on his course had heard Stuart's songs being played on Beat Patrol, and he'd liked the sound of them. The name had come up in class as a possibility for the single they were to release, and Richard recognised it from conversations we'd had. I told him I'd get him a tape, and reminded him I'd hand in one of Raglin Street Rattle too. That was when he told me he played drums. 'I'll play with you both sometime if you're looking for a drummer,' he said. So I told Stuart there was some interest in his music already at the Stow College course, and that Richard had asked for a tape.

Stuart Murdoch (vocals, Belle and Sebastian): Well, you see, I just wanted to get on. It's a good thing to have no idea of what was meant to happen in the music business. I had this feeling from what Stuart [David] had been through that you can try for years to get on a major label, and in the end they don't release your record and nothing happens. And even though I wasn't an innocent at all, because I was a bit older, I'd been hiding away for years. I used to work in record shops and put on bands, and saw the way things worked. And I hated this idea of gatekeepers. I hated the idea of people telling you what not to do. So, when I had an opportunity to do something, I was like yeah, you've got to make it while you can. . . I didn't want to wait for that. For instance, the whole idea of Stow was that you make this kind of demo single so that you maybe get signed. I was making an album! I mean, I've been waiting seven years – you know, I've been ill for seven years. This was going to be the biggest thing that ever happened to me. And I was taking my opportunity. I wasn't missing – I wasn't making a demo. I never made a demo in my life. I was recording flat out. The moment the song was written, it was getting recorded.

The recording was accepted by Stow but in another moment of serendipity, Stuart Murdoch was also toying with the idea of investigating a pre-booked personal opportunity in San Francisco.

Stuart David (bass, Belle and Sebastian): With a firm offer to record the Stow College single on the table, Stuart [Murdoch] began to ask me searching questions. He remained committed to his San Francisco trip, but he asked if I thought the opportunities that were starting to appear for him in Glasgow would still be there when he came back. He seemed convinced they would be. I told him I wasn't so sure.

'Sometimes you only get one shot,' I told him. 'It's easy just to miss your chance.' Richard felt the same. He was certain that if you didn't grab your break when it appeared, it might never come again. He couldn't believe Stuart was going off to San Francisco rather than making the single for Stow.

Stuart Murdoch (vocals, Belle and Sebastian): I remember reading a biography of C. S. Lewis. And he was obviously a very spiritual guy. He was a Christian and I remember the biographer describing how C. S. Lewis lived his life, that he would go with, he would work with, whoever was in front of him. He would never look for anything. He was this phenomenal, creative guy, but in terms of business and getting on, he just lived this life where he would let God put stuff in front of him and that's how he lived his life. And to a small extent, back then, at this moment in time, I felt like God was maybe, you know, good things were happening for once so it was very fateful. And I thought fate is in charge. Let's see what happens. And the people just came out of the woodwork. It was great. So I didn't have to choose anybody. I didn't have to. I kidded it was like *The Magnificent Seven*. In *The Magnificent Seven* Steve McQueen and Yul Brynner go around hunting out people and choosing people. To me, right at that moment, Stuart was there, Richard was just his flatmate and I didn't even know he played drums. He had this little porcelain set of bongos that looked like it was tourist tat from Malaga. That's all he had. I mean there were drummers at Beatbox, there were drummers that played on the demo, but for some reason Richard kept showing up with Stuart and he would just play bongos. And I was like, okay, well, Richard's there. I never saw him behind a kit. He was a snooker player, he wasn't a drummer but he had this little porcelain set of bongos. There was real drummers in

Beatbox that I could have pursued but he was the one that just showed up.

Stuart David (bass, Belle and Sebastian): Stuart, still unconvinced but willing to look into things further, set up another meeting with the (Stow) class and we went in to talk to them. It was a novelty for us to see Alan Rankine standing still, rather than rushing past in a blur in the Beatbox corridor. He wrote some stuff on the whiteboard to illustrate what the process would involve, and he wrote some dates up there too. The budget would cover five days in CaVa Studios. Three for recording, two for mixing. We'd record a single and a B-side in February, and then the class would act as a record label called Electric Honey and release a thousand copies of the single on CD and promote it. Alan explained that the main purpose of it was to give the students experience of everything that was involved in putting out a record, but that it would be a good thing for us too because we would get some publicity from it and it might generate a bit of a buzz for the band. The first thing Stuart made clear was his opposition to releasing a CD. 'Singles have to be vinyl,' he said, '7-inch.' He explained that a 7-inch single was a magical thing, and that CDs were nothing at all. Alan hesitated, but he eventually said we could probably do it on vinyl if we really wanted to. Stuart gave that some thought then shook his head. 'I don't know,' he said. 'How about if we made an album? I think it has to be an album.' The pause before Alan replied this time was a lot longer, and he finally told us he didn't think it could be done. Not in five days.

Stuart Murdoch (vocals, Belle and Sebastian): Even though I didn't have any energy I still had this determination. I really did, at that point, the songs were pinging out of me. And I do specifically remember being in the classroom with Alan and saying that we'd got the thing for Stow. It wasn't Belle and Sebastian at that point but they wanted to make this a record. And I immediately said I want to do an album.

Stuart David (bass, Belle and Sebastian): 'Five days are plenty,' Stuart replied, and he went up to the whiteboard and wiped a space among Alan's doodlings. Then he picked up the marker pen and started writing song titles on the board. 'The State I Am In', 'Expectations', 'She's Losing It'; five in one list on the left-hand side of the board, and five in another list on the right-hand side. When he was finished he turned back to look at Alan as if that was all the proof that was needed.

Alan agreed. The project had swiftly changed from a CD single to 7-inch vinyl to a full album on vinyl.

Stuart David (bass, Belle and Sebastian): After the debate was over, and Stuart was talking to some of the students, Alan told me Stuart's attitude reminded him of Billy McKenzie, the singer in The Associates. 'Bill always knew what he wanted,' he said. 'Great artists usually do. You have to give them room to follow their vision.' And so Stuart cancelled his trip to San Francisco.

Alan Rankine (The Associates; Electric Honey/Stow College): Belle and Sebastian were a Godsend. I've never met anyone who had a voice like Bill's, but with Stuart and his songwriting I'd just never heard anyone that had a body of work that was just so compelling. And this didn't deserve a single, this needed an album. And the fact that it came out on vinyl, that set it apart.

Stuart David (bass, Belle and Sebastian): As word spread around Glasgow that Stuart was going to be making an album, a curious thing started to happen. Suddenly, after years of not being able to find any musicians to play on his songs, almost everybody wanted to be in his band. Just a few weeks after he'd planned to leave for San Francisco because nothing was happening for him, people all over the city began to approach him and ask if they could play on his album. Musicians in Beatbox, musicians in the 13th Note, musicians in the Halt Bar: people who'd always been there and never paid much notice before. I watched Stuart nod at them and make no further response. For the most part, they still didn't fit with the picture he had for his ideal band, but the fact that they'd never said anything positive about his songs in the past wasn't lost on him either. For the time being, there was still only one more person he wanted to add to the line-up, and that was Stevie.

Stuart Murdoch (vocals, Belle and Sebastian): Stevie Jackson never wanted to be in a group. Because he had just been in a group called The Moondials. And I think he had his fill of it – he was kind of done with that for a while. But I'd seen him playing in the Halt Bar up the road. That was another thing, I used to go the Halt Bar and play my songs on the open mic, which was terrifying. But at least if you had the balls to do that on a Saturday afternoon, then you could do it elsewhere. But Stevie was the compere.

Stevie Jackson (guitar, Belle and Sebastian): Some people you can't quite remember when you met but I remember so clearly the first time I met him. In fact, it was the two Stuarts. They turned up [at the Halt Bar] and insisted on a soundcheck, which I thought was great. Later on, when the crowd were in, he came on and he broke into 'Le Pastie de la Bourgeoisie', which was a song we recorded later and about a minute into it he just stopped and said the sound wasn't to his liking and walked off. And that was that. It was quite telling of what lay in the future.

Stuart Murdoch (vocals, Belle and Sebastian): Watching [Stevie] play guitar was like a full meal. It was like a full sound just from him. It sounded like a band, him playing either acoustic or electric. You know, he's a little bit like Jimi Hendrix in a sense, just the full meal. And I thought Jesus, if you had that guy, that is the meat in the sandwich. So he was the one guy I really wanted. And with the Stow College thing, I had a ticket. I had an excuse. I wrote him a letter asking him to do the record with me. I said, you know, it's not a band. You don't have to – it's not a band, you're just helping me out. So suddenly that was a group. A few months before, it had just been me and Stuart but suddenly there was this cohort of funny, funny people. Richard, the drummer that I'd still never seen playing drums. And (soon) Chris Geddes, who Jason MacPhail said knew what a Fender Rhodes looked like.

Stevie Jackson (guitar, Belle and Sebastian): Stuart [Murdoch] is just this extraordinary character, someone who actually has got the balls to just walk into something that's already, fully formed with the format of Stow and change it from three days and a three-track CD to a ten-track vinyl album. Somehow he went in there and made it happen. I thought, that's incredible. He really had a lot of confidence. . . or drive. . . and he still does. A very driven guy, and he had vision. It was great. He came round to my flat and I said, 'Do you like this record?' and I put on 'Something On My Mind' by the Left Banke and he started po-going around my room and I went, 'Alright, okay', that was clear that we liked the same stuff and we had a shared vocabulary.

Stuart David (bass, Belle and Sebastian): One thing became abundantly clear to me: Stevie was hugely impressed by Stuart's songwriting. I'd played with a lot of people on Stuart's songs over the past year, but nobody – except maybe Alistair from Lisa Helps the Blind – had been half as impressed by them as Stevie was. He could already play fragments of them, just from hearing them in the Halt, and he talked about them with a kind of awe. I showed him some of the sections he wasn't sure about, and as he played, one more thing became clear to me: none of the guitarists we'd worked with before could hold a candle to Stevie. He could do just about anything, and it was all free of the rock and blues clichés that even the best guitarists we'd played with had been in thrall to. Stevie's playing was pure shimmering pop.

Stuart Murdoch (vocals, Belle and Sebastian): I definitely had a blueprint in my head. Even though I'm being a little bit coy about everything being fate, okay, the people showed up. But I did have this eight-person plan in my head: I had a mini-Baroque section in my head. That's what I thought, because I loved middle of the road. At that point, I really loved middle-of-the-road seventies hit music. I loved it more than the Small Faces. I loved it more than the the real hip stuff. I was being honest with myself. I had no extra energy to be cool. I liked real bubblegum dross; schlock music – which now if you look back at the songs I'd have as these blueprints, they would now be considered more classic. Things like Hall & Oates – early Hall & Oates –

'Downtown' by Petula Clark, 'Never Let Her Slip Away' by Andrew Gold, these one-off one-hit wonders from the seventies. 'Sealed with a Kiss' by Brian Hyland, which was just reissued – these pop tunes that would stick out in my memory. 'Sugar Sugar' [The Archies] from when I was younger. And I just thought: that's what I love the most. I want to do that. I want to have the sweetness of that, but then there was still the slightly more serious thing. Left Banke was I think uniquely influential on me at that point. For they only really produced one-and-a-half LP's worth, but when I heard them I just thought that was such a glorious sound. . . And that was the Baroque. They had that Baroque thing. I love that sound so much, along with *Forever Changes,* that I thought well why not? Not just have that as string-players but have the whole package. Have the strings on stage.

Stevie Jackson (guitar, Belle and Sebastian): The things that were in common, whether it was the Lovin' Spoonful, it was the Left Banke and The Velvet Underground.

Stuart Murdoch's vision for Belle and Sebastian was now almost realised but there were still a few missing elements.

Stuart Murdoch (vocals, Belle and Sebastian): [Previously] I was jamming with two guys at Beatbox and making four-track demos. They were very cool cats. When they finished the practice, both of them agreed they weren't going to play with me anymore, in the politest way. But they mentioned there's a girl called Isobel Campbell. And they've been playing music with her. And said they don't want to play music with her anymore, either. You should get together. And that stuck in my head. It was six months later that I met her in the queue for the bathroom at a party at Jason MacPhail's house – it was a New Year party, the first day of 1996. And I was standing next to this girl in the queue for the toilet. And we got chatting and she was very sweet. And I wasn't sure whether she wanted to chat. But she started chatting. And then I don't know, for some reason she gave away something about her tastes in music. And then she gave away that she played the cello. And then I was like, that's the girl they were talking about! And of course at that point my radar was going off. I mean I didn't waste any time. I said can you help me out? And that was it. She was in. Yeah, it's fateful.

Jason MacPhail (promoter; vocals, V-Twin): I had a Hammond B-3 Wurlitzer because I liked De La Soul. Stuart knew I had a Hammond B-3 Wurlitzer, but his interest in it wasn't the same as mine. His was Felt; he was looking for Martin Duffy to his Lawrence and he came round and he had the tape. I think it was pretty obvious. . . 'The State I'm In' was a great song, but I didn't want to be in his band. I was gonna do it, but I'd just had the Hammond fixed. It was very difficult, very expensive; incredibly problematic to move. And he wanted to do a gig in the basement of the 13th Note. It was the first incarnation of Belle and Sebastian, I can't remember what they were called. I was like, I can't fucking handle the idea of moving this piano and this organ. I said, there's this guy Simon Shaw knows called Chris Geddes, get him. I didn't want to move the organ. Dodged a bullet. [Laughs.] He stayed with my flatmate, so she ended up just hanging around in a big flat in 14 Ruskin Terrace. Everybody came through that flat at some point. Belle and

Sebastian formed in that flat, at the New Year's party when Stuart met Isobel.

Chris Geddes (keyboards, Belle and Sebastian and V-Twin): My path to meeting Jason as far as I remember was via Simon Shaw, who was in the first line-up of V-Twin. He was in my physics class at university, and I think we ended up on the same day both wearing a Velvet Underground banana t-shirt in our physics lecture and we spotted each other. Okay, you're someone who might be a bit cooler than some of the rest of the people in the class. . . and Simon and I got to know each other. And then a room came up in in Simon's flat.

Simon introduced Chris to V-Twin and Chris would occasionally play keyboards with them when the opportunity arose.

Chris Geddes (keyboards, Belle and Sebastian and V-Twin): My perception at the time was always that Jason didn't really think I was very good and he wouldn't ever really let me play keyboards that much between stuff. . . but he definitely had said to Stuart, 'I know this guy that plays a bit.'

Stuart Murdoch (vocals, Belle and Sebastian): I was pally with Jason, we'd always chat and talk in the Grosvenor. And you know the thing about the Rhodes – Jason had a Rhodes piano and hence the Rhode Island name. I fell in love with this Rhodes piano sound and Chris came into the Grosvenor one time. That felt very fateful.

Chris Geddes (keyboards, Belle and Sebastian and V-Twin): I definitely remember there being a point when meeting Stuart and he said, 'I hear you play a little bit of keyboards.' And I said,

'Yeah, a little bit, but let's have a go at doing something together.' As bizarre as it seems now, Stuart was really kind of scraping the barrel by that point, he was really struggling to find people who were interested in playing on his songs, even though they were, even at that point self-evidently, really great songs. . . I was the last one in so it definitely wasn't, 'Oh do you want to do this and we'll carry on as a band?' It was, 'Do you want to do this?' and then there was maybe a vague 'and then we'll see what happens'.

Jason MacPhail (promoter; vocals, V-Twin): I read books, was interested in stuff and if you pay attention, or if you're curious or maybe managerially minded you see that there's an energy and you just look at it. If you're in a band and every record company in the world comes to see you, maybe you're gonna do really well. Because they're interested and excited, and also like the songs. Like 'The State I'm In'. I didn't want to be in the band. But there was no denying that that cassette was great in 1995. I said to Chris, get this, right. This is amazing. What was happening to him. I was like, 'You're never gonna have to work again for the rest of your life and got a normal job'. He got really annoyed with me. I don't know why it annoyed him. But I was, 'Youse are gonna fucking make a fucking living out of this and you're gonna do it for the rest of your lives, this is going to be your career' and he got pissed off. To this day, I don't know if he thought it was just arrogance on my part that I was predicting the rest of his life.

It was at that Hogmanay party that the band became Belle and Sebastian. Just two months later they were recording their first album.

Stuart David (bass, Belle and Sebastian): We started making the album for Electric Honey on Monday 4 March 1996. We had three 12-hour days for the recording, 10 a.m. to 10 p.m.. Monday till Wednesday, then Thursday and Friday to do the mixing. And the biggest thrill of all was that we were recording in CaVa Studios, the most hallowed studio in Scotland at the time.

Sitting on the edge of Kelvingrove Park, CaVa was based in an old church, with a domed roof and Greek-style columns at the original entrance. It looked very grand, and it was. Most of our favourite Scottish bands had recorded albums there, and the live room was awe-inspiring.

Chris Geddes (keyboards, Belle and Sebastian and V-Twin): At the time, we didn't necessarily think it was crazy to try and record the songs that quickly, because we rehearsed a little bit and the parts were fairly sorted out. So even though we hadn't really played live much it made it seem like, 'Okay, all we need to do is go in the studio and play through the songs. And that will be okay.' And then there was a bit of freedom when it came to trying overdubs. I mean, we're not going down rabbit holes too much but if I played piano on the song, and I was like, 'Oh, maybe I should do an organ part as well' then I could do that quite quickly.

Stuart David (bass, Belle and Sebastian): When Stuart had insisted it wouldn't be a problem for us to record the album in three days, he hadn't quite factored in that it would take us most of the first morning to set up, and for Gregor and Geoff to mic the amps, arrange the isolation booths and baffle boards and organise a monitor mix in the headphones that everyone was happy with. . . We started out with 'The State I Am In' and 'Expectations', just instrumental versions without Stuart singing. Although we were nervous – and there were a few false starts and clanging errors that brought proceedings to an abrupt halt – we'd rehearsed enough to know the structure of the songs well, and we soon had a couple of takes that had gone smoothly enough to be worth listening to. Gradually, things started to come together. The huge wall speakers had been too big a leap for us after the personal stereo speakers we'd been using at home, but as long as we confined our listening to the smaller monitors, and once we had a mix where Stevie's guitar sat properly in place like a glue holding all the other instruments together, things started shaping up.

Because we were recording onto tape, and because multi-track tape was so expensive, we couldn't afford to keep alternative takes of each song. Nowadays, recording onto hard disk, it's normal to keep dozens of takes of each song and decide later which one is best. But using tape, on the tight budget Electric Honey provided, we had to decide as we went, to free up tape for recording the next song. We sometimes managed to get three takes of a song without any disastrous mistakes, then we would go and listen to them through. And although there were usually still overdubs to be done, scratch vocals to be replaced and proper mixes to be applied to the drums and guitars, we'd have to choose there and then which two versions to discard and which one to keep, so's we could move on.

Stuart Murdoch (vocals, Belle and Sebastian): *Tigermilk* had an absolute magic for me because it was the first one. Because of the way it came together. The five days we had in the studio was a dream. This group of people coagulating, or whatever they were – becoming a creative group, was just magical. I'm trying to think how quickly we turned it around. I remember actually doing the artwork before we recorded the record. I used to listen to Mark and Lard all the time: 10 p.m. to 12 a.m. classic slot, Radio 1. And I would always be clearing up. I worked in the church hall. And after all the organisations I'd have to sweep the whole hall. So it took me ages and I'd have the radio on all the time. And they were the first people that played it – we'd sent a few white label copies, not very many – but they played it immediately! And that was the thrill of my life at that point. I couldn't believe it. It sounded magical on the radio. So, yeah, all these these things that happened for the first time. For me they were really magic.

Chris Geddes (keyboards, Belle and Sebastian and V-Twin): By the time *Tigermilk* came out and we did a launch party for it, I'd moved into another flat on Bentinck Street which was literally right across the road from CaVa Studios. So at the end of the launch night I went up to my bedroom and put my speakers in the window and started playing music out to the street as people were coming out from the launch party. . . I knew folk were definitely positive and dead enthusiastic about the band. There'd been records around on the shelves or around the studio so people were just picking them up as they left the building, frisbeeing them around the park. There definitely wasn't a sense that people were treating it as a future collector's item.

At the time of writing, a copy of Tigermilk *is listed on the online record website Discogs for £650. Despite some launch copies being used as frisbees, by this stage media and record label interest in the band was phenomenal, with major labels eager to sign them. Stuart pushed the band to take the unusual step of choosing an almost-unknown independent, Jeepster and immediately recording a second album.*

Alan Rankine (The Associates; Electric Honey/Stow College): There must have been forty record companies up in CaVa where we heard their exhibition to the industry, and people were offering millions of pounds. I tried to say to Stuart, 'Stuart, just have a good time. You know, you don't have to say anything, don't sign anything. Let them take you to London. Let them take you to London in a taxi because you say you're afraid of flying. Let them put you up in a hotel and bring all your laundry and get it done, and get a taxi back to Glasgow. They'll do it because they want you that much.' But you know, Stuart's too much of a good person to be that cynical, but I was trying to illustrate a point to him that these people are so driven when they see something and they hear something and they feel something that is so good. It doesn't come around very often. And that's why they all go apeshit for it. It's not that they're bad people. They're not. It's just, there was just something so special about Belle and Sebastian.

Chris Geddes (keyboards, Belle and Sebastian and V-Twin): A lot of label people came up to the *Tigermilk* launch and Stuart said from the stage, in the in the middle of the set, 'Thanks for coming up from London everyone but we've already told Jeepster we're signing to them, so you've wasted your time.'

Stevie Jackson (guitar, Belle and Sebastian): We thought with those guys [Jeepster] they couldn't control us, because we were uncontrollable. There was a notion that if we had signed to Island or something we'd be coerced into doing something we didn't want to do. I remember being in a café and Stuart going, 'You don't want to sign us, we won't do anything you want to do' and they went, 'We don't care, we want to sign you.' I'm happy to talk on behalf of my friend Stuart here, because as far as I'm aware, after *Tiger* was recorded, he had an impetus to write those songs really, really quickly. And as far as I know, they're all from that same couple of months' period, I don't remember any of the songs existing prior.

Stuart Murdoch (vocals, Belle and Sebastian): Yeah, that was my real golden patch for writing. People say well, you've got your whole life to write your first LP. I wrote the songs for *If You're Feeling Sinister* between February and June, or even March and June. Even when we were recording *Tigermilk,* I was writing *Sinister.* The fact that I had this group had opened the gates for me even further, where I was just ready to go. And they had inspired in me something. Now I know exactly where I'm going. I have the musicians, we have the group. I wrote 'Stars of Track and Field' and 'Fox in the Snow' in the same day. They're side by side in a jotter, just marked the same day in March or something. And that record was sequenced before we ever went in to record it – that's how sure I was about the shape of it. And the shortcomings – even more so with *Sinister* – we were reaching further in terms of production and arrangement but we were doing it too quickly. And there's a slightness and a flimsiness to that record. I find it very difficult to listen back to *Sinister*. Actually, what a lot of people like about that record in the end is what I don't like so much. I wanted it to be *Court and Spark* [Joni Mitchell]; I wanted it to be *Tapestry* [Carole King]. I felt like I had everything lined up, but you don't become a producer overnight. That record overreached. But I don't regret it. I was so determined to keep moving and moving. So I don't regret any of that stuff. I think over the years we've managed to make records that are better sounding and more robust. But I'm still pleased, we did what we did.

CHAPTER SEVENTEEN

Imperial Phase Part Two

The Delgados release their second single (not on Chemikal Underground) and their debut album

In a truly altruistic moment, The Delgados had pulled their Chemikal Underground resources into pushing bis at the expense of their own band. The cost of putting out the first two bis EPs, Chemikal's second and third releases, had left the label's resources depleted. Due to the interest around their 'Monica Webster' 7-inch, however, they had attracted the interest of a major London label who offered them an opportunity.

Emma Pollock (vocals/guitar, The Delgados; Chemikal Underground): To be honest with you, unless you're a band that chimes with the times in the way that bis did at that moment – when they had a huge amount of interest from different labels – then it becomes a very difficult decision to choose who you go with, and what the criteria is that you make the choice with, all of these things. Unless you're a band that strikes gold and has all the choices. We were responding simply to somebody coming along and saying, 'We really like what you do, we'd love to put out a single, let's see how it goes and if things go well then we might put out an album.' Radar did that.

Stewart Henderson (bass, The Delgados; Chemikal Underground): We'd put out 'Monica Webster' and the reason we went with Radar was because we said if we can use the money that we got from selling 'Monica Webster', that Chemikal Underground wasn't about putting out The Delgados stuff necessarily. The idea was we'd got this money back from selling 'Monica Webster', so we don't want to just put another Delgados single out, because then the whole label just becomes about The Delgados. And we want to sign someone else because that way you can become a proper record label... so we'll put The Delgados out on Radar.

Emma Pollock (vocals/guitar, The Delgados; Chemikal Underground): That was perhaps a blip in the master plan, if you like. But it's exactly the same principle as why Arab Strap went to Go! Beat. It's exactly the same principle as why Mogwai went to PIAS for a spell. But what's really interesting to note is that none of these experiences were very positive.

Stewart Henderson (bass, The Delgados; Chemikal Underground): We talked about maybe signing to Radar. I think it was certainly Radar's intention to eventually sign us. But for better or for worse, and I think it was for better, because Chemikal Underground was up and running by this point, we were determined to keep running the label. I think if we had signed to Radar full time, Chemikal would have kept on going. We wouldn't have folded Chemikal and said well, mission accomplished we've got a record deal. We would have kept Chemikal Underground going, it was always the intention. And maybe the thought was if we can get The Delgados onto another label then that might be even better because then we can focus all the resources of Chemikal Underground into the bands that we're putting out. Anyway, we fucked it. We went down to Manchester and played In The City and it was an absolute fucking disaster.

Paul Savage (drums, The Delgados; Chemikal Underground): It's basically an industry convention but bands play at [In The City], a bit like South by Southwest. A bit more corporate than that. So we were booked to play this thing in Manchester, and Radar were like, we want you to be interested in signing to us, but you haven't signed yet. They wanted to do that thing that happened with bis and get the media frenzy going. They said, come and play in front of all these other A&R people.

Stewart Henderson (bass, The Delgados; Chemikal Underground): We talked about it afterwards, you know when you have an absolute clusterfuck like that, all sorts of defence mechanisms kick in. You tell yourself it didn't really matter; it was bad but it wasn't that bad, it wasn't great but it doesn't matter and we'll live to fight another day and all that. As it turned out, it was that bad. Like we had absolutely fucked ourselves in the eyes of the industry.

Paul Savage (drums, The Delgados; Chemikal Underground): We were rushed on stage in this place, I can't even remember the place. It was the dream of nightmares. It's the dream that I have when we were reforming. But it was unfortunately a reality. The kind of nightmare exam dream that you have when you're doing something, or when you've got something really important to do. And you realise you're naked. Something like that. We went onstage and we went to play the first song of the EP, I think it was 'Lazarwalker'. And we were howling out of tune. Like the first chord was like oh my God, that's awful. So, right okay, sorry. We look at each other, who was out? I'm like, I'm fine. Playing chords, and I'm fine. Alright, sorry about that, somebody must have fucked up. And again, 1 2 3 4 – clang. What is going on? Everyone's going, I'm in tune. Right, who's got the tuner? Because we had one tuner. We would pass the tuner around and go, you tune up, you tune up. Really amateur stuff. We couldn't afford a tuner. What had happened is that when someone had passed the tuner to the next person, there's a plus and minus button that's quite hard to see. But somebody had pushed the plus button on it, and raised the tuning thing by one semitone. So some people had tuned in the normal tuning, and some people had tuned exactly one semitone sharp. So it was just absolutely howling. We were on stage for about fifteen minutes figuring this out. And people were beginning to boo. Like, 'Fucking amateurs, let someone else have a go' and we were dying on stage. We had a half-hour set, we finally got going just before fifteen minutes I think it was. By then our nerves were absolutely shot, we played a terrible part of the gig that we managed to play. We fucked our chances with anybody being interested in us.

Stuart Henderson (bass, The Delgados; Chemikal Underground): Radar still wanted to work with us, I think they offered us another single deal and they certainly never told us, 'You know what guys, that was a shambles, we don't want to work with you anymore.' Nobody ever tells you that to your face in the music industry. We were like well it's fine, we've had the bis success, we're going back to Chemikal and CHEM04 was 'Cinecentre'. And then we put out the Cha Cha Cohen EP as CHEM05, and then CHEM06 was 'Under Canvas', the first thing off *Domestiques.*

Emma Pollock (vocals/guitar, The Delgados; Chemikal Underground): The Delgados were often at the bottom of our priority pile. Because we always suffered from a sense of – right, we'll put out the first single: Delgados will be the first single. Let's see how that goes so we don't fuck it up for anybody else. You know, it was that type of thing. And then of course, the very first Chemikal Underground album was The Delgados, *Domestiques*; that was the very first Delgados album. It was the very first Chemikal Underground album, so that we knew how to put out an album. And we took the risk as a band rather than us putting out someone else's album. So we were always the guinea pigs.

Despite their experience with Radar, The Delgados had proved they could successfully put out singles and albums. They'd taken the Scottish labels of the new scene up another level and they'd used the lessons they'd learned wisely.

Emma Pollock (vocals/guitar, The Delgados; Chemikal Underground): As soon as the indie band goes away from the indie label, and starts mixing with the majors, it usually doesn't go terribly well. But there are obvious exceptions where that's the best decision to make. But yeah, there you go. We were enticed for a few months by another label because at the end of the day, we figured they'd be able to do a better job. We figured they'd have more money to spend. But the whole kind of creative instinct is that it's never really right with these things, because I think the strength of indies is the personalities that run them. And the fact that they're actually quite consistent. Whereas your average major imprint has transient staff, unpredictable press and promo, unpredictable interest and passion. Whereas the indie is there because it wants to be. The major is there because it's decided to employ certain people to do a job.

Arab Strap

The huge success of bis with 'Kandy Pop' on the 'Secret Vampire' EP, and the further experience from their major label adventure, had taught Chemikal Underground a vast amount about the inner workings of the industry within a very short space of time. Now, the label struck gold again when Arab Strap unexpectedly appeared.

Stewart Henderson (bass, The Delgados; Chemikal Underground): Here's the thing: you're talking about Urusei and Modern Independent and Vesuvius, all these great labels. What separated Chemikal Underground from them? Well, bis! That's what fucking separated us from Modern Independent because if the guys in Urusei had happened to have been in the position, which they may well could have been, if they'd happened to be the ones that had put bis out, then they would have had the 30-, 40-odd thousand-selling CD single that they would had to have dealt with. And maybe that would have energised them to kick up a level. I'm not taking anything away from us. But there's no doubt that having that experience forced us to kick the level of the label up a notch and thrust us to a higher stratum of the industry than we could have realistically expected to happen on our third ever single. And then Arab Strap came along as CHEM07, and all that came along with that.

Aidan Moffat (vocals, instruments, Arab Strap): We were at different schools. [Malcolm] was at Graham High and I was at Falkirk High, but we were the same age and we had some mutual friends. It's partly that indie scene; the first time I met Malcolm he stole my date. It was in a club called the Maniqui in Falkirk. I was with a girl whose name I probably shouldn't say, but we were having a kiss in the corner and she asked me to get a drink. So I went to the bar, and when I came back, she was leaving with Malcolm. It was a very small pool of people in Falkirk. That's not the first time we ended up having relationships with the same girl, you know, it was a very close-knit community.

Malcolm Middleton (guitar, other instruments Arab Strap): We went to different high schools but knew each other by sight from going to the same pubs and clubs from 1990 onwards. Local rock/alternative bars and indie discos. Through our mutual friend John, Aidan ended up filming my first ever gig and even grabbing a mic and doing some backing vocals. (Rabbid Lettuce at The Argyll Bar, Falkirk, 1991.)

Aidan Moffat (Arab Strap): I never really had this ambition to be a musician in any way. It was a nice idea, I suppose. . . And we did it for just a bit of fun. It was eventually when I was getting tired of working in the record shop, Sleeves in Falkirk. And Malcolm had loads of different jobs. I've only had one job, that was the record shop, five years, four-and-a-half or something.

Because I started that when I pretty much left school actually. Well, I didn't quite leave school, I was asked to leave school. I was about 19 and that was the only job I had whereas Malcolm was working in different places.

Malcolm Middleton (Arab Strap): After we started hanging around together, and not just nodding across the street, we started talking about doing some music. He already had the band name and had made some tapes with Stuart The Postman and Cheg. We went to Stuart's house near the canal in Falkirk on a rainy Thursday afternoon, August 1995, and recorded a couple of songs. Then managed to somehow borrow Stuart's four-track and relocate to Aidan's house where we chipped away at things throughout the autumn and winter. It was nothing serious but I think we both felt that something cool was happening. The songs were funny and the music slightly emotive and changeable. Probably influenced by Aidan's lo-fi American stuff like Slint, Palace and Smog, and by me instinctively not playing anything from my own influences. It kind of worked. Anyway, it was a long fun winter for lots of different reasons. Come February I'd had enough and decided to go to the Isle of Mull to work as a waiter for six months. The plan was to raise enough money to buy our own four-track and then record more when I returned.

Aidan Moffat (Arab Strap): While he was away, I said, look, I'm going to send a tape of some of the songs to people, and I only sent it to three labels.

Malcolm Middleton (Arab Strap): Aidan's job was to send off the demos we had. Drag City, Domino and Chemikal Underground. I think Chemikal got back in a matter of days and then I was called to the red phone box on Mull harbour where an excited Aidan was telling me that a label wanted to meet us and put out our demos as an album, and that I had to come back to Falkirk. I'd only been away two weeks in my new life.

Aidan Moffat (Arab Strap): One was Drag City. One was Domino, which at that point was just a tiny label. Basically, they were sort of just licensing all of the Drag City stuff. And the other one was Chemikal Underground because I knew their music from working in the record shop. I knew they had done their first single. And I was curious that there was this new, independent Glasgow label and I knew they were run by the band The Delgados. Now, had I seen them before I met them? I don't think I had actually, no, I just had the single because the first time I saw them was at T in the Park, which would have been after, and the only reason I was at the T in the Park was because they got us tickets to get in to try and woo us to their label.

Emma Pollock (vocals/guitar, The Delgados; Chemikal Underground): Aiden sent the most beautifully presented demo. A cassette with this gorgeous green cut-out flap cover that had been handmade. I mean, Aidan, from a graphics point of view, as well as being quite a brilliant songwriter and presenter of music, he's an aesthete to the absolute hilt. He absolutely values presentation just as much, I believe. Because at the end of the day, what is music if not presentation of a musical idea? And in order to do that as exquisitely as possible you are creating a piece of art. Which means that every last facet of that – whether it be the cassette with the handmade paper cover, or whether it be the most immaculately graphically designed cover, which Aidan still creates to this day for all of Arab Strap, for all of his solo stuff, for an extensive amount of Chemikal Underground, he is the most wonderfully talented presenter of ideas.

Paul Savage (drums, The Delgados; Chemikal Underground): So Alun [Woodward] played it first and went, 'This is fucking great – come and hear this.' So we all listened and went, 'This is so different, yeah, how do we get in touch with them now? Call them now! Can't call them. We've got to write to them?' So we had to write to Aidan and say we really like the tape, can you get in touch? Here's our number.

Stewart Henderson (bass, The Delgados; Chemikal Underground): We were sure that whoever else they'd sent this cassette to, every single other label would have wanted to sign them, but I think we were the only ones that got back to them.

Aidan Moffat (Arab Strap): I remember the letter they sent me as well. Alun Woodward's handwriting was huge. It was like an A4 – there was only about fifteen words but it filled the whole page, and he wanted to meet up. And we met them in a pub called Behind The Wall in Falkirk. Again, back then it was, 'Let's try something', there was no grand plan even from The Delgados, they were just in their infancy as well.

Malcolm Middleton (Arab Strap): We met The Delgados (minus Paul, he was recording Mogwai and couldn't make it) at a pub in Falkirk, Behind The Wall (upstairs). They bought us some drinks and then I think we maybe signed something. Can't remember. We said our album was already finished (the demos) but they insisted we go into the studio with Paul and record them properly. We did, but didn't really, as we had rules like 'no reverb' and 'no second takes'. Stupid stuff like that, which I guess makes the album sound the way it does. (Not great!)

Paul Savage (drums, The Delgados; Chemikal Underground): I think it was only Alun that could meet them that first day. I said, how did it go? And he said, well I was driving so I didn't have a drink, but the two of them had a few drinks. And he said, I think they might like us – they might be up for it, they might do it. I said, what makes you think they'd do it, did they say? Alun said no, but Malcolm stole me some firewood from a garage. So I think that means we're okay. [Laughs.] I was fascinated, I was like, who are these people? That they're doing this kind of music. It's so raw. I'd never heard lyrics like that. I remember playing it to various people and my dad was one of them. We were going, we're so excited about this, have a listen to this. And he was like, you're mad. What is this music? It's crazy.

Emma Pollock (vocals/guitar, The Delgados; Chemikal Underground): Because Paul was now able to record, he basically said to Aidan and Malcolm, look your demos are really, really promising, but wouldn't it be nice for us to actually go into the studio and see what comes of it? And of course that's exactly what happened.

Aidan Moffat (Arab Strap): All those songs on *The Week Never Starts Round Here* had been properly – well I say demo'd, but the demos don't sound that much different to the LP because we didn't even want to re-record them. Like when Chemikal asked us to do the album we presented them with an album's worth of stuff we'd done on the four-track and because I was enamoured with that sort of lo-fi scene and American stuff, I was like 'Fuck it, just release them. I don't really want to do them again. I feel like the work has been done.' And they insisted that we go to the studio – it became the CHEM19 studios – it was called MCM at the time, they were sort of in partnership with them and Paul was working there as an engineer.

Paul Savage (drums, The Delgados; Chemikal Underground): So they signed to us. And part of the deal was, I had been working in a local studio and I could get cheap rates for the studio, for the label. We'd said the album was great, they'd sent us a four-track version of the album, but how about you just come in and we do the album again in the studio with proper mics? Less of a four-track thing. They were a wee bit cagey about it. And they were a wee bit cagey with me when they turned up, they were like, 'We don't want you to fucking steal our soul'. I said I'll keep it really, really simple; really raw. They really liked the drum sounds we were getting, because it was more like the records they loved, like maybe a band in a room like Slint. They were like, this is great, we can get this kind of sound. And I think I had to slowly win them over that I wasn't going to polish it and make it sound like all glossy or all studio. So they were very like, right, no overdubs. This is all it is. One take of this, one take of that. Keep it stark and keep it simple.

Malcolm Middleton (Arab Strap): The distinctive sound at the start was not having a tuner for a few years, and not knowing anything about guitars etc. I was mainly a bass player but ended up recording guitars on the demos. I come from a metal background, so most of what I do is power chords and open strings.

Think Iron Maiden at 33rpm on an acoustic guitar. I think we did it all in four days, all the songs were already written and there wasn't really much on them.

Aidan Moffat (Arab Strap): So we'd finished the album and they were happy with it but they said we should maybe start with a 7-inch single to try and gauge how many albums we think we can sell. And it was not that we didn't want to do a single off the album, there just wasn't a single thing on the record you could releases as a single. [Laughs.] So they said can you try and maybe do a one-off single? You don't have to put it on the album but we'll see how it goes and then gauge the market. I mean, I don't think anyone was actually wanky enough to say 'gauge the market' at that point.

Malcolm Middleton (Arab Strap): The album was finished minus 'First Big Weekend', then Chemikal asked if we'd record a standalone single to put out before the album to 'test the water'. Probably a polite way of saying we didn't have any singles on the album. Which we didn't, because we weren't even a band really.

Paul Savage (drums, The Delgados; Chemikal Underground): We said, well is there anything else that you maybe could do? And Aidan and Malcolm were like, I see what you mean, there's nothing there. But what about that one, Malcolm had a guitar line or something, and Aidan had a drum machine pattern. And that was it, and they said, right okay we could do something, there's this song kicking about that we haven't finished yet. But why don't we book in next week? So I said, fine I'll book in Monday. And Aidan's like, right, I'll write the words at the weekend and

I'll come back in on Monday and we'll see how it works out. But maybe that could be a single. Right, fine, that's great.

So Monday morning comes around, I'm like, right, okay let's go, let's start laying it down.

Aidan Moffat (Arab Strap): We went in, and we already had the B-side. That was an album offcut. So it was just the A-side we had to do. So we thought we'll try something with a dance beat.

Paul Savage (drums, The Delgados; Chemikal Underground): And Aidan's like, listen, I'm really sorry, I was out all weekend. I don't have any words, so I can't finish it. And we said, okay, well what we'll do is – why don't you just take a break? You've put down the drum machine stuff. Me and Malcolm will do the bassline and the guitar. And if you have anything, give us a shout. . . And he said, fuck it, I'm just gonna write about the weekend. So give me an hour.

Aidan Moffat (Arab Strap): I just wrote about the weekend we'd had – it wasn't planned or anything. The chorus, 'went out for the weekend' – but Malcolm wrote that in the studio. We just felt something had to happen at this point. It was like 'hold on, I've got an idea'. Did this wee weekend chant and stuff.

Paul Savage (drums, The Delgados; Chemikal Underground): And he just came out with that. So it was all about meeting on Friday, or Thursday, booked in the studio for the Monday; he goes out the weekend that he's supposed to write a song. Has exactly that weekend that happens in the song, comes in on Monday morning and goes, I don't have a song. So I'll just write about the weekend. And there you go.

Aidan Moffat (Arab Strap): It certainly stood out as most unusual and I think that's why it ended up in the album. It kind of sticks out in the album quite badly but it works because it's like a sort of tent pole thing in the middle where all the other songs around about it seem to be about coming down and being miserable and having a hangover. And in the middle there's this big party. So we decided it worked and put it on the album.

Malcolm Middleton (Arab Strap): I remember Aidan did the drums first, then I played some guitar down the phone (landline!) and maybe sang the chorus? Not sure. We were probably still recovering from the said Big Weekend. We recorded it in a day I think.

Paul Savage (drums, The Delgados; Chemikal Underground): It was the most natural, unplanned thing. Malcolm did two takes on the bass and I remember the first take I was like, I don't think he knows what he's doing. I don't think he knows what's going on. And then the second take was the full one on the record. It was unbelievable, like, oh that worked! Okay, that's done. Next: guitar. There you go. It was as simple as that.

Emma Pollock (vocals/guitar, The Delgados; Chemikal Underground): Utterly unique. I mean, utterly unique. What Aidan and Malcolm still do now is something that is completely different to anybody else. It's very difficult to know if they are influenced, I'm not really sure I'd be able to tell you who it was; they do make such a unique sound. And Malcolm's got a very distinctive guitar sound and playing style, and Aidan of course has got this delivery and these lyrical ideas. He's also a fantastic drummer. Yeah, it's a really quite unique coming together of sounds to create something that I think a lot of record companies at the time would have thought twice about because it didn't sound enough like anything else to know what they had. Whereas we were actually dead excited about the fact that it was so unique.

Stewart Henderson (bass, The Delgados; Chemikal Underground): When it came out, nobody had heard anything like this. You've got all the kind of lazy *Trainspotting* things and all that but we had the discussion at the time: do we need to manufacture 20,000 copies of this single? And we were like, no we're not going to do that. Again, for right or wrong, we may have made a mistake with this. But we decided that we weren't going to press up loads of singles, we were going to limit the single: that it was about the album. And we limited the manufacture of 'The First Big Weekend'. Way below, way, way, way below what it could have sold. I think we limited it to a few thousand. The idea being that we didn't want to have *The Week Never Starts Round Here* just become all about 'The First Big Weekend'. In the way that bis at that time had become this kind of 'Kandy Pop' phenomenon, where it was just about, God forbid, that one-hit-wonder thing. We didn't want Arab Strap, who were a brand new band nobody had heard of, to go that way. So we chose to limit 'The First Big Weekend' and focus more on the album release. And the album did really well. It got great reviews. And it worked really, really well.

Aidan Moffat (Arab Strap): With all these things nobody knew what to expect. We'd got the 7-inch single. It was much like work to me because we had to go and fucking put all the stickers on all them in Paul and Emma's flat. So we had a thousand 7-inches and me and Malcolm were sitting putting fucking stickers on. So it seemed a bit laborious to me. It was great though. The test pressing was the best thing. I've still got it. I've got my own personal test pressing. I did a version of the sticker that eventually came so I glued that to it, and it's hand stamped. It's all messy and fingerprints. That was the exciting thing, definitely, the test pressing. But the actual final record was just like work. Back in the record shop, the manufacturing line. And then it came out and to our great surprise I remember we all heard it on John Peel. At this point my dad had converted the garage in my house into some sort of a pool room. It had a wee pool table in it and stuff. And we're all in the garage and they're having a drink when John Peel played it. John Peel was the first but the important one was Steve Lamacq because he picked up on it. He was doing the Evening Session at the time, which had been so instrumental to all that Britpop stuff. And he and Jo Whiley were doing that at the time, and they picked up on it. And that's really where it became successful. It wasn't playlisted but they were playing it every night. And that was the big help. Hearing Peel play it though, I mean that was the moment. That was the only ambition I really had, was to be part of that world that he seemed to be at the centre of.

Malcolm Middleton (Arab Strap): We were amazed when Peel played it a couple of weeks later, then Lamacq etc. It was pretty unreal.

Stewart Henderson (bass, The Delgados; Chemikal Underground): I think it's still the most consecutively played track that the Evening Session ever had. For all of Lamacq's love of

Britpop and all those guys, no song was ever played more times consecutively in the Evening Session, than 'The First Big Weekend'.

Aidan Moffat (Arab Strap): And it went from there. Then people heard the album and realised that not all our songs were joyous and a celebration of life. [Laughs.] And I don't know what happened after that. We were forced to do gigs. We didn't play. Chemikal Underground said you have to go and play a show, it's absolutely essential. So we cobbled together a band. Me and Malcolm, and Gary Miller and David Gow. David would end up in Sons and Daughters later on.

Stewart Henderson (bass, The Delgados; Chemikal Underground): They were a band that had never been a live band. Just Aidan and Malcolm. So they brought Dave and Gary in and extended the line-up to play shows. Their shows were shambolic as fuck, but good. They were just one of those bands that really came along at the right time. The zeitgeist was very much the case. But right from the get go you could tell Aidan and Malcolm were going to be more than that. They really were going to continue to develop, there was no doubt about that.

Aidan Moffat (Arab Strap): I had this great idea with 'The First Big Weekend' that I could always constantly improvise it. But that was too much work. And then one night, we were touring and supporting Mogwai. And the entire song ended up with just me and Stuart from Mogwai having a wrestle on the stage. I can't remember how that happened but there just weren't any words. You know, it just became tiresome. It was a really nice idea that I thought I could pull off. Never could.

Malcolm Middleton (Arab Strap): We never wanted to be a traditional band, it was mainly the enjoyment of messing around with four-tracks. And I don't think we had any plans to play live until Chemikal said we had to do a Peel Session live on air from King Tut's a few weeks after the album came out. We could only find a drummer and bass player so I got bumped to guitar. It took us a few years to get any good though.

CHAPTER EIGHTEEN

More Yummy Fur

The Yummy Fur record their album

In 1996, The Yummy Fur finally recorded their debut LP, Night Club, *a defining record, in all respects, of Glasgow's indie scene at the time. It stands as a fascinating counterpoint to Belle and Sebastian's two iconoclastic albums of the same year, by being everything they are not. In short, it is a truly blistering burst of energy that has very few antecedents in that era of Scottish music. Unusually, it was released by two of their previous labels – Slampt, who put out their first 7-inch, together with Guided Missile. But in another bold move, the band decided to release a 10-inch EP first, with another label.*

Brian MacDougall (guitar, The Yummy Fur): *The Male Shadow* 10-inch EP was first. According to the sleeve it was recorded over five rain-soaked days. I had been eager to bring The Yummy Fur to Vesuvius. I think Marc and John were initially reluctant but I pressed for a release and we settled on a 10-inch, in the style of the Fall's *Slates,* which was by far everyone's favourite format back then. We had a £500/£1000 budget for recording and decided to record it at Stuffhouse Studios where many

Vesuvius bands rehearsed as it was cheap and had absolutely no mod cons like heating. We had a week recording and a week mixing where we recorded seven tracks. Stevie Doyle was engineer and his 16-track desk there was a big step up from the home-basement recording of *Night Club*. This, with the addition of Mark Gibbons' keyboards to the band sound, all helped put flesh on that skinny scratchy sound that was more by default of what we could access than by any design on our part. A much-needed upgrade for The Yummy Fur sound that might yet be equal to the Sleazy's jukebox.

Lawrence Worthington (drums, The Yummy Fur): The Vesuvius record was all recorded on an eight-track at our friend Spongle's flat on Bank Street. Nobody knew about Dolby on/off so there is a buzzing throughout I think.

Brian MacDougall (guitar, The Yummy Fur): It also features the only track where I have a full writing credit on 'Colonel Blimp'. It was one of a handful of song fragments that I took up to John's flat one time and we hashed it out on the four-track. I expected this collaborative approach to become more prevalent but instead the songs after this album just became more open, leaving plenty of room for me to do whatever I thought might work. I have no formal music training and still don't really know the names of all the chords but I could usually cobble together my own parts based on John's lead. The back of the sleeve nods to the crediting of songs on the album. 'Original songs by those credited greatly enhanced by additional melodies, rhythms and sheer intelligence of the other guys in the group.' It must have been a raw nerve.

Pete Dale (Slampt Records): We invited them to do a split LP with Kenickie (who had supported them at one of the Yummy Fur gigs at the Broken Doll, which was Kenickie's first gig in fact, around September 1994) because the two bands had a mutual admiration thing going on and we loved both. Both parties agreed but after lots of press and label attention, Kenickie (who had done a single on Slampt in early 1995) backed out, so we got talking to The Yummy Fur about an LP all of their own instead and they requested a split release with Guided Missile who had done their second single. We had known Paul (Guided Missile bod) for a while through mutual friends Prolapse so we happily agreed to this. The Yummy Fur were given £500 to record (£250 from each label), with which they bought an eight-track reel-to-reel and installed it in somebody's flat. Wish we'd had more money to get it recorded better, in retrospect, but it was a great album I thought – absolutely loved The Yummy Fur, me.

Paul Kearney (Guided Missile Records): Slampt discovered the group around the same time I did. They'd beaten me to the release of their debut 7-inch and I did the next one. We both really loved them and wanted to help them put an album out and after chatting with Pete from Slampt it was fairly straightforward how to do it. As I remember Slampt were a vinyl-only label at the time and didn't want to make a CD version of the album, whereas the band and me were happy to – so we did it as a split release with two catalogue numbers for each format but with a SLAMPT prefix appearing first on the vinyl and a GUIDE catalogue number on the CD.

John McKeown (vocals/guitar, The Yummy Fur): So album policy right off the bat was even between two record labels,

Slampt and Guided Missile. I honestly think the recording budget was £500. I know it's the old money but even then – so we thought that's not going to fly. And then somebody was selling an eight-track recorder. And we thought fuck it, we bought an eight-track recorder. . . and set it up in my mate's flat in Arlington Street just next to the Arlington Bar, in his living room.

Brian MacDougall (guitar, The Yummy Fur): The album was a joint release between Slampt and Guided Missile. They both wanted to put out an album and somehow it was agreed that they would release it jointly. They both put forward some money to record, which we used to buy an eight-track quarter-inch tape recorder and desk. Mark Gibbons reckoned he could record the whole album in the dank basement of the flat he and Tom and Philippa (from Dick Johnson and Lung Leg) shared in Arlington Street, Woodlands. So we did. No-one really knew what we were doing and the recording quality attests to that. Lawrence and I designed the sleeve, the front from Tom's *Big Book of Russian Constructivist Architecture* and the back a nod to Alfred Jarry, who Pere Ubu had presumably led Lawrence to, with additional drawings by the both of us.

I remember *Night Club* was on the CD Jukebox in Nice N Sleazy's for a while. To me this was mind-blowing, like *Top of the Pops*-level stuff. You could play a Mogwai track, which would soar and fill every corner of the bar with its 24-track glossy production mids and lows then follow it up with 'Chinese Bookie', which would wheeze tinnily from the exact same speakers, struggling to rise above the patrons' Thursday afternoon rhubarb.

Pete Dale (Slampt Records): People loved it, including me. . . skronky wonk pop, maybe? With really short songs. Less skronky later though, with longer songs: I still loved 'em and bought everything they did (except some kind of EMI-related CD comp that I thought was a sellout – I was really uptight in those days!). I would describe John (at that time) as a scrawny little punky type with a really bright mind and a great knowledge of music: he stuck out really, although I should add that I always got on great with Lawrence and Mark, both were lovelies! I think one time they phoned me and asked for a gig, so I booked the Broken Doll but then forgot all about it. On the day, I was blissfully unaware and went to Whitley Bay to get a tattoo! Got home around 5 o'clock to an answerphone message saying, 'We'll be there around. . . 5 p.m.!' They rocked up to my flat and I had to apologise that, although I had a venue, I had no PA booked, no support acts and no audience – the drummer was fuming (this was before Lawrence joined) and I believe he quit the band as a result, with Lawrence taking over after that. What a fucking idiot I was! Amazing that they agreed to carry on with Slampt, really.

John McKeown (vocals/guitar, The Yummy Fur): It's a real thing, it's an object. It's physical. Or at least like having your film played in a real cinema. Other than that I don't remember how we ended up making that record. That flat was a basement and I remember we were coming over, and every morning we'd start, and Philippa and Mark who lived there – their whole quilt would be covered in slugs. Slugs would come in the window and they'd have to pull off the slugs first before we could start the day. We were jostling for who could get nearest to the wee three-bar Calor gas fire – it never had three bars on – that was crazy. Just jostling each other to get closer to the one bar. It was freezing. Hard to play guitar.

Despite the retrospective plaudits and obvious influence over many subsequent Glasgow independent bands, the album's release at the height of Britpop did not endear it to the London music press at the time.

John McKeown (vocals/guitar, The Yummy Fur): Aye, it got an end-of-the-year thing in *Melody Maker* and stuff. I did a total Jake LaMotta with that. You know in *Raging Bull* when he's hard done for cash? So he smashes the belt open to get the jewels and when he takes it round, the guy's like, if you just brought the belt round. . . the jewels are worth fuck all but the belt is worth thousands. I can remember cutting a wee picture of the album out, a wee review. But not the whole page that told you the story of who was Number 1 that year, who was Number 2 – I was only interested in me. [Laughs.] I don't know. We didn't have the same catchy songs in the way that The Delgados did. Theirs were very hooky. Ours were hooky more on the guitar parts and repetitious. . . more refrains and things. I knew it wasn't going to set the world on fire but the people who were into it seemed to be really into it, they seemed to really get it. The people that we met who'd say, 'Ah! I've been waiting for something like this, you know we haven't had anything like this since The Fall and the Fire Engines and Contortions.' And a lot of other people found us quite kind of – I don't know, I thought it was fun music but I think people found us quite aggressive.

Pete Dale (Slampt Records): I thought it was superb although the snare sounded a bit weird to me. 'Roxy Girls' was my absolute fave, but lots of other belters. It was the last thing they did with Slampt but I absolutely loved them – arguably the best British DIY group of the 1990s.

CHAPTER NINETEEN

Mogwai Young Team

Mogwai Young Team meet CHEM019

Mogwai released their debut single, 'Tuner', in 1996 on their own Rock Action Records. Rock Action also released a single by Trout and a further two by Pilotcan before lying dormant until the early 2000s when it sprang back into life to release Mogwai's own work, and a mixture of new and essential reissued songs by their favourite artists.

In 1997, after releasing of a number of acclaimed singles on various labels, mostly produced by Paul from The Delgados, Mogwai finally signed with Chemikal Underground and recorded their debut album.

Mogwai Young Team sleeve

Stuart Braithwaite (guitar/vocals, Mogwai): Paul from The Delgados and one of the Chemikal Underground owners is an engineer, and he actually recorded a lot of our early music. I think apart from that first 7-inch, he did almost everything. He did the 'Love Train' single, he did the Ché split single ['Angels vs Aliens']. And another guy, Andy Miller, at the same place did the Wurlitzer Jukebox single ['New Paths to Helicon']. So we knew Paul, and we got on really well. And we all knew about bis because that was a big thing to happen for the Glasgow scene. A band that we all knew and played with, getting on *Top of the Pops*. So we knew their label was going places. And I remember Paul let us hear 'The First Big Weekend', the first Arab Strap single – we were all like, wow, that's brilliant, that's totally different, that's next level. So we're really excited about it. And I guess at one point, Paul asked the rest of The Delgados about maybe putting our music out. We'd been courted by some of the London labels and none of it really seemed that appealing.

I had a sneaky feeling that they would try and change what our band sounded like, which I've seen happen to bands. It was probably a founded worry. So we went with those guys and it was great.

Aidan Moffat (Arab Strap): I suppose musically we were closest to Mogwai to a degree, although we sound very different. I think there's the influences. The first time I heard Mogwai I didn't know of the first single, which I think was 'Tuner'. It was when they were recording 'Summer'. And they'd been doing that with Paul Savage while we were in recording something. And Paul said, 'Do you want to hear this band Mogwai that we'll be doing? I think you'd quite like them'. So he played us the mix he had in the studio, which he probably shouldn't have done. It's probably against the code or something. But it was amazing, it was brilliant. And then we became aware of them doing gigs. The first time I saw them was in Sleazy's. That was the first time I met Stuart and after that, it was just a case of always being around each other, and bonding over the same records. I think we show love for the same music.

Paul Savage (drums, The Delgados; Chemikal Underground): Everything that we always did, we would go, okay, that's taking a step forward, so what can we do? I like to do this for the studios. If I know that Chemikal Underground is going to pay CHEM19 [the studio] to record a band, and it's going to be a set fee, it's obviously a great deal – I think that album was recorded for £1,500. Six weeks' worth of studio time for that, it probably is pennies, you know, the daily rate is crazy. But for that, because I knew it was coming in and I knew it was upfront I said, well, if I can get this automation system for the desk that I had at the time, it means I can do all these things with faders moving that I couldn't do before. Fader automation, where I could do a pass of a channel moving up and then cutting back down and coming back. And before that, it had to be four or five people at a mixing desk with each of them responsible. It was really clunky the way we used to do it. So with the Mogwai record, it was quite hard to do all that. So I thought, okay, if they're going to pay for this thing, I want to get this automation system for the record. Let's do that. We bought this system, and it allowed me to play around with that. The first song has got a recording of when the drums come in, you'll hear a little ting, a little noise, it sounds like a tiny symbol. It happens every bar or so. It's basically Dominic flicking in a two pence coin. So we'd go: ting, catch, wait, ting, catch, and I don't want the catch. I just wanted the ting, but it was before digital recording. So I had this automation system and was going, we can do this now because I'm just going to mute all the catches. The ting is the coin flying past the microphone and then coming back down.

Emma Pollock (vocals/guitar, The Delgados; Chemikal Underground): Here's where the serendipity lies between a band forming a record company, who also wants to run a recording studio. Because it realises that's where the artistic control might lie, it's where budget control might lie. And it's also exciting because I run both. Nowadays I run both Chemikal Underground and CHEM19 – I never really saw that coming. It wasn't something that I ever planned, because it can be quite a lot. But in 1997, we had the opportunity to buy the studio MCM. The original studio MCM, which is where we recorded the very first Delgados stuff, is where Paul recorded Mogwai's debut. And of course that came out in [facing other way] 97. But before that we started working with the band and put out the '4 Satin' EP as a precursor in June '97 as a precursor to *Mogwai Young Team*, the album. Paul had recorded this and he got on with the guys really well. They were also Lanarkshire-based. What's really interesting about all this, with the exception of bis, is that the majority of the artists that we've worked with have not come from Glasgow city. They've come from round about.

Stuart Braithwaite (guitar/vocals, Mogwai): It was quite a weird one because with most bands the first album is the easiest one because they've got all the songs they've been writing since they were 15 or whatever. But because I'm such a big Joy Division fan I didn't want any of our singles on it. So it was more like what it's probably like for most bands making their second album. It was actually kind of stressful. We hadn't written enough songs. We'd had this release there that we, for some reason, didn't realise you could probably change if you wanted to. Because we'd already put out the Wurlitzer Jukebox single and an EP that year, then waited till the summer to make an album, we only had like two or three songs for it. So it was a pretty intense experience. Brendan also joined the band. And to be honest, Brendan was super-helpful because he'd made loads of records with Teenage Fanclub and with Telstar Ponies, who are another band that we were big fans of. We actually thought it was crap so we were pleasantly surprised that it went down pretty well. But yeah, it was a really intense experience, a very intense period for the band.

Paul Savage (drums, The Delgados; Chemikal Underground): It's certainly not dinner table music. We wanted it to be that thing where people think, is there something going on there? Turn it up, turn it up a bit more. I can't really hear the guitar. And then they forget about where they put it. And then the big bit comes in. They [Mogwai] were always saying, I know that's loud, but can you make it louder? Can we go further? Can we push it even further? That was great fun, doing that. They were just fun. There's a bit at the start of 'Tracy' that you can hear the Hamilton West train, because the studio was right next to Hamilton West train station. I got all the cables in the studio and said, do you know what, it'd be great to stereo mic a train – so we'll stretch these cables out and we'll put one at one end of the lane, and then the other one at the other end. We knew when the trains were coming in so we would time it and start recording. I knew the train was coming so I started recording and you could hear the train pulling away in stereo. Almost platform lens stereo, panning. And then other things like John riding a bike with a squeaky brake round about in that tune, past the mics. Just fun. Lots of stupid things. And the phone call about them fighting, and stuff like that. All totally made up. It was just a lot of fun doing it. But the most important thing was the bedrock of it was they were just a fantastic band, you just set it up and just go, there you go, play it.

Aidan Moffat (Arab Strap): Mogwai are the ones we definitely socialised a lot with, and when they'd signed to Chemikal, we'd just seemed to be in the same place at the same time. And, obviously, more importantly, the same gigs. That's when you would see everyone you knew, and then you'd go and see a band, maybe downstairs in Sleazy's, and then you'd end up sitting in a pub all night afterwards, and that how any scene starts. . .

good venues, good pubs that are going to be open, and open to sometimes ridiculous behaviour. And that just lead on to singing on their album, I did something on an EP with them. And then they started to take off so we went and did a tour with them, which was the second tour Arab Strap ever did.

Malcolm Middleton (Arab Strap): Yeah, that was fun. We'd toured with them a bunch first and then they became label mates. We both appreciated what each other was doing and we were in the pub a fair bit too. It was a great time for Chemikal. They're still one of the best instrumental bands to come out of Scotland, and the fact that they're also our label bosses now is pretty cool.

CHAPTER TWENTY

Lung Leg Meet Beatbox

Back to Beatbox

Beatbox, where Belle and Sebastian had their genesis, had further importance to the scene. Hubby had become the de-facto producer of many of the bands who were recording. His experience from engineering at the Kazoo Club had led him to become very much in demand. And Beatbox was one place that allowed much of this recording to happen.

Annie Spandex (guitar, Lung Leg): At the time, there was a place called Beatbox at Anderston, where there's a big SkyPark place now. There was a recording studio there that was linked to the college. And Hubby was doing the sound engineering course there. At weekends you could get in for nothing. He had the keys so we could go in at the weekends and record – somewhere better to record than somebody's basement. It was a proper recording studio but you had to be out by the time the students came in on a Monday morning – leave no mess, no trace. That's where Lung Leg first recorded the album, over the weekends in there. It's everyone all helping each other out again.

RM Hubbert: I'd been doing live sound for all these bands and because of F&J too, I'd help them record. But really, I was able to do that because of Beatbox. It was hugely important. Beatbox wasn't run by the government but it was funded by the government; it was a recording studio. The whole reason it existed was because in the mid- to late-1990s there was a government scheme put in place called the New Deal For Musicians. It was basically a scheme to lower unemployment figures, but you also got an extra £10 on your dole cheque and nobody ever asked you to go for job interviews. It was basically you saying, I'm going to be a musician, I'm going to be an artist. And because you were on this scheme, you weren't counted as being unemployed any more. But also, they wouldn't harass you to find a job. Also at the time, you could get 100 per cent of your housing benefit paid. For a long time all of my income came from music. For a very long time in the nineties. It was a poor income but it was enough. As part of that the government funded schemes like Beatbox. It was this crazy little place. It was underneath the parking ramp of an industrial park's car park. It was wedged shaped; it was bizarre. . . After the course was finished, I did a deal with them where I would come and help teach and help organise things, in exchange for access to the studio at the weekend. I would help them out during the week, make their life a wee bit easier. Then at 6 o'clock on a Friday, I would load a band in and we would record non-stop until 9 o'clock on Monday. That's how all those records were made. . . most of them. If the bands had money to pay me, I would give a bit to the guy at Beatbox who'd let me stay there all weekend. I would love to say that I ended up producing those records because everyone saw this inherent talent in me, but a lot of it was,

Hubby's got the keys to a studio at the weekend – if we give him £200 we can make a record. And that's what we did. It was great, but it's just pure luck and circumstance that gave us access to that; it's just not the type of facilities that kids like us would normally have access to. That's how we managed – we made some great fucking records in there. Those Yummy Fur singles are still great. The Lung Leg album. I love the version of that Lung Leg album we made.

Lung Leg record their album

After a series of beautifully abrasive 7-inches, Lung Leg were given the opportunity to record their debut. In a Fast Product- like art project, the mechanics, recording and release of the album meant it was one of the most unusual – possibly unique – albums ever to emerge.

Jane McKeown (vocals/bass, Lung Leg): The Lung Leg album evolved up until 2023. I mean, it's now in its third evolution. But the first evolution of it was that we had Pat and Brian from Vesuvius wanting to put out an album. And I can't remember what came first, chicken or egg, but these two people that worked for an EMI subsidiary in Japan wanted to meet us because they were doing an indie label as a subsidiary of EMI in Japan. These two Japanese people came over to see us and they said they wanted to fund the album. It was agreed that we'd need about £1000, which is crazy. They were like, 'Go ahead, record the album', but we were like, well we don't have any money. We don't have £1000. It's quite sad actually in a way, but they went back to Japan and they said, 'We'll personally give you that £1000 from our own money just until we get the money from EMI.' And then, as with many labels and big things like that, all of a sudden their subsidiary label just got dropped, cascaded. And we were skint, Scottish punks. So we were like, 'We're keeping that fucking money and recording an album'. And they were Japanese and too polite to ask for it back.

But you know what? I think they're so cool because we could have just been assholes and just spent the money. What's that thing – honour among thieves? We held ourselves accountable and recorded the album with Hubby. He was doing some sort of scheme in this recording studio, which is behind SkyPark. So we gave him the £1000 and he produced the album for us. And we had the songs. We'd evolved by that time more. We had Maureen, me, Annie, and Todd had joined. And we recorded the album. Just, whenever, steaming, didn't know what we were doing. The song, 'Maid to Minx', we had musically; but we didn't have any vocals for it; any melody for that – and we went in and recorded it with no vocals. And our friend Danny Saunders went into a cupboard in the recording studio and wrote the lyrics and the vocal melody and just gave it to us. We were like, okay, thanks. And it sounds fantastic. I think that's why the song sounds so good. Anyway, recorded that. Put that out on Vesuvius. At which point we'd played with Sonic Youth and met The Make-Up through Sonic Youth.

Annie Spandex (guitar, Lung Leg): We supported Sonic Youth, and we were the first support act. The middle support act were The Make-Up. And they were helped by John Loder who did Southern Records. He was on tour with them just as a jolly.

We really hit it off with John Loder and he said, I want to help you guys.

Jane McKeown (vocals/bass, Lung Leg): John said I'll sign yous, so he signed us to Southern Records. He said I'll sign yous but we're going to re-record that album, down in Southern.

Annie Spandex (guitar, Lung Leg): So we went down to London and spent two weeks with Harvey Birrell, who was in Alien Sex Fiend of all bands, re-recording the album. But by that point, Maureen had left before we did that. She'd left to go and have a baby and different things. So we roped in Philippa [Smith], who was in Dick Johnson, as her replacement and we re-recorded the album. But he painstakingly separated all Maureen's vocals from the original so that we kept Maureen. But Philippa re-recorded all Maureen's guitar parts, so it's a kinda hybrid.

Jane McKeown (vocals/bass, Lung Leg): Hubby produced the fuck out of it, and produced the fuck out of us. And I love it. I'm so glad we did it with him because songs like 'Maid to Minx' he really gave it the bombast it needed. I think it was only us and The Fall at that time that had done that: put an album out with two completely different recordings.

Pat Crook (Vesuvius Records): I think John Loder wanted his own version. They're very, very similar, to me they seem almost identical. They basically were recreating the album. But I think it was so that they had the rights. I think it was something around that, possibly. I think he thought that it was going to be a big hit. But – he wanted to be able to control it a bit more, but that might be unfair. I don't know. I feel like maybe that was it.

Jane McKeown (vocals/bass, Lung Leg): Pat and Brian were told they were not allowed to sell the Vesuvius version anywhere. Really interesting. So two different versions of the album. . . not a lot of people know that. Because most people who have the album just think that's the album, but they have the Vesuvius version, or they have the Southern version. And they're two completely different records. . . And now there's the Last Night From Glasgow label version, which is the Southern version but it's got a couple of extra tracks on it, and different covers and some different photos and stuff.

Dick Johnson

Dick Johnson were another band with releases on Vesuvius and Guided Missile. They were far more influenced by the garage scene but, like many other Glasgow bands, had formed as a side-project. Jane from Lung Leg was the drummer, with Philippa Smith (now in Lung Leg) and Tracy Vandal, the singer.

Tracy Vandal (guitar, Dick Johnson): They named the band after a favourite Pussy Galore song ('Dick Johnson') so they were definitely an influence but more so it was a Link Wray vibe and Philippa had a penchant for Howlin' Wolf and Black Sabbath at the time. My influences I brought were more from a female singer torch song sort of vibe with a dash of David Lynch, and I'm not sure about Jane. At the time I remember very much there being two scenes: the Pop Kids and then the 13th Note one with Alex Kapranos, that I was more from. But we all mingled together and created a scene from which came loads of great bands obviously and definitely the most weird and long lasting friendships. At least for me, I can say I'm still friends with a lot of them now.

We always had a great reception because we were loud, a super loud chaotic shambles, two Fender Twins (or whatever shitty Peavey was going spare and even an old Selmer Philippa found in the skip once), turned up to the max, no pedals, just raw painful volume.

Only gig I remember where we were very unwelcome was a gig at The Red Eye in London where the few people that were there at like 7.30 p.m. fucking hated us. The rest of the time it was pure mess, mostly from us dressed up to the nines, speed, drinking whisky before the show to get courage for stage, with the crowd right up to the front staring at us as if we might perform magic (or play in time with each other).

The band's debut single, 'Dawn at Death Creek', produced by Hubby, was released by Vesuvius.

Tracy Vandal (guitar, Dick Johnson): 'Dawn at Death Creek' was recorded on a four-track in Philppa's basement in Ruthven Street. I think I wrote that song but it's so long ago I struggle to be 100 per cent on that, but it seems more like my kind of vibe that I still write now, that slow miserable love song vibe; and the other two songs I think was all of us together, maybe based on riffs Philippa came up with.

I remember the first night we held the single in our hands, fresh out the box, was also at Ruthven Street and I don't think I, at least, let on even how exciting it was for me, but I imagine without a doubt we got very drunk that night.

In Glasgow I think we were so surrounded by our own types

that sexism didn't feel like too much of an issue in the beginning. By the time we played in London however, and the *NME* reviews started coming out, we were absolutely dealing with some toxic attitudes towards being three girls in a loud noisy band, which is easier to see now in retrospect to be honest, reading back over one review, especially, that was dug up not long ago.

One time in Newcastle, after a gig at the Broken Doll we went to a bar where we were playing pool and some sponk stuck their hand up my arse as I bent over and I think I hit him with the pool cue and a fight ensued, ending with us waking up to our van having four slashed tyres in the morning. That was a van Dick Johnson and The Yummy Fur used. But I have to say, generally I don't think we got it too bad, maybe because we just weren't exposing ourselves much to those kind of people and generally kept safe in our own kind. Now, I can definitely see there was probably a bunch of disrespectful things that went on but at the time I was a teenager, just excited to be where I was and doing what I was doing. I think now things actually might be worse, at least in the past few years.

The band's last gig was Upstairs at the Garage in London. I had moved to London by that point and it was just a natural thing to move on. There were no fights or falling out. That last gig we were so hammered that my clearest memory is noticing that the drumming had become minimal for a bit and I looked around to see Jane was drumming with one stick but was bending down – I thought to try to find the other stick. However, she rose back up with a bottle of vodka in her empty hand and kept going, and for me that was the most genius bit of drumming I've seen to this day. Triumphant.

CHAPTER TWENTY-ONE

All That Glitters is Not Gold

Urusei Yatsura begin to burn out

The trajectory of early stars of the scene, Urusei Yatsura, continued. They had a Top 40 single in 1997, closely followed by their debut album to excellent reviews. As far as they could, as they had always done, they aimed to help their friends as much as possible. But there was extreme pressure to produce a follow-up album at the same pace.

Elaine Lawrie (bass, Urusei Yatsura): The time between finishing our first album and starting our second was a whirlwind of touring really. We were very dedicated to being a live band and delivering a visceral live experience. We toured with lots of our friends (Eska, Mogwai, Pink Kross) and did festivals in Britain and Europe and toured in the USA with The Wedding Present. In and around this we recorded our second album with Chris Allison producing. It was hard to balance touring, recording and the lifestyle of being in a band with no money. We had never had a manager and it was a bit out of our control. It was chaotic and became about satisfying what we thought other people wanted rather than ourselves.

Graham Kemp (vocals/guitar, Urusei Yatsura): We recorded *Slain By Urusei Yatsura* in London, at Ray Davies' studio, Konk. We wanted to be somewhere a bit more central so ended up there at Chris Allison's suggestion. We had done the 'Fake Fur' and 'Strategic Hamlets' singles with him and were really happy with how they turned out. Chris worked on *George Best* for The Wedding Present, so we just continued the practice of working with people involved with our favourite albums. We had a really strong set of songs for it but it had been delayed for a year due to record company nonsense. The recording went pretty smoothly as I remember and we got to see the inside of some pretty swish studios for mixing (Olympic). We were maybe a little out of place but it was nice to have a go. It felt like we'd made it. Well, we got the record out and we toured it and we got a Top 40 single out of it, so I feel we did okay. We were always beset with delay after delay due to what was happening with music business people at a level above Ché, so our involvement with major labels was not a happy experience for us.

Fergus Lawrie (vocals/guitar, Urusei Yatsura): The dream of being in a band starts to run into the reality of what it's actually like to sit in a freezing cold transit van all day for weeks at a time and play the same songs over and over. Luckily we loved playing and travelling and made an effort to promote other Scottish acts as we went, bringing Eska, Mogwai, Pink Kross and Moniak out on tour with us. The more we played the more our confidence grew, we knew we were a shit-hot live act and could crush it wherever we went. I found playing live totally cathartic and addictive. There was free booze on the rider and people would buy you drinks. The adrenaline was phenomenal and you would end up drinking two or three times your normal intake because you didn't feel it. Things started getting a bit manic and my behaviour became increasingly erratic. We had great live reviews and audiences were going crazy. We started to get a bit cocky and believe some of the hype around us.

The pressure the band were under, minus any managerial assistance, began to increase dramatically. Eventually, Urusei Yatsura effectively ground to a halt.

Fergus Lawrie (vocals/guitar, Urusei Yatsura): It gets difficult to talk about at this point as things started to unravel as quickly as they had come together. We had met Primary in Manhattan and they had two managing directors and one intern in a massive office full of empty desks. They told us in a year it would be filled with A&R guys and press agents. In fact in a year they were shut down. Ché had cashflow problems, which slowed everything to a snail's pace, and they didn't have the industry clout or financial firepower to promote us consistently or book enough tours. Trust within the band and between the band and the label collapsed. It took nearly two years to get the second album out, by which time a lot of our original fans had moved on and the initial buzz around us was long gone. Sire was taken over by Warner and they fucked up the European distribution for the album and didn't bother to promote it in the US. The air started being let out of the whoopee cushion until the noise was overwhelming. By now we were out of the city a lot and losing touch with the Glasgow scene. One of the bands at Babelfish turned out to be junkies and started ripping off gear so we had to move to a more secure but characterless rehearsal space. A lot of my university friends had moved away and I started drinking by myself every day, coming back from the pub and having a bottle of wine or some beers watching *Noisy Mothers* and *Club Nation* at three in the morning.

Fergus Lawrie (vocals/guitar, Urusei Yatsura): There were some real high points, like working with Shona Marshall of the Space Kittens, who drove and helped out on tours, and also James 'Jaffa' Jarvie, tour manager extraordinaire. Playing festivals in the UK and Europe, touring across the US with The Wedding Present and Magic Dirt, gigs with Super Furry Animals, Ash, Teenage Fanclub, Pavement, Number One Cup etc., but the sense of specialness and inevitability was draining away. Britpop and Cool Britannia were in full swing and becoming an oppressive and nauseating monoculture of Union Jacks and binge drinking. Being in London a lot is very corrosive: you work with people who clearly view you as just another band, another paycheck, and there is pressure to conform to industry expectations.

We didn't have a manager or lawyer and weren't business-minded and basically didn't know crap in that environment. It started to play out along the lines of Steve Albini's famous article comparing the music industry to a trench full of shit. The late nineties was probably the worst possible period to be in an indie band. Ché had had a last throw of the dice trying to get us into the charts with the second album and then went into liquidation. It was a car crash and everyone got their hearts broken. *Melody Maker* started calling us the 'Most Indie Band in Britain' then they closed down as well. Festivals and venues began doing sponsorship deals. The music industry was consolidating around monolithic bands like Muse and Coldplay and becoming even more corporate. Majors had bought out most of the indie labels during the guitar boom and then started shutting them down and dropping bands across the board.

Our record deal with Sire somehow limped on to a third album but it was torture. We were still trying our best to turn out good songs but everything became increasingly toxic and dysfunctional. The stress levels were unbelievable and I didn't know why I was in a band any more. My drinking was out of control and I felt like I was having a nervous breakdown in public. Getting dropped and breaking up was a huge relief but also felt like having my heart dragged out through my mouth with fish-hooks. I was a burnout. I stopped going to gigs. I got a job in a bar, it felt right serving people and tending to their needs in small ways after all the hubris and selfishness of being signed. In 2014 I embarked on a two-year course of medication for alcohol addiction and finally got sober.

CHAPTER TWENTY-TWO

Veganism Meets DIY 2

Club Beatroot

Back at the 13th Note, the growth of the Kazoo Club led to other nights and label opportunities. The next experiment combined Craig Tannock with a record label: the 13th Note met Flotsam & Jetsam and created Club Beatroot.

Craig Tannock (13th Note venue owner): Alex had the idea of doing another night, but this time having a charge on the door to help take it a step further. It was called the 99p club and that was Thursday nights. The idea was only two bands, and bands that played the Kazoo, could then move up to the 99p club night. But we had lots of other nights. We had a great revolving Wednesday night. I did something called Club Beatroot (sometimes spelled Beetroot).

Annie Spandex (guitar, Lung Leg): It comes from the 13th Note and Craig Tannock. That's the centre that everything comes back to for a lot of us. Without the 13th Note, loads of this wouldn't exist. Without Craig Tannock's input. Because it was all bands that had played at the 13th Note. Club Beatroot was all 13th Note people that had played there. And mainly at the Kazoo Club that Alex had done. And then Hubby recorded it.

RM Hubbert (Hubby) (F&J Records): The project we did that was best known was the Club Beatroot stuff that we did in conjunction with the 13th Note.

Gordy Davidson (F&J Records): T'was in the second era of Kazoo. . . after a good few of the bands that had played those early club nights were either signed, or on their way to being signed, or had members who were in new bands that were signed. . . when 13th Note proprietor/guru Craig Tannock approached F&J Records with an ambitious proposal. Craig himself was in a band at this point, called Beatroot, and his idea was to put on a year of monthly Club Beatroot nights, each of which would be hosted by Beatroot and feature a couple of handpicked bands from Craig's throbbing contact book. Each night would be recorded straight off the desk, from which recordings the guest bands would then each pick their preferred live track to release as one side of a split single with the other bands.

RM Hubbert (F&J Records): It was the brainchild of Craig Tannock. It was also a little bit of self-promotion but he basically wanted to do the same idea as the Kazoo Club, to do a series of gigs, record them and then release the series of 7-inches from bands playing at the 13th Note. He paid for them all and there are some incredibly rare records that we released. PH Family and Mogwai. The Lung Leg and El Hombre one is pretty rare now as well.

Craig Tannock (13th Note venue owner): The high concept was that we'd do a live recording every month and release it as a split single to launch at the following gig. We never managed them all. But we managed about seven out of the thirteen planned. We've still got all the recordings – we might finish them one day, we'll see; but we managed seven releases. It was a three-way thing, it was 13th Note, Flotsam & Jetsam and Apollo Recording. We did the live recordings on site and then Calum [from Apollo] mastered them. That was the Apollo Recording bit, I did the design and the funding and Flotsam & Jetsam did the release and liaised with Harry from SRD: it was a team effort.

Gordy Davidson (F&J Records): The money spent pressing up the first single would be recouped by selling it at the next Club Beatroot night, and then go towards pressing up the second single, which would then be available for sale on the third club night, and so on. This process was to continue for thirteen singles, and then there would be an album, and a grand final gig. Importantly, each single would be restricted to F&J's standard batch size of 500. This choice was both budgetary and a recognition that some of the bands Craig had on the hook for his scheme were signed elsewhere, and were more likely to be allowed to stray off-contract if it was just for a solitary live track on a limited edition release. From the outset, Craig was talking about some bands that F&J would have had no hope of releasing in our own right, so we were very keen to do it, and perhaps did not think too deeply about the possible problems as a result.

It was Craig's project, so it was his choice of bands, and the pairings of those bands, and he was being gleefully random about that part of it. We had Lung Leg and The Yummy Fur and The Karelia and Mogwai and Poison Sisters and the Space Kittens and El Hombre and Pink Kross, who were all home team players, y'know, but he threw in curveballs like Olympia, who were his pals from France, and the Primevals. Swelling Meg? Cora Bissett is now an award-winning playwright. . . she did The Glasgow Girls I think. . . but Swelling Meg was a very introspective high-concept thing, based around brutalising a cello. And I can't tell you a single thing about the Radio Sweethearts.

Craig Tannock (13th Note venue owner): Jane Chalmers (Pink Kross and Amphetameanies) did Skank 'n' Pickle, which was a ska night. The Pastels did a night, on a Wednesday night, it might have been under Geographic; Douglas MacIntyre from Creeping Bent did a night. So Wednesdays were great. All sorts of special things happened there.

Gordy Davidson (F&J Records): Club Beatroot had been founded on the unrealistic notion that the seed cash would recycle monthly. When it quite predictably didn't, the schedule started to stretch as there wasn't another £500 spare every month to turn into vinyl. And that meant that the bands were getting to live with their recordings for longer, and the immediacy of 'this was recorded last night and it's off to the pressing plant this morning' was replaced with 'this sounds a bit rough in the cold light of day, maybe we can take it into a studio for some over-dubs. . .?'

I understand what Craig was going for. . . it was typically ambitious, and a touch idealistic, even utopian. And you need people who think like that. I can't remember which band it was that first broke the Club Beatroot rules, and either doctored their gig recording before it was sent for pressing, or just substituted an alternative recording altogether. I genuinely don't recall.

It wasn't Mogwai. Their Beatroot release sounded to me like someone had gone to Glasgow Airport and held up a mic as a transatlantic jet started its engines. That was pretty much how they had sounded downstairs at the Note. I'd speculate that the rebellion started with Lung Leg. I don't blame them. If someone says, 'I'm gonna pay to put a record out for you. . . but you aren't going to sound your best', the natural response is to try to keep the first bit and change that qualifying clause. I am sure if you listened to all the releases in order, you'd spot the point where the recordings stop sounding so rough-edged. And, of course, once that 'live recordings only' principle had gone, it was no longer someone from the 13th Note handing me the production DATs. . . I found myself chasing various bands for tracks. Between agreeing to take part, and actually having to submit a track, The Yummy Fur had gone into abeyance somehow, so when I went looking for a track, their cupboard was bare, and no one wanted to answer the phone to tell me that.

Alex stepped up on that occasion. Even while he was busy with the Amphetameanies, he'd started playing with The Yummy Fur live, standing in on bass I think, so was sort of part of their team. Enough so that he could get access to a bunch of old recordings, and maybe some unfinished bits, riffs and beats they had lying around, and he then cobbled all that up into a single track that was sort of intended to cover The Yummy Fur's career, and that is what then got released under their name.

Nowadays, that'd be a pretty standard thing to do. . . a producer remix. . . but back then it was totally off the fucking wall, and felt quite transgressive. The Yummy Fur were a comparatively big name, after all, and here was their substitute bassist putting that name (albeit with John's cooperation) against a bedroom-studio mash-up of their out-takes. AND he titled it 'This Is Andrew Sinclair', which is of course [Amphetamenies band member] Rat's real name, and this was round about the time Rat was retreating from the 'Meanies, so there was definitely some devilment afoot there.

For all the effort that went into its creation, the Yummy Fur/ Olympia Club Beatroot release was not the big seller we'd all hoped for. It actually lost us quite a lot of money, because another distributor had stepped in to the fund the production, and he was having that money back whether or not it sold, and wasn't going to accept it in the '18-months-of-dribs-and-drabs' that was our usual business model. We really weren't even remotely professional in how we did things. . . and on that occasion, sloppy optimism cost us dearly. By the time it was clear that the big finish we'd been hoping for, with bis or The Delgados or whoever, wasn't going to happen. So it ended with me pretty blatantly using Club Beatroot 9 as a vehicle to release another track off the 'Meanies' first album, *Right Line In Nylons,* 'cause by that point, the 'Meanies were rocking, and I knew at least that would make its money back.

CHAPTER TWENTY-THREE

The Party is Over

The landscape changes

The landscape that had been centred around the Kazoo Club and the 13th Note was now inevitably changing. Many of the original bands had called it a day as the initial excitement of the scene started to fade. Careers, real life and a change in income support had hugely impacted the livelihood of the majority of the youthful musicians.

RM Hubbert (Hubby) (R&J Records): I stopped being involved probably around the time I stopped recording stuff. Gordy kept the label going for a very long time after Sandy [Black] and I stopped doing stuff. It turned into more of a proper record label, with Amphetameanies, Newtown Grunts, things like that. The early years with people like The Finger Creams and The Commercials. It's bizarre having a discography that's got The Commercials alongside Nostril. Nostril was a one-off thing I did with members of dawson and Stretchheads; it was very varied. I loved it for that.

Gordy Davidson (F&J Records): The Kazoo crowd was being pulled and stretched away from the centre. All the folk involved had been young (even me, relatively speaking) and had been doing music with the overt intention of getting signed, getting released, getting an 'Access All Areas' pass on a lanyard, and then ascending to a higher plain of existence. Some of them might have had a proper plan, a strategy even, but I think the majority were just kids who reckoned if they learned how to play, learned how to write songs, and then combined the two with a bit of style, the rock'n'roll ecosystem would naturally select them for greatness. Which of course is not always the case.

bis had taken off, which hadn't been a surprise to most of us because they'd long been this perfect wee pop unit, but nonetheless, it's a splash of cold water to your musical ambitions when the very youngest folk you know are suddenly on *Top of the Pops*, being vastly energetic.

I think around then *Tigermilk* had come out, and although that was a slow burner, the name Belle and Sebastian was being whispered everywhere, and their powerful presence was coalescing out of the mist like Brigadoon, as if they'd always been there, y'know?

And of course Mogwai were on the march roundabout then too. Stuart Braithwaite had been in the Kazoo as far back as I can remember, as the drummer in Eska, so was a familiar face. I'm not good at quickly accommodating change. The notion that he was suddenly a guitarist alarmed me. Like Bill Murray in *Ghostbusters*, I was anticipating an apocalypse of shattered boundaries, 'dogs and cats, living together' etc.

Before then, Alex had repurposed The Blisters as The Karelia, with some line-up changes and a change of tone, although several of Blisters' best tunes had persisted, and they had been signed to a European label on that basis. Roadrunner Records? But that hadn't worked out, or at least, it had run its course and nothing much had come out of it.

By then The Stanleys/Tonic had thrown in the towel, having quite genuinely had those 'musical differences' one reads about in rock biogs. The recordings we had released hadn't attracted any outside attention, and although we were rocking it live. . . I think our last gig might well have been supporting Hugh Cornwell of The Stranglers at a sold-out Glasgow Garage. . . attempts to write new stuff just made it plain that our various preferences had diverged. There was, of course, all sorts of personal stuff going on, the usual build-up of complications that human relationships accrue, but none of that would have been fatal if we'd stumbled upon a new song that we all enjoyed playing, y'know? But we didn't, so the unit drifted apart.

Annie Spandex (guitar, Lung Leg): I think a few contributing factors were political and sociological. Tony Blair's government made it harder for folk to get dole money (I know a lot of musicians signed on) as they made you actively apply for jobs etc. Tuition fees were also introduced so many folk could no longer afford to go to university or college. . . so there were financial reasons that meant folk had less time or money to do music. A lot of the art places lost funding here in Glasgow so it was less of a hive, there were less places for like-minded folk to meet. The art and music scenes always had previously cross-pollenated.

I also think for a lot of the folk here, lives moved on – weddings, babies, proper jobs – as you couldn't make music pay an income, this was for a lot of the people who drove the scene. Also, guitar, indie music had become less favoured, fallen a bit out of fashion; it seemed mainstream was all about dance music, vocal bands and reality shows like *Pop Idol.*

Bosque call it a day

As the decade drew to a close, exhaustion and loss began to take their toll on Bosque. Two close friends and collaborators, Alan Crichton and Mark Gibbons, both died in 1999. The label slowly went quiet after that.

Tom Worthington (Hee Haw, Starstruck, Bosque Records): Alan Crichton died, and Mark died in early '99, not long apart. That was it for me. I broke. With the label I did only what I'd already promised and nothing beyond. The dream stopped.

Tom identifies his proudest and fondest moments from those years.

Tom Worthington (Hee Haw, Starstruck, Bosque Records): Our two nights at De Val's felt like we'd braided it all together – films flickering, bands roaring, a paper trail of a fanzine left behind. Not just a cool band at the 13th Note, but a way of using our freedom to go somewhere new.

Making music with Mark – the happiness of sound in a small room, instinctive art with someone who saved me from being a mediocre architect. I met him in my first week at college: the unbelievably cool gothic poet at Edinburgh College of Art.

Tom still has boxes of tapes, letters and unreleased recordings from that time. He occasionally thinks about bringing them back into the world, but he remains wary of nostalgia.

Tom Worthington (Hee Haw, Starstruck, Bosque Records): People talk about Gilded Lil again; I'm hearing from old friends, opening boxes with Mark's handwriting, deciding what is and isn't for daylight. I'm not nostalgic. The past is interesting, but it's not somewhere to return to.

His final reflection could stand for an entire generation of Scottish DIY musicians who bridged the 1980s and 1990s.

Tom Worthington (Hee Haw, Starstruck, Bosque Records): Do it yourself, with friends, and don't wait. If there's a door, open it. If there isn't, put a hinge on a wall and call it a door. That's what Bosque was, when it worked – not a business plan so much as permission.

Ben Wallers (vocals, Country Teasers; guitar, The Male Nurse): Alan Crichton was very gregarious, extremely good company. I was the opposite, too shy, Kajagoogoo. But to quote one of his girlfriends, 'Alan you are basstard! But you are lovely basstard!' She was from Europe, hence the grammar. Heroin solved his problems, created new ones and then finished him off. I dunno man, I'm not a bloody mind-reader. Lots of great bands during The Patriarchy have been basically two blokes who have an intense bromance, write one great album or maybe two and then hate each other, sound familiar? Like most marriages. The Male Nurse, after Alan's heroin use got out of control and made him impossible to be around, felt very free when he left. We basically pissed ourselves with joyful enthusiasm in our band practices and improvised hours and hours of great music, just like all these krautrock bands in the seventies it turns out. Under Alan we were constricted. We had to play our songs tight; I remember someone saying, 'I don't want to play any more shite gigs'. Country Teasers was based on the idea that shite gigs were a fact of life and if they were shite enough you could actually entertain an audience for EVEN LONGER than your tight show of hits. Alan wanted to avoid his destiny, which he feared, ending up back in Kirkcaldy signing on. He did avoid it.

On the other hand, Alan's departure meant a lack of direction. What the fuck does that mean you idiot! I dunno. Suddenly I don't think I really know what I'm on about! I have his amp in the garage, I think it was his sister Nicola's, it's a heavy H&H and very loud. No, it's a Carlsboro, sorry. Heavy to schlep around. But very loud and a great sound. Quite often he appears in dreams, usually clean, always very mature and sensible. My favourite personal memory is when he was sleeping on the floor behind the sofa in my room in Lochrin Place, Tollcross, which I rented off the landlady who lived in the big room. I used to drink a quarter bottle of Grant's [whisky] and a six-pack of Sweetheart Stout, a dark sweet ale which was probably not too strong, roughly every day. Anyway it was bedtime, I expect Alan had made stovies (corned beef hash) and we were both in our beds. I was reading *Naked Lunch* and I laughed aloud and he said 'What was that bit?' and I read it, from the Interzone riot scene. I'll paraphrase: 'A coprophage calls for a plate, shits on it, eats the shit and says "Mmm, that's my rich substance!"' I recall Alan's chuckle, how it would have raised his upper torso off the floor as his lungs inflated with laughter, and I chuckled aloud too, both of us somewhat wary of not waking the landlady, or not giving a shit.

Some people might say, 'Ooh don't say that out loud Ben,' but I think the main factor destroying the scene or the bands or The Male Nurse and maybe even preventing Country Teasers from achieving full bloom back then is HEROIN. Not drugs or too much to drink, just heroin itself. But then again as I said before I was unaware of any scene at the time and didn't care anyway, I just wanted to be famous, with my band or on my own; I didn't give a shit about any scene. I felt at the time that The Male Nurse were very unlucky, and that what should have happened was that someone should have come along and made us successful, based on how good our songs were and how cool we all were. Hey ho! I didn't know that you had to sort of 'work hard' at it and undergo all sorts of ups and downs. I thought it just happened like a stork delivering a baby.

Country Teasers

Keith Farquar (vocals, The Male Nurse): Black humour and absurdity were rife. We did very leftfield gigs, some with spontaneous art: in central London, we painted a huge mural of a mountain. Liam Gallagher had said in the press that music was a mountain with The Beatles at the top. We took him at his word and painted it, complete with features you might see on a music mountain such as Nick's cave or Kate's bush. 'The Beatles' in cut polystyrene letters were balanced on its peak. We bought and glued together an Airfix Chinook helicopter and hung it in front – this was The Male Nurse being airlifted from the mountain – 'Get us off!'

We were invited to play at the book launch for Simon Ford's *Wreckers of Civilisation* at an obscure ex-TV and VCR shop in the Elephant and Castle shopping centre. That was a memorable gig. Thousands of plug sockets in grids on the walls to plug into. Memories of smashing holes in the floor of the Wee Red Bar, naked with guitars and getting banned. Supporting Jayne County at the Cas Rock. Playing in front of a hundred Hibs casuals in the Cowgate, when they infiltrated the club where we were scheduled. We survived. Playing at Jimmy Boyle's wedding (without me).

So, there was always excitement but not much trajectory (maybe tragedy). A lot of chaos, and in the end, hopefully some moments of beauty.

CHAPTER TWENTY-FOUR

But Not for Everyone, Imperial Phase 3

Belle and Sebastian: A series of EPs and *The Boy With the Arab Strap*

While many of the bands who started in the early 1990s were slowing down significantly, Belle and Sebastian had been working relentlessly, despite Stuart Murdoch's health concerns. A series of EPs dominated 1997 and early 1998 with songs not included on albums, in a nod to The Beatles, Joy Division, New Order and The Smiths. The first release of 1997 for Belle and Sebastian was the 'Dog on Wheels' EP, made up of tracks recorded at Beatbox previous to the recording of the band's first two albums. It's a testament to their quality control and prolific output that these EPs would have made very fine LPs for lesser bands.

Stuart Murdoch (vocals, Belle and Sebastian): By the time we finished *If You're Feeling Sinister* I wanted to line up the next recording straight away because I still had this glut of songs. But singles were always a big thing for The Smiths, for New Order, Cocteau Twins. . . the independent, 12-inch singles. And so I thought, okay, that's what we should do next. But we had an album's worth of songs that we recorded. We had twelve songs and we sat around trying to decide which would be the best A-sides.

The first was the 'Lazy Line Painter Jane' EP.

Stuart Murdoch (vocals, Belle and Sebastian): It's funny, I only just really mentioned this recently. I was driving through a village in Ayrshire, called Galston. I'd been scouting venues for a live concert video that we wanted to do, so driving between Motherwell and Troon. So I tweeted that I was in Galston because one of the first letters we ever got from a fan or admirer of the band was from a girl from Galston! She worked in the village shop, and she wanted a poster so she could put it up. So that sparked off an image for me. That was enough, I didn't need much in those days to start writing a song. I immediately wrote this song, 'Painter Jane', about a girl who comes from a provincial town – I knew what those times were like. And she came to the city to be who she wanted to be really. And we recorded it in the church hall where I worked because that was the difference about doing the EPs. Suddenly we were exploring different recording techniques. We wanted to capture the echo, and we also wanted to record more live. I remember doing that and it was excellent for that song because it had a big dome ceiling. So we've got this reverb. It's like a mesh of sound – a little bit like getting Spector's Wall for free. And I just didn't feel my voice was cutting it because it was a bigger sound.

Enter Monica Queen.

Stuart Murdoch (vocals, Belle and Sebastian): How did I know Monica? I'd met Monica when I went to America. I met her at a Teenage Fanclub concert. I'd gone to America a few years before to try and get better from ME, to spend a winter in California, just hanging out. The Fanclub were playing and I got in to see them. And Johnnie (Smilie) and Monica Queen (both from Thrum) happened to be in California as well. I'd become sort of buddies with them since that point, but I knew she had a great voice so that was a no-brainer. But I had Isobel and I didn't think about asking Isobel to sing, which shows at the time that I was fooling myself. I didn't look forward, I didn't have much tact. I was a little bit tactless, because I was so full of myself with the songs and everything. It never occurred to me that it might annoy Isobel that I was going to ask Monica. But at the same time, I just thought Monica has got a voice like a guided missile, shoot, she'll be great. So we got her in. It was just a meteor, it just fucking worked. We already had the track up and running. The second that she sang, it was great – the church hall with that booming effect. So immediately that became an A-side.

'3.. 6.. 9 Seconds of Light' followed in October 1997, the same year the band recorded the album The Boy With the Arab Strap, *which came out in September 1998. It was their most commercial release, its title understandably causing a little tension with the band of the same name.*

Malcolm Middleton (Arab Strap): Aidan was angry about it but I found out from Stuart Murdoch years later that Aidan had drunkenly given his permission in the pub and then forgotten all about it. Or something like that. It was all fine, no one really fell out. The only downside is that we still get asked by people if we named our band after their album. Grrrr. Lovely guys though.

They invited us through to Glasgow and London to play with them a few times when we started, which we still appreciate.

Aidan Moffat (Arab Strap): Our second gig was supporting Belle and Sebastian on what I think was their second gig, it was in the Mitchell Library. It was the first gig we did as a four-piece band and Stuart had made these wee cards and put them on the table to warn the audience that some of it may get a bit racy. [Laughs.] I wish we'd kept those. It was a sit-down gig. I can't remember how it was set out because it wasn't in the actual proper theatre where you sit, the one that looks like a proper theatre with rows. It was in a room at the Mitchell with tables and on the table there was these wee cards saying, 'Just to warn you, it might get a wee bit fruity when Arab Strap play'. So that was when we first met them.

Stevie Jackson (guitar, Belle and Sebastian): ['The Boy with the Arab Strap'] was the title track of our biggest selling album, when people still bought records. . . it got to Number 12 in the charts, it sold 100,000 copies. It's a big tune. It's kind of like our 'My Generation' or something. We can't not play it. It's the only song that we play every night. It's become a sort of fan song really because it's the one where everyone gets up on stage to dance.

Stuart Murdoch (vocals, Belle and Sebastian): I remember Isobel. . . I remember playing it to her in the church hall on the piano, and her saying in her funny, cute way, 'It's a bit Chas and Dave – it's a bit whiffy'. She didn't see the good in it at all. But we went ahead and recorded it. It wasn't a single, and it wasn't like an immediate thing. But I guess over the years, it's had this natural thing. I can't remember who was the first person the first person was who came on stage to dance to it. But that was a very gradual thing. It was just somebody managed to get up on stage. And that added to another, it took it up a gear. And from that point onwards, that just seems to be a stalwart in the set. . . Yeah, it's good it's happened because even though it's got that quite straightforward rhythm, the Trojan horse is that the words are saying quite a lot. And people have latched on to that.

The writing of the album was a significant departure from the way previous albums had been written. Stuart encouraged the other members to write themselves, even taking over lead vocal duties in some instances. Stevie wrote two tracks that have become fan favourites, 'Seymour Stein' and 'Chick Factor'.

Stevie Jackson (guitar, Belle and Sebastian): That third album, we started in 1997, and then worked on it for a bit then stopped and went back. I just thought it was taking too long. But then it came out. With regards to 'Seymour Stein' and 'Chick Factor', when I look at them now, they're almost comments on what was happening, or you know, *Tigermilk* and *If You're Feeling Sinister*, Stuart's songs, and they seem to encapsulate this kind of self-contained world if you like. It was clear that he had got to break out of that and not be a self-contained world anymore.

Chris Geddes (keyboards, Belle and Sebastian): We kind of started to be a normal band, and then we realised that we're not normal.

The previous four or five years had been unrelenting for Belle and Sebastian, with a continuous upwards trajectory. The band recorded Fold Your Hands Child, You Walk Like A Peasant *in*

2000 after touring, then took a temporary break, after which founder member Stuart David left to focus on his own project, (the excellent) Looper. His reflection on his time with the band, especially their earliest days, and how unique and uncompromising their approach to being in a band was, is fascinating.

Stuart David (bass, Belle and Sebastian): I think most of the frenzy about us in the record business had been initially stirred up by Alan Rankine. We didn't have a following. We were barely a band. And we hadn't built even the beginning of an audience. But in retrospect, it's quite clear that what happened next is that we became one of the first bands to go viral on the internet. In Beatbox, one of the tutors – Neil Cameron – had taught me how to make websites, so I made one for Belle and Sebastian in 1996. There were only 100,000 websites on the internet at that point. Today there are about 1.2 billion. There were no platforms or anything. But we went viral in the newsgroups and on the email lists that existed, probably after the record had been played a few times on Mark Radcliffe's evening show on Radio 1.

I suddenly started getting over a hundred emails a day coming in to the contact address I'd put on the website. From Japan and Brazil and America. Only ever one of two messages: 'When will you play my town?' and, 'Where can I find a copy of *Tigermilk*?' So that's why we needed the manager, Neil Robertson, to turn things down and refuse promotion opportunities and fend off record companies and interview requests and say no to gigs and tours and TV appearances and all of that.

It was a full-time job. He got an office in Central Chambers and turned things down all day long. Jools Holland appearances, tours with Radiohead, front covers on all the weekly and monthly magazines.

As a band, we didn't even all know each other all that well yet. Stevie still wasn't even fully in. Chris and Isobel were full-time students, Stuart wasn't all that well, and we were trying to protect this vulnerable thing that was just being born – that we had just found while we were making *Tigermilk*. We were trying to look after it and work out what it was in the midst of a bomb having gone off. So a whole other myth developed in the outside world about who we were and what we were doing and why we were doing it, because of that situation. But that myth isn't even fully coherent to any of us who were in the band. We can't really see what it looks like from the outside. We were really just trying to learn to play, in the church hall, while Neil sat in Central Chambers with his feet up on the desk, keeping the world at bay.

Belle and Sebastian had done something rare in music: they had created their own myth, one that was infectious for certain fans throughout the world. The band had created a hyper-real Glasgow, a fantasy indie paradise that still attracts and intrigues people everywhere. But now, they needed to take a pause after the years they'd spent and the energy they'd expended to achieve it.

Stevie Jackson (guitar, Belle and Sebastian): At the end of finishing *Fold Your Hands,* Stuart wasn't feeling too good with CFS and requested a year off but that didn't last very long. He phoned with a song idea a week later. Stuart David left the band about then. We didn't do a single gig in 1999/2000 so we were quiet anyway. In 2001 we started playing live in earnest but, with Bob [Bobbie Kildea] there, it felt like a new group in a sense.

Arab Strap: *Philophobia*

Chemikal Underground and Arab Strap were in full flow and the band's second LP proved to be another high point.

Stewart Henderson (bass, The Delgados; Chemikal Underground): [Arab Strap] were just one of those bands that really came along at the right time. The zeitgeist was very much the case. But right from the get-go you could tell Aidan and Malcolm were going to be more than that. They really were going to continue to develop, there was no doubt about that. And that was realised fully I think with *Philophobia*. *Philophobia* was a terrific record. And it was a great progression from what they'd done with the first album. The first album was quite sparse in how it was all put together, but that's just the way it was. Then *Philophobia* mirrored in lot of ways what was going on with Mogwai. Their album, *Young Team* – I don't know, can you say that *Young Team* was to *The Week Never Starts Round Here* what *Come On Die Young* was to *Philophobia*? I don't know, maybe that's overly simplistic, but in terms of the trajectories of the bands, it's definitely the case that these were really strong first albums and then a real creative development in the second record. Without losing any of the vitality or the singular sound or vision that they had as bands, none of that was lost on their second records.

Aidan Moffat (Arab Strap): I think this album became more focused, and we became the band that we would become for the next few years. It became a lot more focused once we knew we could actually make this. I mean, that's the first step when someone says, do you want to make another record because your first one did quite well? Fuck. Those first songs on the first album were deeply autobiographical. I never even knew anyone else would ever hear them, didn't think anyone except our local friends would understand them. So it was great to be offered that again. I think I realised what I've been trying to do, which was to write these brutal love songs, about honesty; and the important thing about them is that I'm always the worst person in the room. I think that's why, even if I'm writing about someone who's hurt me, it's important that, I don't want to sound like a victim is what I'm saying. It wasn't people treating me bad, so much as me being a fucking arsehole. I think it's important in those songs. And ever since throughout life, if you're going to write about certain things, it's important mthat you're not trying to make yourself out to be the hero, or you're not making yourself out to be infallible, I suppose that's what I'm looking for. So all of these songs on *Philophobia* talk about infidelity, and some ugly aspects of being young and in love. But I'm as bad as anyone else, I'm in among it, I'm part of it, I am not trying to make a moral judgement on anyone. And I think that's what I realised, when we started writing those songs. It's like I want to write a bit about the messiness of it all in an honest way. And the ugliness as well. But also do it with humour. Which probably came naturally as a defence mechanism. It's like, you'd better start seeing something funny here. Otherwise, people are going to turn the record off. That's, that's an important part of it.

Malcolm Middleton (Arab Strap): It was a strange one for me, because we recorded it over a year, going into the studio between tours etc. So I didn't see the big picture. It's probably taken me about twenty-five years to appreciate it. I was always surprised by the praise the album received, but yes, we'll take it. It's strong lyrically for Aidan, but I've always thought the music was a bit patchy. Miles ahead of our first album, but still not where I was aiming for in terms of making a good-sounding record. Also, I did have a couple of songs that I'd written for *Philophobia,* but Aidan didn't think they fit with the mood so they were left off. (Cue some silent seething.) 'Devil & The Angel' was one, so it kind of lit a fuse in making me to want to do solo albums. Which turned out to be good/bad.

Aidan Moffat (Arab Strap): Malcolm sang a lot songs on the first album, but he just drifted away from it. I can't remember why, again, it wasn't a conscious decision. I think he just said, 'You know what, I'm just gonna sit back, let you do that stuff'. Certainly phase one of Arab Strap was realised on *Philophobia,* as opposed to the first album because. . . obviously, everybody's first album, they have fond memories of it, and I do. I've got a lot of love for The Week Never Starts Round Here. But it's a messy record, you know, it's not focused at all. And then I think *Philophobia* was when we started realising that we were making albums, and I still have that attitude to albums. I don't see an album as a collection of songs. I think it's something that can transport you to another world. It became a job prospect at that point as well. Suddenly we're playing tours, we've got records on the radio, they're writing about us, the *NME* and *Melody Maker,* not necessarily that flatteringly? You know, it's funny, because you think of those things. We were in the papers quite a lot, but the way journalists wrote – even if they were giving you a four-star review, they were snidey bastards. Like, even the good reviews. Utter pricks, man. So suddenly, the second album to me almost seems like the actual start.

Paul Savage (drums, The Delgados; Chemikal Undergound): It was an incredible time. I don't think we realised what we were doing and what was happening. We were trying to keep hold of the bands; we thought we'd done a great job with all of those records. We felt, in some ways, vindicated that they had chosen to do it. Certainly Mogwai could have been on any label in the UK at the time. And they chose to come with us. There was a feeling, I suppose, to be honest, that we were trying to entice them to stay. (We all were – I mean, we'd signed outside of Europe to Beggars Banquet.) But a lot of it was to do with educating ourselves and the label and seeing what we could do, and it would also help all the other bands. But we were acutely aware of the amount of attention Mogwai were getting; Arab Strap were getting. They had both agreed to do another record with us, but that was it. It was like, we'll do one more and then we'll talk about it. Okay, fair enough, it was always a 50/50 deal with them so that was part of the thing that appealed. They were going to get fair compensation for anything they did, and they still do with those records. So that was appealing to them but there is always going to be somebody in your ear in the industry, when you're playing to 1,500 people in London, and none of the Chemikal Underground are there. There's somebody taking you out and saying, just imagine what you could do if this happened or if you had this kind of set-up behind you.

The Delgados: *Peloton*

The Chemikal Underground highs continued, this time with The Delgados themselves and their second album, Peloton, *released in June 1998. It revealed a hugely ambitious soundscape and more mature songwriting, and was one of the highlights of the year. The fact that the band were focusing on themselves in this hugely productive period was welcome. The album also continued their convention of using cycling-related titles.*

Emma Pollock (vocals/guitar, The Delgados; Chemikal Underground): I guess it became a little more oblique as the years went by but Alun's always been a massive cycling fan. He was a big cyclist when he was a kid, when he was younger. I've got a road bike – I go out every now and again. I really enjoyed that from being a child. It was a thing that came out of how we got the name. 'Pedro Delgado' was put in a hat along with another few things. We literally pulled that one out and we became The Delgados and that was it. And then Domestique and Peloton of course are two important aspects of the Tour de France. . . And the name suited the absolutely frenetic pace of *Domestiques*, which was a band that was trying to pack in all the ideas at a hundred miles an hour, all the ideas into the one song, written by two people.

Paul Savage (drums, The Delgados; Chemikal Underground): There was a big difference between the singles that we did at the start, and then soon we found ourselves with an audience that we almost didn't expect. People were liking us and we were kind of fast punk-pop songs. But that wasn't always what we wanted. There was a side of us that we wanted to show, and we started to show that side on the first album, with some songs bringing in cello and bringing in some slower stuff, but most of that first album was quite erratic and fast and edgy. When we released our first album, I remember our press agent trying to get us stuff and I don't think the *NME* were particularly keen on us.

Like many of their contemporaries, The Delgados were often overlooked by the mainstream music press, although Peel was always a huge supporter.

Paul Savage (drums, The Delgados; Chemikal Underground): 'Under Canvas Under Wraps' was a John Peel Festive Fifty Number 1, I think? That got us a certain amount of kudos within a certain scene, but when the album [Domestiques] came out it was basically ignored by a lot of mainstream people and certainly the *NME*. The Blur and Oasis thing was happening at the time; Britpop was in full flow. We've always joked about our second single: the 'Lazarwalker' EP was released on the same day that Blur and Oasis were head-on. Like, why are you talking about these two? There's a third band in this contest here. So of course, we were ignored by Britpop. That was a good example of it. We always felt we had nothing to do with Britpop. It was a horrible scene. And it was one that we never felt really part of. Still don't. So there was that kind of thing happening at the time and when we came to do *Peloton*, we were kind of reacting to the way that people thought we were just a John Peel band, or just a pop-punk band, just shouty stuff. There was a lot more to us than that, but we hadn't really shown it. So we started dabbling with strings, we got a

Peel Session together. This was in 1997 because we didn't do anything in that year, we were just writing *Peloton* and getting ready. We got a string section involved and we started writing these songs. 'So Everything Goes Around The Water', 'Pull The Wires From The Wall', 'The Arcane Model', and a song that was a B-side called 'Mauron Chanson'. And that was the four in the Peel Session. I remember driving down and going, is this career suicide, that we're bringing a string quartet into this sound? We were just basically a pop-punk band. The response to the Peel Session was amazing. There was a couple of things that happened. It gave us the confidence that we should just continue with this for the album, but also a guy called out of the blue, saying he was the manager of a producer called Dave Fridmann. And he said that Dave had heard a tape of the Peel Session and loved it, and wanted to work with us.. . . and we said, is this the Dave Fridmann that does Flaming Lips? He said yeah. And we said fuck, we love Dave Fridmann. Peter, his manager, sent us an advanced copy of *Deserter's Songs* by Mercury Rev. There's a Mercury Rev connection as well. We had loved Mercury Rev's stuff as well so we thought, this is amazing, he's great, but we were in Glasgow, and we can't afford it. So we can't work with Dave, but we said we'll keep him in mind for the next one. But we can't all get over to America to do this. So we'd been happy with the response to the Peel Session, then we recorded the album without Dave, but, you know, we put it out and we got a new press agent at the time. We spoke to him about our ambition for the record. . . He was going, this is the record that people are going to go nuts for. We got this guy, John Yates, to do press; Bad Moon was the name of the press agent. John was amazing, and he sat us down one day and says, look, I love this record. I think it's amazing. But I have problems because when I talk to people about you guys, they're just saying the same thing over and over. They just think you're a twee indie band that does pop shouty music. A bit like bis without the synths, and clearly with this record you're not like that at all. So I'm finding it really hard to sell you to people. So it was quite a tough time. But John was really good at working on people. Slowly he got people to realise that we had a lot more to us than what the first few singles may have shown. We got Single of the Week in *NME* for 'Everything Goes Around the Water'.

Emma Pollock (vocals/guitar, The Delgados; Chemikal Underground): I think a lot of that was to do with Alan Barr becoming our cello player. Becoming more a part of the writing process. We began to slow things down a little bit. We began to become more comfortable with space. And a three-four time signature. And it was a real gateway album, I suppose in a way that paved the way for what would be the first orchestral commitment, if you like, of *The Great Eastern*. As a band, we didn't feel like we had to fill up every single corner with fuzz and speed and frenetic guitar playing. We were becoming a bit more comfortable with the sound that we wanted to make and could make. And we were probably just getting a bit older and a bit more mature as songwriters. But yeah the cello was a huge element of that, because it encouraged the use of space, because you wanted to hear that thing. You wanted to hear the texture that it brought, without being frightened of slowing things down. I think when you're young it was the energy, literally the energy in the room when *Domestiques* was written is what you hear in that record.

We were so excited. And songs are written, like, Alun would have an idea and I would have an idea and we would literally force them together until we had a song.

Stewart Henderson (bass, The Delgados; Chemikal Underground): I don't think Peloton was as hard a pivot away from what we did with *Domestiques* as some people might think. It's also funny how these things come about. We had Alan Barr who played cello through all of our records. He had a wee sign up in MCM studios, 'Cello player looking for stuff. . .' So we brought Alan on board for *Domestiques*, there is cello on that album. I met a girl called Camille Mason, who I went to primary school with and went to high school with – she was in Alan's class as well – at the bus stop in Motherwell one morning. I got chatting to her, and I said, 'Are you still playing the flute?' And she was like, aye. 'You should maybe come to one of the practices. It'd be interesting to hear if there's anything you could do.' And she said okay.

Emma Pollock (vocals/guitar, The Delgados; Chemikal Underground): We were literally forging these joint songs together at the hip. By finding ways that musically they could work together. It was a really interesting way to do it. But then things began to change a little bit. I mean, things like 'Everything Goes Around the Water' on *Peloton* was a really, really, really important song. That was also a joint thing. Alun wrote the verse, I wrote the chorus. That was another kind of segwayed song if you like. But then you've got other songs that are fully written by one or the other of us. And the one or the other of us becomes much more prevalent from that point on.

Peloton *wasn't as commercially successful as* Philophobia *but it reached a very respectable Number 57 in the UK charts and received favourable reviews, including in* Pitchfork. *For me it remains one of the defining Scottish albums of the decade.*

CHAPTER TWENTY-FIVE

Another Generation

Camera Obscura

As progress towards mainstream success slowed down for the first generation of nineties acts, a new band appeared on the scene: Camera Obscura.

Tracyanne Campbell (vocals, Camera Obscura): I met John Henderson (singer/songwriter) at college while doing a sound and video recording course. After seeing Juliana Hatfield live I decided I wanted to start a band and write songs, We put up an ad and recruited Gavin. I think the influences named on that ad for bandmates would have had to be The Pastels, The Velvet Underground, Lee and Nancy and probably Felt and The Supremes.

Gavin Dunbar (bass, Camera Obscura): [I saw] an advert in the 13th Note. People looking for like-minded folks with the same influences (I think the ad named Stereolab, The Lemonheads, Pastels and Yo La Tengo) to start something. Tracyanne and John were at college together, I'd been playing with another guitarist, but we were looking for other people.

Tracyanne Campbell (vocals, Camera Obscura): In all honesty we were just making it up as we went along. From an early age I was always interested in dressing in clothes from charity shops and trying to present as a bit retro. I suppose I was always a bit in love with the past. I liked looking at old family photos, listening to my nana's records etc. so a retro aesthetic was inevitable. As far as the Super 8 thing, that would be down to Blair Young (Forest of Black), who has made our videos from the beginning. He's been instrumental in our visual aesthetic. We met when we were very young and enthusiastic and impressionable. We somehow managed to cobble together a feel, a look, a vibe.

['Park and Ride'] was probably one of the first songs I ever wrote. We recorded it on a cassette four-track in Gav's basement where we used to rehearse and it was released on Andmoresound Records.

Gavin Dunbar (bass, Camera Obscura): Andmoresound was run initially by Lindsay Boyd and Allan McCallum, who were in a band called Mac Meda together (the first release on the label had been their first single). They had seen one of our ads and had thought our influences list had been really interesting, so they got in touch and asked us for a demo tape. We sent one off, which would have had 'Park and Ride' and 'Swimming Pool' on it, along with another four or five songs and they really liked it and asked us if they could put it out. We said yes. I don't think we re-recorded the versions on the tape, they just put them out as they had been. When it came to do the second single, 'Your Sound', we recorded onto a digital multi-track and then after that, we finally got into a studio.

Tracyanne Campbell (vocals, Camera Obscura): Lindsay Boyd basically called us up after seeing the ad we put up in John Smith's for a guitarist and drummer to tell us he liked the bands we named as influences and told us he had started a label and wanted to put out some 45s and asked if have any songs we wanted to release. We said yes and I guess that was sort of the start of it all. I believe Beat Patrol [BBC Radio Scotland] was the first show to play 'Park and Ride'. I do remember feeling very excited to hold the record in my hand and of course to hear it on the radio. It was always very exciting back in the day to hear ourselves on the radio. I vaguely remember we met up in my flat and listened together while drinking cheap plonk. We should do that going forward. I suppose we've become blasé. I remember going to John Smith's to look at it among the 45s and Stuart Murdoch was standing talking to Stephen Pastel with two or three copies in his hand. I got all shy I remember and left the shop immediately! When we had four or five songs written we decided to play The Halt on Woodland's Road's Saturday open mic. Richard Coleburn and Stuart Murdoch [of Belle and Sebastian] were in the pub and came over after to tell us they liked our songs. Before we knew what was happening, Richard was drumming for us and Stuart was sitting in on our rehearsals at the church hall. They were always really supportive of us, as were The Pastels, both bands being favourites of ours, which was amazing to us. Stuart was a real champion and very encouraging. We could barely play by the time we played the Bowlie Weekender. . . I guess he put us on at the church a few times to get us match-fit, playing with bands like Snow Patrol and Astrid.

Stuart basically encouraged us to ditch the four-track and get into the studio. He heard a demo of 'Eighties Fan' and wanted to arrange it. He produced by default almost. He generously just gave us a lot of his time and we've always felt a close connection to him and the Belles.

Gavin Dunbar (bass, Camera Obscura): We hadn't played live at all really. We did a couple of open mic afternoons at The Halt and that was where we met met Stuart Murdoch and Richard Colburn. Richard offered to drum (he was already playing in about five bands at once) and Stuart asked us to come and rehearse in the church hall in Hyndland, where they lived (and indeed were caretakers at the time). Stuart produced two of the tracks on the first album, 'Eighties Fan' and 'Anti-Western'. He had come to us with an arrangement idea for 'Eighties Fan' and wanted to take us into the studio and do it properly. We'd never been near a proper studio before, so it was a really exciting time. Especially with string players being brought in as well. I think we had one day in the studio to get 'Eighties Fan' down. After that it just made sense to keep going. We had moved into Maryhill Burgh Halls for rehearsals, which at the time had a couple of bands sharing the space (The Starlets and Palomino) and leaving gear set up to be ready for rehearsals a few times a week. We pretty much spent 2000–2001 holed up in there rehearsing up the first album in what could only be described as faded glamour (it had once been the base of Wet Wet Wet's Precious Organisation label), but by then it was a run-down large damp room, that if you left your amps in for too long, they went a bit mouldy. But we prepped a record in it, and after 'Eighties Fan' was recorded, we had enough songs prepared to just keep going.

Tracyanne Campbell (vocals, Camera Obscura): I guess we got encouraging press and we always had folk at the shows in the beginning. Folk like John Peel definitely helped our profile which we'll be eternally grateful for. We felt like part of the family, we even played his 70th birthday and went around to eat haggis with him on Burns Night once. We were very shy and probably didn't make the most of the opportunity but he seemed to like us despite our social short comings.

Gavin Dunbar (bass, Camera Obscura): We'd been at it for three years by the time we sorted out the band having a full and settled line up with Kenny [McKeeve] and Lee [Thomson] having joined, and us finally feeling like a real band. It took another two to get the album recorded, so we'd spent a long time in our own wee world. We were fairly confident that we'd made a good record but really didn't know how it was going to go. In reality there were a thousand records pressed and a few thousand CDs. The week that 'Eighties Fan' came out, we played Glasgow, Dundee and London. Literally seven people and a dog turned up in Dundee; Glasgow (Hyndland Church Hall) was sold out; and then London was also a sold-out show at the Spitz. So we got to keep our heads fairly well adjusted with nice doses of reality mixed in with the excitement. Just after that we got asked to go to London for a Peel Session which was broadcast just before the LP came out. That was a proper joy, getting to go down to Maida Vale and experience recording in a totally legendary space. Even took time to wander round and found the old Radiophonic Workshop room, which was sadly defunct by that point, but a total thrill to see for a Dr Who geek like myself.

Tracyanne Campbell (vocals, Camera Obscura): I had a lot of anxiety in those early days. If I could have chilled out, I could have enjoyed it a bit more at the time. Looking back I feel really blessed to have done all the things we did, and to travel the world over and over. Getting to do Peel Sessions always felt special. I guess the first time we got to do those at Maida Vale was special. To be honest though I just love thinking about how in love we all were with doing it. Making music together has always been the special glue. We don't always get on and we've been through the mill, but we are solid together. Carey [Lander] once said we're weirdly close for a band. I guess she was right.

Gavin Dunbar (bass, Camera Obscura): Anything was possible. I don't think we were ever particularly ambitious, but we just wanted to make good music, communicating with each other and letting the music talk for us. Before we made a record, we were happy recording in the house. We were too nervous to play live, but that never bothered us really. I guess we developed a bit of a group mentality as a band: none of us would have ever seen ourselves getting up in front of an audience in the early days, but together we managed to gee ourselves up into doing something that was in equal parts totally and terrifyingly out of our comfort zone and exactly what we needed to be doing. We made our first single and we didn't have a drummer on it, took five years to finally make an album. Probably learned to play properly as a band on the third album, but every step was an adventure together.

CHAPTER TWENTY-SIX

New Horizons for Arab Strap and Mogwai

Arab Strap leave Chemikal Underground

As had happened in the twilight years of the preceding 'indie' decade, the nineties independent scene started to slow down as lives moved on and maturity struck. But some clearly established careers had emerged. Come On Die Young *by Mogwai and* Elephant Shoe *by Arab Strap were two of the more prominent albums to be released in this late period. However, while* Come On Die Young *was released on Chemikal Underground,* Elephant Shoe *appeared on a major label.*

Aidan Moffat (Arab Strap): Well, the PR man, Steven Bass, who went on to found that indie label Moshi Moshi, approached us very early on while we were making *Philaphobia*. So, it wasn't like they suddenly swept in at any point. There was a long relationship where we would meet up and talk. There was never any chance we weren't going to do *Philaphobia* with Chemikal but we were discussing it at the time and then we met Ferdy Unger-Hamilton. There's a good working-class name. But he was great. We got on with him really well. He was the head of

Universal for a while. At the time, he was running [the indie label] Gobi. And the label had Portishead, who I loved, and also Gabrielle who I also loved too. And I was like, fuck it, you know? I was already convinced. Yeah, I thought that was great. . . Then we made an EP for Chemikal Underground, '(Afternoon) Soaps', well it's just called 'Arap Strap', but the lead track was '(Afternoon) Soaps', which was a remix of the *Philophobia* track, and that was our sort of goodbye message. And everything was all friendly. Chemikal Underground were like, 'Take a chance, do it, why not? Let's see how it goes.' And it went well. You know, in the old CaVa studios, suddenly we weren't in room two but in room one, you know wee differences like that. We were like 'Alright!' And I don't know why, because there was still only mostly just two of us making the record. We didn't need the fucking room one, it was ridiculous. They wanted to throw money at us.

Malcolm Middleton (Arab Strap): I think we both benefitted! We wouldn't have homes now otherwise, and we still made a decent album and managed to tour a fair bit.

Aidan Moffat (Arab Strap): I was really conscious of not making this total sell-out record. And I think that was why we ended up making probably the most difficult record we've ever made when we went to a major label, which I'm not saying was a mistake, but there was a kind of wilful thing in my mind where I can't be seen to be making an album of 'First Big Weekend's which is I think what Go! Beat wanted? They loved *Philophobia* as well but I don't think they had any notions of that sort of thing. And they were very supportive of the record [Elephant Strap]. It did us wonders in Europe. We did this big tour in Europe, supporting the Tindersticks, which cost tens of thousands of pounds, which we could never have afforded. It took us to so many different places. And we made new fans there. It did really well in that respect. And it's funny, because in the UK, people lost interest because we'd signed to a major label, but it gave us a bigger platform all across the world after that. It really, really helped us. So I have no regrets about it.

Emma Pollock (vocals/guitar, The Delgados; Chemikal Underground): I remember being quite upset about it. We were down in London at an Arab Strap show to do with the *Philophobia* tour, so this would have been April 1998. And at this point, we were in the middle of a really purple period. Those first five years of Chemikal Underground were also. . . as well as us being relatively new and growing quickly. . . when Arab Strap decided to leave to go to Go! Beat it was because of the assumption that they were on this little indie in Glasgow. And also it was quite a buoyant industry at the time, so Go! Beat would have offered them a pretty nice advance – there's no doubt about that. A lot of it would have been to do with the money. The lure of the London record company. All the trappings that come with them. It would have appealed! So of course they wanted to try it because there's an assumption that if you start with the local indie that maybe you're going to get a break and maybe you're going to be able to jump onto a London major. And before you know it you're going to be selling not just tens of thousands of records, you're gonna be selling hundreds of thousands of records. As it happened, that wasn't the case. Go! Beat didn't do a very good job. *Elephant Shoe* came out in 1999 on Go! Beat. Apparently the genre is 'sadcore' according to Wikipedia, which is pretty funny.

Aidan Moffat (Arab Strap): The reason we left Go! Beat was that. . . I mean, it sounds kind of petty now that I think about it, but I was absolutely against those parental advisory stickers. I was like, nobody buying an Arab Strap record's going to be offended by what's on it. Like at this point, I would like to think they knew, which perhaps was a bit naive of me at the time. But the point was, we were promised there would never be any stickers on it. And then lo and behold, I saw it in the shop and there were stickers all over it. And that's because they would tell me, well, we requested that there'll be no stickers on it. And I was like, okay, and then someone else makes that decision. And the fact that they apparently had someone who listened to it, who would then decide if there's going to be a sticker. Yeah. I mean it fucking annoyed me, and other things as well. Like, they spent a lot of money on a full-page ad in *Q* magazine. We'd never had a good review in *Q* magazine. I mean, the first album got like two stars or something like that, like, they fucking hated us. And I'm like, why are you spending this money? It was that sort of thing that we were so used to being so hands-on with the release to suddenly have that taken away from you. It really didn't work for me at all.

Malcolm Middleton (Arab Strap): Things went wrong when major label guys appeared and suggested trying to market us. Then we just clammed up a bit and started resenting everything. It was a fun time, but the best part was definitely the fact that Chemikal didn't pause in taking us back and there were no hard feelings.

Emma Pollock (vocals/guitar, The Delgados; Chemikal Underground): They came back because it'd been a bit of a disaster by all accounts. So that's absolutely fascinating. Absolutely fascinating what happened. And then they ended up putting out a fair number of records with us after that. That was like part two of the Arab Strap story on Chemikal Underground. So yeah, that did feel pretty horrible. But it was understandable.

Aidan Moffat (Arab Strap): But then Chemikal, who offered us a fraction of the money, said they would take us back. And so we went to Chemikal, just because we knew we would be happier there. And then the album we did with Chemikal, *The Red Thread,* did really well in Europe, not least because we'd done that big tour.

Malcolm Middleton (Arab Strap): It was great when we returned. I think we did a John Peel night at the Garage by way of an announcement. And a Tennent's Brewery tour. I think we'd gotten our cake and eaten it, and then gone back for some biscuits. That's what it felt like. We'd all stayed friends but it was nice to hang around in their office again and not feel like a dick.

Aidan Moffat (Arab Strap): There wasn't any hard feelings [with Go! Beat], there wasn't any battling, it just wasn't suited to my way of working and Malcolm's ways of working. It just wasn't us. We would much rather be involved with decisions like the *Q* ad thing. . . It was great being on a major label for a bit. They afforded us things that we could never have done on an independent label.

Mogwai record their second album then also leave Chemikal Underground

Mogwai recorded Come On Die Young, *their second album, with Chemikal. It is often regarded as their masterpiece. But they were also lured away.*

Stewart Henderson (bass, The Delgados; Chemikal Underground): It was a tricky time. Generally speaking it all ended amicably. Mogwai left after *Come On Die Young*, because while they could have stayed on at Chemikal, I think in retrospect they were perfectly within their rights to leave and go to another label and have more resources put into them. That's fine. And likewise with Arab Strap, it's just one of these things. Over time you look back on it and it's like who cares? It is what it is. But at the time it's quite a fraught process. You feel like you've put a lot into it, you put a lot into their career. But it was okay, we were happy with it.

Stuart Braithwaite (guitar/vocals, Mogwai): We had a lot of momentum. We were very passionate about our music, we still are, but especially back then I think that we were probably a little bit cocky as well. So probably thinking yeah of course people think it's good. [Laughs.] We were just a bunch of wee dicks. But yeah, it was a very exciting time. And I think the whole thing with the first album being a bit shambolic, we wanted to do the opposite thing with the next one. We really rehearsed that one to death, and demoed it and all that kind of stuff, and ended up going to America and recording it with Dave Fridmann, who'd just made *Deserter's Songs* by Mercury Rev, which we all really loved.

Paul Savage (drums, The Delgados; Chemikal Underground): Mogwai were quite a demanding band, and rightly so because they are incredible. But they're not the type of people to just go, yeah, do whatever you fancy. There was a certain amount of expectation that we would push. The campaign for *Come On Die Young* was so ambitious, and so costly – I can't put figures on it, because we had problems in the early 2000s when we had to sort ourselves out. And we probably realised that we'd spent most of the profit that we had in the first five years on maybe thinking that we were a major label with ultimate control. Putting these really weird and wonderful and homegrown records out, but going, we want to deliver it to lots of people. And we weren't a major label.

We weren't necessarily being wasteful with money, but we were certainly stretching what an indie label would do. I can totally see why Factory Records went bust. You get a little bit of success with a band, Happy Mondays for instance, for them, I think they notoriously were the ones that broke them. I wouldn't say any band in particular was the cause of any problems that we subsequently had. We luckily never went under. But the point is that we started to – we were so pushed and spread, with the label, with the band – we lost sight of some bills that we had to pay, or maybe once a whole campaign comes to an end, and you've got a profit and a loss, and the expenditure is way more than it probably should have [been]. There was a period where we had to learn from those mistakes, and to survive we had to change a few things. But the one thing I would say is that Mogwai and Arab Strap probably benefitted quite a lot from that – our taking the eye off the financial ball.

Stuart Braithwaite (vocals/guitar, Mogwai): It was that kind of idea that if you go to a bigger label, you'll do better. Which isn't actually true. [Laughs.] PIAS, the label we signed to, are great too; I'm not saying anything mean about them at all. But I'm sure we'd have done just as well if we'd stayed on Chemikal. There's always an idea that if someone's got more money, the more money you spend on something, the better it's going to do. And it's not always the case, especially with a band like ours, which is kind of weird. If you said to your average man or woman in the street, what do you think of this? They're not going to go, 'Oh I've never heard that, why are they not as big as, I don't know, Muse?' Most people would probably think it was a bit odd. But that probably didn't occur to us at the time.

Paul Savage (drums, The Delgados; Chemikal Underground): Maybe Mogwai's management and all these people that were in the industry going, right we're fucking having this for *Come On Die Young*. This is going to be huge. So we thought, we're going to show people how to release an independent record with clout, with creativity. . . The teaser ad for *Come On Die Young* that just said 'Come On, Die Young'. A black ad for flyposting in London. So for two weeks before the next wave of ads came out, all over London in places where you could flypost, there was this thing that said, 'Come On, Die Young' and didn't mention Mogwai. So that was the idea: you 'tease' people – like, what does that mean? Next it was 'Mogwai' with the same font, and the date. And then the third one was the full poster with Dominic's face on it. And it was like, major label shit. We were throwing money away at this, because we knew that you've got to do it, this is going to be an important record. They got front cover of the *NME* at that point. They were headlining the John Peel stage at Glastonbury. They were doing a headline tent, or headline stage at Glastonbury. It was just all going well for them. And we were about to almost mortgage the houses to make sure that this happened. Like, right, we're all in – we'll do it, we'll do it. We didn't mortgage the houses but you know what I mean. It was like, we'll go with this because we were being assured by everybody that it's worth it. And hopefully the band will see it and they'll go, you guys are great. We're gonna stick with you. Unfortunately that didn't happen. But I don't blame them and we still have a great relationship with them and a lot of respect for them.

CHAPTER TWENTY-SEVEN

Another Generation 2

Huckleberry

Huckleberry had started to release singles as far back as 1996 but by 1998 had become one of Edinburgh's more prominent independent bands.

Vic Galloway (vocals/guitar, Huckleberry): Huckleberry was formed in Edinburgh in 1995/1996 by James Wright (now known as songwriter James Yorkston) on bass guitar and backing vocals, Reuben Taylor on organ and keys, Dave Simandi on drums and myself on main vocals and guitar. (I'm now a BBC broadcaster of twenty-seven years.) Dave was replaced on drums by Stuart Bastiman after the first Huckleberry release, the 'Halo Jones' EP. We would then go on to release the 'Idiot Listening' EP and an album called *Hard Luck Stories* – all on Edinburgh-based independent label, Copper Records. Huckleberry also home-recorded extensively and made many more albums-worth of unreleased music. We played highly melodic, organ-driven, garage rock with punk, prog and pop flourishes, and as a band we were trying to push things in terms of songwriting and LIVE performance. We definitely stood out from the crowd at the time. I suppose sixties Nuggets, psychedelia, Cardiacs, The Damned, The Kinks and the big man, Johan Sebastian Bach, were on the playlist, alongside everything that was being released at the time.

James, Stuart and I had previously been in an Edinburgh band called Miraclehead from 1991 – our first band out of school – who played a frenetic type of punk-funk influenced by Nomeansno, fIREHOSE and, dare I say it, (early) Red Hot Chili Peppers! We built up a sizeable following in Edinburgh and could fill The Venue by the end of our lifespan. Latterly we had also started veering away from the 'funk' side of things, and begun to write more classic-sounding songs in the vein of XTC, Madness and The Kinks. Naturally, as with so many other groups, the band imploded as we peaked in popularity and went our separate ways in 1994. Stuart and I hooked up with Kenny Anderson (King Creosote) and played with Khartoum Heroes, James formed an acoustic punk band called Agapapa, while singer Cliff Simms stopped making music altogether.

James and I soon reignited our friendship and met in pubs, talking loosely about forming a Violent Femmes-esque acoustic punk band with both of us writing songs. Soon we became slightly more ambitious and developed stylistically, so we brought in virtuoso organist and keyboard player, Reuben Taylor, who had been recommended to us. I'd once seen him in an acid-jazz-style band called Hot Sausage, and knew how good he was. With Dave Simandi, fresh from the band Wonderboy Buckley, on drums; we started writing, rehearsing, gigging and eventually went on to record the 'Halo Jones' EP, which was then released on Copper Records.

Being from Edinburgh was probably a hindrance for Huckleberry. Glasgow has always been, and probably will always be, the epicentre of music and pop culture in Scotland. Edinburgh shone for a while post-punk, and has had all sorts of success stories throughout the years, including some legendary acts such as Incredible String Band, Fire Engines, Rezillos, Exploited, Idlewild, Boards of Canada and Young Fathers. Although we love Edinburgh with all our hearts, ultimately it probably didn't produce the quality and consistency needed to break through at the time. Glasgow has a far larger population and a local music culture that promotes and encourages people to form and play in bands. It also has the infrastructure of music venues, managers, publishers, promoters, agents, clubs and industry, in a size and volume that Edinburgh simply doesn't. . . or didn't. I think things are slowly changing, and Edinburgh is holding its own more now but in the nineties it was all about the Bellshill bands, Chemikal Underground and the Soma clubbing scenes. All of which were great, but didn't include an organ-driven garage rock band from Auld Reekie. We [Huckleberry], and almost all other bands outside of Glasgow, were kind of excluded at the time by the media and industry. We couldn't get arrested in the west!

The band with James, Stu, Reuben and I lasted until around 1999, when things started to splinter. We had officially released two EPs, a full-length album, two singles and various B-sides. We'd been played by John Peel and Steve Lamacq, performed at the Transmusicales festival in Brittany, toured across France, played Reading Festival and T in the Park, supported Carter USM on tour, and joined a *Melody Maker* 'Maker Breaker' tour. We did our absolute best to break through to a bigger audience, but it wasn't to be. Ironically, the 'Maker Breaker' tour actually broke us, and James left shortly afterwards. I look back on our music quite fondly, although I generally think James's songs were better than mine, to be honest!

I was lucky enough to join the BBC as a presenter on a new BBC Radio 1 show, *The Session in Scotland*, with co-presenter Gill Mills. I would then move on to presenting weekly shows on BBC Radio Scotland, BBC 6 Music and the World Service, as well as doing various TV programmes. I've also become a music journalist and written two books so far. James would go solo and sign to Domino Records as James Yorkston and is having a brilliant career, with a string of superb, acclaimed albums right up to this date. Reuben would go on to play on the first two JY albums in The Athletes, and has played with other bands including Meursault and Storm the Palace. Stuart left Huckleberry and joined various groups including Rancher, The Serial P.O.P and Clean George IV – making superb music, but to no tangible success. He also played on the U.N.P.O.C album *Fifth Column*, released on Domino, and now runs a brilliant restaurant in Somerset.

Reuben and I continued with Huckleberry for a while with heavy-hitter Cymon Aretz on drums and Paul Mustarde's brother Steve on bass. The music got heavier, proggier and more riff-based, while keeping the garage feel and the melodic suss. We had a song included on the 'Rock Mess Monsters' compilation, but eventually changed our name (as bands tend to do) to Hail Caesar! and my brother Alan Galloway replaced Steve on bass. From there, we had a second lease of life in a way. One day we got the call, asking us to support The Damned at the Liquid Rooms in Edinburgh. They had been childhood heroes of James and I, growing up in Fife; and our very first LIVE concert as kids was seeing The Damned in Edinburgh Playhouse on 1 June 1985 – it is still etched into our DNA to this day.

In a way it was unsurprising that The Damned, especially Captain Sensible and Dave Vanian, loved our band! Maybe it was their influence on us, or our love of sixties garage and psych, but we ended up supporting them both as (late period) Huckleberry and Hail Caesar! in Edinburgh on various occasions and even in the Glasgow Academy once. I personally have got to know them a little too. Mind-blowing for a young me! Fast forward to 2016 and I even made a documentary for BBC 6 Music on them called 'New Rose & 40 Years of The Damned'

After gigging further across the UK and playing Alan McGee's 'Death Disco' club in Notting Hill Arts club, Hail Caesar! called it a day around 2002/2003. It just kinda fizzled, and all momentum was lost. We're all still involved in making music and we're all still mates, thankfully. Looking back, it was (mostly) a lot of fun!

Copper Records

Vic Galloway (vocals/guitar, Huckleberry): Copper Records was set up by an entrepreneurial friend of ours called Paul Mustarde. He had no previous experience of the music industry, but had been a fan of Miraclehead and then Huckleberry, and decided to invest some money into starting a label. He signed Huckleberry and another futuristic trip-hop band called Petrol 3 (formerly The Fugue). Paul worked hard and attempted to scale the peaks and troughs of the music industry with an ambitious, independent label. However, being based in Edinburgh and with two groups who weren't part of the 'zeitgeist', it was tricky for him and eventually he threw in the towel and left Edinburgh for

New Zealand, and eventually the south of England, for a quiet life. In some ways, no-one could blame him! It's a thankless task running a label, pouring loads of your own money, time and effort into a bottomless pit.

Amphetameanies

Gordon (Gordy) Davidson was still running F&J, as he does to this day. He followed The Stanleys/Tonic with a vastly different band: The Amphatemeanies. The band had a huge revolving roster of members over the years, which included Alex Kapranos from The Karelia and Jane Chalmers from Pink Kross.

Jane Chalmers (vocals, Pink Cross and The Amphetameanies): I was in The Amphetameanies for twenty years, from 1997 onwards. . . so it was concurrent to Pink Kross. We used to say I was 'on loan' to The Amphetameanies when they asked me to join them. It was always the side project, but then it lasted ages. It was great fun, there hadn't been a ska band in Glasgow or Scotland for quite a time when we started. We had a lot of members, but for the first seven or so years there really wasn't a lot of personnel changes. The gigs were brilliant fun, as it was just great to have people dancing to your tunes.

Gordy Davidson (The Amphetameanies): Misremembering as I may well be, there was one grey afternoon when myself, Alex, Stan [Millar] and a few others of the great unsigned remainder, were sat in the 13th Note contemplating our fates. Tuesday Kazoo gigs were still happening, as were nights at its Thursday satellite, 'the 99p Club', and there were plenty of bands coming forward, but maybe there was a slight feeling that the eclectic tide upon which Urusei, bis, the Bellenders, the 'Gwai had risen had begun to recede, leaving us back in our own wee rock pool.

In '96 I turned 30. In my head, that was the magic line where there was no longer any point even attempting the 'studied cool' expected of an aspiring indie star. Fuck it, I said, let's start a ska band, have a bit of fun for a change.

Now, ska wasn't a verboten topic among the Kazoo crowd, at least not my end of it, 'cause two-tone had always been my thing. I battered on about it relentlessly, and any time anyone left a stereo unattended at a party, I'd sneak some on. And, of course, in our parallel life as scooterboys, myself and Shane and Stan heard a lot of it, as the national scooter rallies round the English seaside towns, and the Scottish scooter club dances around the miners' welfares and first division football ground function rooms of the central belt, thrived on DJs who strictly adhered to the formula of playing three 2Tone/Trojan tracks, followed by three Northern Soul tracks, followed by three mod-revival numbers, followed by three psychobilly or old punk tunes, then back to 2Tone/Trojan and repeat.

That dance-orientated sixties and seventies melee had all been as much a part of our social life as the Kazoo, and the likes of Helen and Tracy and Alex had come along to dabble in that with us. . . but it hadn't ever crossed onto the Kazoo stage.

But the magic ingredient in the 'Meanies was Joel Gray. He'd been there all along. . . working behind the bar at the 13th Note, but keeping quiet, musically. He must have seen many of those Kazoo gigs, probably more than me, doing shifts pouring pints. Stan and I had been vaguely aware that Joel's past life had included being drummer in a Glasgow ska band called Capone and the Bullets, who'd been quite a force in the early eighties. They'd been a very convincing two-tone outfit at a time when the original two-tone bands had more or less moved on, but there was still a big crowd for a multi-racial band with suits and saxophones and shouty bits. But Capone's original line-up had dissolved in acrimony, and Joel wasn't playing for anyone. So after a few weeks of whispering among ourselves, me and Stan sidled up the Note bar, and asked Joel if he fancied joining our ska band, although we'd never actually played ska ourselves, so what we were really asking was, can you join our band and help make it ska. Of course he could. Joel played offbeat drums completely naturally. It was his rhythm, and he could circle round a big ska jam forever, with a great dancing beat and lovely fills at just the right spots.

Unfortunately for him, the musical brains of the 'Meanies were never gonna tolerate big ska jams, and he ended up having to cope with some very fast songs, with timing changes and some very odd stops and starts, so it was an achievement that he kept the songs danceable despite the songwriters' best efforts to complicate things.

The line-up of the 'Meanies that emerged. . . Joel, Stan singing alongside Jane from Pink Kross, Alex on keys, Stevie Jones on rhythm, Rat on lead, me on bass, Jenny from Ex Cathedra on sax, then very shortly after we started, Mick Cooke from the Bellends on trumpet and Lindsey 'Meanie on trombone, then Helen muscling in on keys. . . was just a great combination of people. Several natural comedians, several brilliant songwriters, several really good musicians, and enough previous history so there were friendships in there that'd been through a few bands already, and a certain amount of wisdom regarding inter-band diplomacy.

From the first gig, it just took off. We debuted downstairs at the 13th Note, possibly at one of the 99p club nights, alongside Bangtwister I think, and all we had was a few covers. . . 'Last Night' by the Mar-Keys, with the traditional scooterboy singalong of 'Bollocks!' at the top of every bar, The Specials' 'Stupid Marriage', a Pietasters cover. . . and a few half-finished tunes of our own, but it went off, as the saying goes, like a box of fucking firecrackers.

We'd told some of the scooterboys what was coming, so they'd jumped the invisible fence to come down and see us, and actually danced, which was not something that generally happened at Kazoo scene gigs. I remember us all squeezed into the beer cupboard 'dressing room' right afterwards, all sweating and high as kites that we'd got such a reaction. There was no doubt at that point that this thing, which had very much been a last experimental throw of the dice for me, was going to continue.

Alex had been an enthusiastic supporter of the project, 'cause he wanted to do all that Jerry Dammers swirly wonky Hammond keyboard stuff, but also 'cause it was a whole new sandpit for him to play in musically. He'd had a trumpet player in The Blisters, but he'd been there as a soloist, and that hadn't gone too well, as I remember. And The Stanleys had a trombonist, but never a clear idea of why. But with the 'Meanies, we had this brass section, under Mick who was already a strong musical arranger, who weren't there to show off individually, but loved playing tight interlocking section stuff.

Initially, songs got written at practices, so there were big sprawling things like 'Ghost Bus' and 'Arizona Highway Patrol', bolted-together collections of parts contributed by everyone as they got used to playing in this style.

But then Alex wrote us a new song called 'Last Night' that was a simple wee thing which put that brass section in the spotlight and it worked beautifully. . . Then Mick rose to the challenge and wrote pop songs, 'Driving Home' and 'Life Without You', with big brass section parts, and Alex and Jane came back with '60 hours in Albuquerque' and pretty soon we had a setlist of our own stuff that stood on its own with no need for two-tone nostalgia.

The gigs got bigger and bigger, and we couldn't really sensibly play the Note given the boisterous crowd we were getting, so we'd often do Sleazy's, then King Tut's; and when you do well at Tut's for a few gigs in a row, the promoter, DF, starts considering you for other stuff.

While we were getting a lot of skinheads and punks, there were also lots of indie kids turning up, 'cause the 'Meanies had that heritage, so it was never a threatening crowd, and brought together some previously disparate scenes. . . bits of the Kazoo, bits of the old ska'n'scooter scene, the southside punks. . . with no one being particularly precious about the old conventions of each, 'cause we were just having a bit of a post-modern party with all of it.

I do remember though that some of our old Kazoo counterparts might have been a bit sniffy about it. . . we'd played the ska card. It was like interrupting a serious seven-year game of Dungeons and Dragons by pulling out a water pistol.

Equally, folk like Belle and Sebastian were very generous with their support. Stuart Murdoch had been a wee Specials fan himself, and we got a slot at the first Bowlie Weekender (which became All Tomorrow's Parties) down on the south coast at some holiday park or other. That was indie ground zero. We were on before The Flaming Lips, for fuck's sake.

Then some of the band and hangers-on totally disgraced themselves around the chalets. Pinging butter at passers-by with breadknives. Climbing on the roofs. All good clean fun.

I remember driving back up from that, on the motorway, in a hired minibus, we got synchronised with The Pastels, who were folk we really didn't know, them having been the generation just before us, but their van was similarly underpowered, so there was miles and miles of us overtaking them, very slowly, with two-fingered gestures, then them getting up an extra half-mile-an-hour of speed and overtaking us, reciprocating on the gestures of victory. That helped pass a long journey.

The Belles had us back to a Bowlie in 2010, when All Tomorrow's Parties brought them in as 'curators'. I think we were maybe a bit more civilised by then. That would almost certainly be one of the numerous occasions when Alex jumped back onstage with us for 'Last Night', to show off how much better he could play the guitar solo by then.

John Disco [Clark] from bis had joined us maybe 2002, after Alex had indicated he might miss the next couple of dozen or so practices 'cause he'd be busy with his side project. Disco fitted in great from the outset. By the time Alex bowed out, we'd already lost Rat on lead, as he was working very hard as Craig Tannock's right-hand-man during an expansion of the Note empire, so John sort of slotted into the triple role of being the band's sense of humour and rhythm and lead.

In that era, bis had their wee 7A studio up in a converted council shed near the river in Cathcart, so we got to record there, and the Belles, with a lot of drive from Mick, had turned their offices and practice room up Finnieston's Hidden Lane into a proper recording studio, so we could record there too, if we didn't make a mess. Or at least, if I cleaned up any 'Meanies mess before any Belles spotted it.

A bit like the early Kazoo, we just took all this for granted. OF COURSE we can draw hundreds of folk to our gigs. OF COURSE our pals all have recording studios. OF COURSE we can stand there playing a song written by the guy from Franz Ferdinand, with a brass arrangement by the guy from the Bellends, and the guy from bis throwing cool guitar shapes stage right. Another blessed era.

There was a gig up the Art School Vic bar, I can't recall the occasion, but Disco was well settled in by then, we were on form, and both Alex and Stuart Murdoch were there, quite well-known chaps by that time, dancing down the front, with a big semicircle of folk behind them, watching their moves, rather than watching us. But that was alright. It was still the scene, the same camaraderie it had all started with, and it was great to look out on your pals, famous as fuck, dancing about to my donkey bass playing.

CHAPTER TWENTY-EIGHT

A Happy Ending

The Delgados: *The Great Eastern*

The Great Eastern sleeve

The disappointment of losing two of their star bands had been frustrating for Chemikal Underground, amplified by their disappointment at the reception for The Delgados' own previous album, Peloton, *two years earlier. But the band's fortunes were about to change as they harnessed the determination they had drawn on to steer bis, Mogwai and Arab Strap towards success for their own band.* The Great Eastern *is rightly regarded as their great achievement, both commercially and critically. Though it was not an easy album to create.*

Stewart Henderson (bass, The Delgados; Chemikal Underground): We threw everything into *The Great Eastern*, we really did. And I think there was a sense that – Mogwai had left, Arab Strap had left – it was probably going to be the last record we were going to do. It felt like we were approaching the end of something. And it turned out it wasn't. But it was one of those records that was borne out of a very tumultuous period for the label and for the four of us, personally, individually. The four of us often bore the brunt of it, and there was a lot of projection that went on, I think a lot of the stresses and strains of the label. We often took it out on each other a wee bit. So personally it was quite a hard time for all of us making the record, keeping everything moving forward. It wasn't always the easiest, I have to say.

Emma Pollock (vocals/guitar, The Delgados; Chemikal Underground): We recorded the songs but we just couldn't get the mix right. And this was all at CaVa, this was all in Glasgow where we recorded *Peloton* – the whole thing in CaVa; recorded and mixed in CaVa. *Domestiques* was recorded at CHEM19, or what was MCM at the time. But with *The Great Eastern* we had the songs [recorded at CaVa] but we weren't getting the mix right. And we remembered that Dave Fridmann had said the only thing wrong with *Peloton* was that he didn't make it. And so we reached out. I mean, that's a way to get a band to come in. If you want to court some business

Paul Savage (drums, The Delgados; Chemikal Underground): Although we had convinced people that [*Peloton*] was worth listening to, to an extent, we've never reached a mainstream audience. We kept on having people at the time saying, this is it, this is going to break, it's going to be huge. We were always proud of the records but they never seemed to transpire (how we wanted them to). But working with Dave (Fridmann) was great because we couldn't afford him for *Peloton.* We had already gone down a pathway, I think we were already recording at CaVa with Tony and it was just a little late. But when it came to *The Great Eastern,* we got to work with him. But also, before *The Great Eastern,* Mogwai were saying, we want to get away from Glasgow to record. We want to record with someone else. Do you have anybody in mind? And we said, actually we've just been contacted by Dave Fridmann. So we could maybe hook you up with Dave Fridmann. Maybe he could do your next one. And they were like, yeah, that sounds great. So they started a relationship with Dave after the contact that we had after the *Peloton* Peel Sessions. They went over [to the US] and worked with Dave and said, oh he's great.

We kept in contact with Dave and then when it came to finally mixing *The Great Eastern,* we took it over to him. We needed to because we were really stuck with it in Glasgow. We felt that we couldn't see what was going on. It was such an ambitious record, but we couldn't do it. . . And the weird thing is that the people that went to Dave to mix the record – and when I tell people this, to this day, they go, 'This is really bonkers, you guys are weird' – were myself and Tony and Stewart the bass player. Alun and Emma didn't go over. They weren't part of the mix. So the drummer, the bass player, and the engineer from Glasgow went to Dave's for two weeks and drank beer and listened, poked our head in and went, 'Fucking hell Dave, that sounds amazing.' And then went back to drinking beer.

Emma Pollock (vocals/guitar, The Delgados; Chemikal Underground): Stuart and Paul took all the reels over on the plane. And Tony Doogan, who recorded it. And they mixed it at Tarbox, and he [Dave Fridmann] did an absolutely wonderful job. And he would send over these mixes by post. And we would listen to them, Alun and I, and marvel at how fucking bold Dave's mixing was. And then talk about it over the phone. Yeah, it was an amazing experience. That's how [Dave] got involved. He did an astonishing job. And then of course the same with *Hate.* It's a kind of post-mixing production rather than a full – I mean, it'd be dead interesting to record from start to finish with Dave Fridmann. I wonder if one day we might have the opportunity. We'd all have to save up our pennies I think. But that would be an amazing thing to do.

The Great Eastern *wasn't just a critical success; it elevated The Delgados to the mainstream – and secured them a Mercury nomination.*

Stewart Henderson (bass, The Delgados; Chemikal Underground): It's not always cool to say it's important to get these kinds of nominations. But at that time it was really important for us. I think we'd maybe sold about 14,000 copies of *The Great Eastern.* And then the Mercury nomination came along, and it kicked it up to about 25–30,000. So it made a huge difference just in terms of the amount of people that bought the record, or the amount of people that had heard of the band. Ancillary benefits that came along were you got a slot on *Later* with Jools Holland. You get your fifteen minutes of fame with it. And it was important. It was also fortunate and early enough to at a time in the industry where the multiplier effect of these nominations was still in place. I think you could probably get a Mercury nomination now and it wouldn't make a blind bit of fucking difference in terms of how many records you might sell. So that's changed, but that's just the nature of things now. At the time it was a big thing. It came along at a time when the label needed it as well. Financially, economically, it was important. And it was also quite nice – again, fuck it, it's true. I can't speak for Alun, Paul or Emma. But at the time with Arab Strap and Mogwai and their successes, it felt good for The Delgados to get told that we were good as well. It was, for me.

'The release of The Great Eastern was a high benchmark of Scottish independent label success.

Stewart Henderson (bass, The Delgados; Chemikal Underground): It's a record I'm proud of and it's nice to look back on it. And you realise again, it still fell within that five-year period of the start of the label. It was a fucking crazy five years. Absolutely crazy five years. I think we got the nomination in June of 2000. 'Monica Webster' came out in February '95. It's nuts what happened in those five years.

Paul Savage (drums, The Delgados; Chemikal Underground): It was an incredible time. I don't think we realised what we were doing and what was happening. We were trying to keep hold of the bands; we thought we'd done a great job with all of those records. We felt, in some ways, vindicated that they had chosen Chemikal Underground. Certainly, Mogwai could have been on any label in the UK at the time. And they chose to come with us.

Stewart Henderson (bass, The Delgados; Chemikal Underground): I think Mogwai have extended levels of courtesy and patience to us as a record label that we frankly wouldn't have been able to survive without; they're incredible. The same with Arab Strap. I just think it's not honest to have these conversations and not accept the fact that there were tensions at the time. How on earth couldn't there be? I wouldn't want to overblow them, but I wouldn't want to sweep them under the carpet and pretend they didn't exist either. . . It's difficult because you've got a lot of different dynamics at play at the same time. You have the successes of both of those bands, the more modest successes of The Delgados, who also happened, ironically, to be their label bosses, for want of a better word.

So you've got all these kinds of tensions and dynamics at play. You've got the coaxing away of bands from Chemikal Underground – 'Well, hey, look what you've done with Chemikal, can you imagine what you would do if you fucking came to us?' So you've got a lot of honey, a lot of white being whispered in people's ears. You've also got the tensions that we will have had with them as artists. We weren't able to say yes to everything that they wanted to do. You've got costs and budgets; you have to say, I know you want to do that but we really think it would be better if you do this. . . You put a lot into their career. And it was okay, we were happy with it but I know that we delayed going into the studio to do *Peloton* so that we could put out the Mogwai record. So, selflessly as a band, as The Delgados, we made sacrifices for the sake of other bands. But as it should have been, for the greater good, because these bands were bigger than we were and it was important that we did commercially as well as we could. So I suppose really that for a label like Chemikal Underground to have gone through those five years and to have reached that pinnacle – the fifth birthday party at The Garage, John Peel DJing at it – it was pretty much the pinnacle of where Chemikal Underground had gone. And Mogwai had already left I think by that point; Arab Strap had gone as well. Or were they back? I fucking can't even remember.

It was a period of upheaval for us to have got to where we got, to see Mogwai move off the label, to see Arab Strap move off the label. And again, it was one of those those key moments that I've talked about: there are certain things that happened with Chemikal Underground that were really important. It just so happened that after Mogwai and Arab Strap left, we had the success that we had with *The Great Eastern*. That was a really important moment. For us. For me personally, I felt it was something that I really needed. That The Delgados had a little spell in the spotlight, that we felt that we'd made our mark with that record, and I'm still proud of it.

Paul Savage (drums, The Delgados; Chemikal Underground): Those first five years, there were monumental changes happening every month. It was such a weird period and to think about any five years subsequent to that, it has nothing near the amount of huge occurrences. Hear ourselves getting played on the John Peel Show for the first time, our first Peel Session was a big moment. I suppose the context is important. The biggest things aren't necessarily always the biggest in your mind, or the most important. Although the Mercury's something that we can have a discussion about with somebody who doesn't really understand the music that we put out. Or, you know, an auntie and uncle, when they ask about what have you done – are you still in that wee band? Which we used to get in our twenties: 'Have you not got a proper job yet?' I could say, well, we've been nominated for a Mercury Music Prize, or we played *Later with Jools Holland.* And those couple of things would be like, oh right okay, well I'll let you off the hook for another couple of years. But if you don't get to Number 1 soon I'm gonna start calling you a waster. It's the way that people identify things like Mercury prizes and *Later*, where they maybe don't understand hearing your first single getting played on Radio Scotland by Peter Easton is equally as big.

Stewart Henderson (bass, The Delgados; Chemikal Underground): I remember saying to Alun at the back of the tour bus at the time when we were putting out all these records, 'Running a record label is a fucking doddle.' [Laughs.] 'It's an absolute piece of piss, if we'd fucking known it was going to be as easy as this we should have done it years ago.' Little did I know, obviously, how things were going to go. It did feel like there were other forces at work, not that we realised it at the time, but I think anyone with an interest in the historical landscape of the music industry and how things go, will recognise 2000 and 2001, the turn of the millennium, as being like a pivotal moment – all just starting – it was all in the foothills. You had Napster, MySpace was starting to come around, you had the whole digital thing with iTunes and the iPod; all these things were starting to come along. And obviously we've been talking about that five years from 1995 to 2000; the next five years to 2005 (up to the point when we called it a day actually as a band), you had the beginning of the change of the industry transitioning out of the whole analogue thing and into the foothills of the digital landscape. All the social media stuff. We split up in 2005 and I think Twitter and Facebook were launched 2005–2006, round about that time. The industry, not that we realised it at the time, was going through a real revolutionary process – the whole of society was.

The twenty or twenty-five years that Chemikal Underground has been going really straddled that analogue/digital switch. The kind of explosive growth and all of the landmark moments that we've talked about that happened in those five years [1995–2000], would have been diluted immeasurably if they'd happened five years later. You've got all of these things that have happened in your life, it's great they happened, they happened out of things being good and being worthy of attention, but you realise it's so much to do with timing. Timing is fucking everything. If everything had started five years later, if 'Monica Webster' had come out in 2000, it would have been a different story entirely.

Our timeline finishes there, with the ascendence of Chemikal, and The Delgados rightly receiving recognition in the shape of a Mercury nomination. It was richly deserved after they had done so much to help their friends and colleagues. Mogwai, Arab

Strap and Belle and Sebastian would all go on to have more than two decades of success, and to this day continue to make great music.

But there is another happy ending in a perfect example of how good things happen to good people.

CHAPTER TWENTY-NINE

Another Happy Ending

The birth of Franz Ferdinand

Alex Kapranos from the Kazoo Club, who had spent so many years nourishing and developing other people's talent, went on to huge international success with Franz Ferdinand. As we started this book with an extended section on Craig Tannock, it feels appropriate to end on an extended section on the birth of Franz Ferdinand.

John McKeown (vocals/guitar, The Yummy Fur): When I was about 17 or 18 I was at a party and I played in a band, that were like Sonic Youth, sort of late eighties. And we were playing some demo we'd made, and a girl said to me: 'You have got the worst singing voice I've ever heard in my entire life. It's so awful.' Thanks a lot. And I never sang again. I never even tried to sing again until about the mid-2000s, with The 1990s. I honestly took that to heart and just thought well, I guess I can't sing. I knew I could shout like The Fall. You know, I knew I could do that Fire Engine stuff but I'd never even tried. I remember we were in the studio – we did a 7-inch called 'Stereo Girls' and on the back was a cover of 'Always

Crashing in the Same Car' by Bowie. And I remember trying to sing it, and Alex was going, 'You're singing it really, really good; you're singing it in tune, it's fine.' But I felt really self-conscious and I thought I can't – I ended up, like, scared of it. Scared of singing. But Alex was not like that. Nobody told Alex when he was 15 or 16 that he couldn't sing and he sang beautifully. And he strapped his voice to strong melodies, vocal melodies. I just thought if you shouted 'Policeman!', with catchy guitar, that was catchy enough. No, you really needed to sing something. So he did that. Franz Ferdinand is like. . . I can imagine if we'd grown up a wee bit, we may have ended up in that zone. But I'm happy that he did it, otherwise I'd have spread myself too thin. I don't want to include his success in my CV!

I remember after The Yummy Fur and they had Franz and we formed a band called The Mars Hotel. I think their [Franz Ferdinand's] second gig was with us at Flourish Studio and I remember thinking they were alright. I thought they were okay. They just seemed like an indie band. I thought we were better. And that we were much more likely to do well. Turns out nobody liked us at all, and everybody loved them. Not that night, but a few weeks later. And then by the time 'Darts of Pleasure' came out I think it was clear that they were going to do really well. But when 'Take Me Out' was in the charts, it wasn't Number 1 was it? It was Number 2 or so? But it might as well have been Number 1. And I'd just come through a divorce. I was working in Safeway, next to Central Station. Everybody in the place was walking about humming 'Take Me Out', and I was at my lowest of the low and I think I actually remember Alex coming to visit me, or he came in anyway – bumped into me while I was working, stacking shelves. It could not have got more low. I've nothing against the tune, I knew it was a good tune, but I just thought – just fuck off. [Laughs.]

As Stewart Henderson discussed earlier, the music industry was at the end of an era. Not just the Glasgow music scene but the entire industry was about to go through another change – and Franz Ferdinand were at the front of the queue.

Their story begins in an abandoned Glasgow warehouse that hosted parties, art installations and early gigs.

Alex Kapranos (vocals/guitar, Franz Ferdinand): It sounds like a cliché saying it now but you always read about other people's scenes and think it sounds so much more exciting than your own because it's of a time and place which are impossible to visit. I was obsessed with Berlin, and I was obsessed with New York. The idea of Warhol's Factory, or that Lower East Side scene of the late seventies. I'd be reading about people talking about the lofts that they had and the things that would happen; you could just have this space. I wanted to do something like that. I didn't know exactly what it was but that was the inspiration. This idea that we could take it over and make it something that didn't have to fit in with the conventions of what was expected of a live performance.

Alex took inspiration from what he saw in New York when he returned to Glasgow.

Alex Kapranos (vocals/guitar, Franz Ferdinand): There were lots of artists that we knew who were looking for places to work, so one floor was given over to them. The upper floor was kept for the music. The idea was that we had bands performing and people showing their work. Very good artists as well; really strong artists.

It felt exciting again, for the same reasons that the 13th Note scene had seemed exciting, which was: potential. There's nothing more thrilling than knowing something exciting, something with substance is happening, but you don't know what it is yet. It's one of the most thrilling experiences you can have in your life. Being in a situation where you know all your senses are tingling, it's about to happen. It can happen when you're writing a song, it can happen when you're playing with people for the first time, it can happen when you go and see a performance for the first time. Particularly, it happens when you have a combination of personalities at a particular time and place where you just know it's gelignite. It's going to explode, something is going to happen here and you don't know what it's going to be. You don't know if it's going to be a massive mess, or whether something great is going to come out of it. The idea of trying to predict what's going to come out of it is perverse. You've just got to wait and see what happens. That's what it felt like at that time in the early 2000s.

As with the Kazoo Club nearly a decade earlier, this new scene spread throughout the city, most memorably at one of the empty building parties.

Alex Kapranos (vocals/guitar, Franz Ferdinand): Word had got around and maybe there was a little bit of a buzz happening around Franz Ferdinand at that time. People were coming down and it was heaving with folk that night. I guess the police just watched people coming in. I thought we'd get away with it for a little bit longer. Because we didn't have a licence or anything, no licence to play music or anything like that. Somebody had told me that if you sold booze you could get away with it by making it a raffle. We'd bought a bunch of wine from somewhere like Lidl, so we were selling wine and beer but giving people raffle tickets. We'd decorated the place and found all this rope in the basement. We'd made nooses and they were hanging from one of those sprinkler systems with pipes running around over the ceiling. We didn't have any lighting but in the basement of this place, from one of the companies that had been there at one point in the early to mid eighties, it had a showroom or something for sunbeds. There were all these fluorescent sunbeds in the basement and we'd taken them all upstairs and lined them up at the back of what became the stage. We put them on their ends so they were like standing vertically up, and plugged them all in via four-ways connected to each other into this one socket that was illegally jumped. The whole thing was a fire hazard, it was terrible. We found that if you just turned the socket on and off, the fluorescent tubes randomly came on at different time intervals. It looked amazing. Eighty sunbeds, if you imagine, fucking hell – God knows what radiation was coming off those things. We literally had sunburn at the end of the gig.

We played. I've got a feeling Sons and Daughters might have played and Uncle John & Whitelock played as well. It was really great. But I think towards the end of Uncle John & Whitelock's set, the cops arrived. I remember these two cops burst in and there was one younger guy, I'm guessing in his late-twenties and an older guy, your archetypal tubby copper who was really pissed off, wheezing away having climbed up six flights of stairs. Furious, like who the fuck are these assholes, dragging me up all these flights of stairs. He was like, what the fuck's going on here, are you selling booze? What are all these tickets thrown on the floor, are you gambling as well? It was like, no, no, no, no – and then he goes, what the fuck is that? And points at the nooses. 'Is this some kind of perverse sado-masochism thing going on?' I was just stuck, like, oh no it's just a group of artists showing their art, like an art piece. The guy's like WHAT? And then the other cop just goes, oh you mean like a Richard Kern thing? I just remember looking at this cop, like whaaaat? Yes, exactly! So it was good cop, bad cop. We managed to talk them down; they didn't charge us with anything but they said that if they caught us there again, they would. So that's when we looked for another place. That's when Nick found the other place.

The next place [The Chateau] was the old East End CID police headquarters but it was built in the 19th century and it was quite a multitasking building. It was the police station, but it was also the courtroom. There were also cells, and there was also a morgue.

It was a very creative time. We used the courtroom as our studio and rehearsal space. Then it started raining and we discovered that it was completely useless and we were just getting soaked. We ended up using one of the cells, which if I remember rightly was ten foot long by seven feet wide. It was pretty small. We set the entire band up in this tiny little cell. I think we had a mattress in there to try and soak up the sound a little bit. I sometimes think that had a lot to do with the evolution of the band's sound, because when we were playing in the big courtroom it was very tempting to use the reverb and have lots and lots of space in the music. But then suddenly we're in this extremely enclosed space, very close to each other, and it made for this sound that no sustain to it, where everything is fast and repetitive rather than long, long tails. There was an immediate evolution in the sound as soon as we moved into that room. We started doing nights there as well. The first night we tried to do there, I got the Country Teasers up. They were in London at that time, so they were one of the bands I had in.

The intention of the band was part of a set of ideas that had evolved at that time. It was completely at odds with any idea of mainstream success; it wasn't until we did a gig in a mainstream venue that we actually had to get a name because there was a poster. Everything we'd done up until that point had been entirely by word of mouth. I love this idea of it all being word of mouth.

Simon Henderson was booking for this place that became The 78. It's in the West End, in Finnieston. It's a wee venue. It was called Way Out West. It was another place that was owned by Craig Tannock. Simon was involved in the latter stages of the GMC. Simon was booking the bands at that point, he'd seen us play and asked if we want to play The 78. We were like, I'm not sure if we're into playing real venues. But I liked Simon and he was a cool guy so we decided to play there. We needed a name, and that's how we ended up getting called Franz Ferdinand, because he needed to put a name on the poster.

We had no idea or drive to have commercial success. I'd presumed that that wasn't going to happen. Then word seemed to get around about the band. How did that happen? We'd done some recordings, in my flat and in Nick's flat. They were cool, the recordings were great. I think I'd realised. I'd found the recording experience with The Karelia not particularly satisfying – it didn't sound like how I wanted it to sound. Part of the evolution of what was happening at that time was, it was performing; recording as well within this context – the idea was we were going to build our own studio in one of these places and record ourselves. I'd had a few ideas and started my own production stuff with a few other recordings.

There was a period in the late 1990s, around 1998, when I was playing in The Yummy Fur. The Karelia was still going, but making a very different kind of music. I had the studio that I shared; I was really into the idea of having a studio and I guess that's where my interest in production developed to a certain degree as well. I wanted to continue that in among what we were doing with these old buildings. We imagined that we would record ourselves and maybe release something ourselves. I thought maybe we'll put out a 7-inch, and go about things that sort of way. Even though my experience of releasing things was not a particularly great one. Somebody would find somebody who might do it. Maybe Paul from Guided Missile. I'd been friendly with Paul, he'd released one song that was under the name of The Karelia, even though it wasn't really a Karelia song. It ended up on a version of our second album actually. Anyway, Paul was in the back of my mind, I liked Guided Missile. We thought we'd maybe do a single at some point and that we would record it.

We'd done these recordings in the flats and I'd given a burnt CD of these to my pal Todd, who had been the drummer of Lung Leg. He'd started a band called The Beatings – in the early 2000s there was that garage revival for a bit. The Datsuns, and

The Libertines were also part of that. Todd was in London, very much part of that scene. He'd got a manager and he played him the CD that I'd given him. Like, oh my pals in Glasgow have got this band together, they sound really good, I think you'd like them. This guy Cerne (Canning) got in touch with us straightaway and said, listen, I really like your band, maybe we can work together. I liked him, he seemed cool. I was suspicious at that time. I was suspicious of everybody in the music industry. I just didn't trust anybody in the music industry at all. Especially the London end of things, I was very anti-London. It even came through in some of the lyrics of the earliest songs: 'Shopping for Blood' has a very anti-London perspective. I think that was quite a Glasgow-wide perspective, not just at that time, but throughout the nineties as well. I think it informed a lot of what happened with those releases in the nineties. The formation of Chemikal Underground, it was this anti-London sentiment, this idea that it can be done up here.

I was a bit suspicious of meeting this London music industry guy. But I liked him straight away, I liked his enthusiasm. I guess I was doing what I'd always done, which is going on my instincts, the same thing I'd done when I booked the bands in the 13th Note.

I felt this guy was coming from the right end of things. Suddenly he connected the band with all these record labels that we hadn't even thought of approaching. That's how we ended up doing stuff, it was through Cerne. There's no way we could have done anything like that on our own. We weren't capable of it. And not really interested in it. If it wasn't for Cerne, I don't think the band would have been drawn in that direction, it probably would have stayed very underground and then fizzled out after a few years, which is what tended to happen with bands. We probably would have tried to make some recordings in a very DIY sort of way and botched it. So it was really Cerne that connected us with people.

It did feel truly original, in a way I'd maybe never felt in any of the other bands I played in before. I loved all the other bands that I played in, they were great bands and I had great times with the people. But, when the band started off Nick was playing drums and Paul was playing guitar, and it was shit. It sounded bloody awful but it was a great laugh. Then one day I persuaded them to swap places, and from that point on it just sounded like something I'd never heard before and something exciting. Something I'd never felt in a band before. I knew that it was something that was potentially bigger than anything I'd ever done before.

It flipped around about the time of the *NME* tour. We were opening up the bill on that tour. There were inklings of it as we went along. We released 'Darts of Pleasure' and I couldn't believe that it charted. If I remember rightly it got to Number 42 in the charts, not the indie charts, but the actual charts. It got to Number 42 and it blew my mind. I knew that Belle and Sebastian had done stuff like that. I knew that The Delgados and Mogwai would have done that kind of thing as well but just the idea of being in a chart, it kind of blew my mind. Like, fuck, I wasn't expecting this, this is insane. I guess that was the first thing. I also remember making the record was very satisfying. It felt like the culmination of a lot of ideas of mine that had been developing for a long period of time, I guess from the mid nineties up until that point in 2003. Particularly, in a more concentrated way, that stage between early 2000 up to 2003, which is from my personal nadir, my year zero. Because there was a period where I wasn't interested in making band music at all. After the year zero thing, I was still playing with the Amphetameanies but that was because they were my pals and I was doing it for fun. In terms of actually making something, I didn't want to make anything in a band.

Unlike much of the story of Scotland's nineties independent music scene, the success of 2003's 'Take Me Out' was completely unexpected. And it changed things dramatically for all guitar music, not just in Scotland but London and elsewhere too. In contrast to the differences between London and Glasgow during the Britpop years, the timing of Franz Ferdinand was perfect. There was no jumping on any bandwagons; this new scene simply aligned perfectly.

Alex Kapranos (vocals/guitar, Franz Ferdinand): I remember sitting with Jonas [Odell, director of the video for 'Take Me Out'] and showing him all the references we had, the things that informed us, the places where the band was coming from musically and aesthetically. It had all come from [the] lectures I used to sit in on at the art school. That's where I got introduced to all that stuff. It's basically first-year art school stuff, and it's so fucking exciting. I love it. Dada, constructivism, it changed my perspective on music and aesthetics. And I wanted to see that in the videos that we were making. There was a guy who was the lecturer in design, it was his lectures. He was obsessed with bicycles.

In the middle of that tour, I got an email saying that there was a rough cut of the video [for 'Take Me Out'] and I could go see it if I wanted to. I didn't have a laptop or anything like that, I had to go and find an internet café to look at the video. There was a brief period in the early 2000s where McDonald's had these really basic internet connection services. They had this really basic keyboard that was set into the furniture. You couldn't take it out or anything like that. I think if you bought a cheeseburger you got half an hour on the internet. So that was the first place I saw the video. I remember watching it, seeing the culmination of all those ideas and the music, and just thinking, fuck, that's powerful. I knew then that it was going to have an impact and knew that it was something. Making the 'Darts of Pleasure' video was really fun but it could have been any band's video really. It wasn't anything radically different. Nothing I hadn't seen in the video before, even though it was a funny video and a really good one. But when I saw the 'Take Me Out' video and I heard the music together, I was like, I've done something that's going to have a bit of impact here. Then when it came out, it went mental.

The first record I had in my hand would have been *The Kazoo Collection*. . . I remember being very excited. I couldn't believe I'd done that. That's something else. The first time I was genuinely really proud of a record would have been 'Darts of Pleasure'. All those years later. I'd done other records – The Karelia never came out on vinyl, it only ever came out on CD. When I first got 'Darts of Pleasure', I remember having the 7-inch and 12-inch. I just remember it was a different kind of excitement. It's not like the kind of excitement that you have when you go on stage. It was a much quieter, peaceful type of excitement. It was closer to contentment than the visceral thrill of the joy of being on stage. It was much more like the contentment and satisfaction of having something that I knew was good, both musically and aesthetically. It felt solid and it felt satisfying because it came after a lot of failure.

It was the physical manifestation of a lot of years of thought. It wasn't just something that I'd flung out. I'd spent a long time thinking about what I was doing and formulating ideas, throwing them around, carving away the excess and the bad until what was left was the raw essence. I think that's what my artistic evolution has come to. It's the difference between the Franz Ferdinand years for me and the Kazoo Club years for me. It's like a maximalism versus minimalism. When I was doing the Kazoo Club I just wanted to hear everything. I wanted to absorb everything. I wanted to give everybody a chance. I wanted everybody to have a go at doing their thing. And I wanted to soak up every idea, I want to talk to everybody. I wanted to listen to everything. So maybe that's what I did for the first decade. And then the second decade, I took the scalpel out and cut everything away way that I didn't want. That's when I was left with what I did want.

I think so much of my formation came from the friends that I had and the people that I hung out with. Particularly in those two scenes – the 13th Note scene and then the scene around the art school of Glasgow. They were very formative for me. And my friends before that happened, Andrew and Glen, my friends from school. Because they're the ones that you share your ideas with. And ideas are always way more exciting when you share them with other people. Because when you share them with other people, they see it from a different perspective. They become different ideas.

The way I was referring to record releases was as flags by which we measure a landscape. They're like orienteering points by which we can understand the landscape. But they're not the landscape, they're just flags on a landscape. I know that's definitely true for me as an artist, and the things that come out are just the bits that stand up above the horizon. I also feel like that about some of the features of landscapes that didn't get flags put on them. I sometimes feel this terrible sense of guilt in a way about the good minds that didn't have a more lasting mark. I think about those bands that played in the Kazoo Club and those names that I mentioned before like Superslinky and Eska, another great band. Trout, The Stanleys, Glen or Glenda, The Girlfriends, Poison Sisters – all amazing bands, and none of us knew it was going to be the guy from Deadcat Motorbike [Stuart Braithwaite, later Mogwai] that was going to have such a big effect. Quite rightly so he should because he's amazing. But everybody was on the same level at that point.

I still feel slightly guilty that they didn't (all) get the kind of recognition that I know they wanted. And maybe I did. Because there was a period where I felt like them. There was that period in the late nineties where I felt I'd fucked it. It made me quite despondent. I'm not talking about financial success, we're talking purely about other people around the world recognising that you've done something that has an element of artistic merit to it. Even the scene afterwards, around Glasgow in the early 2000s, those are the bands that we played with, like Rob Churm, what he was doing and what Uncle John & Whitelock were doing. There were other people at that time that should have had more of an impact. Anyway, you could go on for hours talking about that. You don't have to feel guilty about everything, do you Grant? The thing is, in my mind it always felt like going to a good party, after a gig or something like that. You want to take everyone with you, like let's all go, let's all go to the party. I think that's what I felt with all the Kazoo Club stuff. I wanted to take everybody with me. Maybe I felt a bit bad that not everybody managed to make it.

CHAPTER THIRTY

Reflections

Emma Pollock (vocals/guitar, The Delgados; Chemikal Underground): Those first five or six years were absolutely golden. Not just because we were new, not just because the industry was utterly buoyant – particularly the spotlight in Glasgow was strong. But also because the industry was going through its last flourish of health and buoyancy. And nobody knew what was coming. And then the noughties was this horrible, slow, wilting. And then the decade after it was a fucking catastrophe. So from 2010 onwards, we just didn't know what the fuck had hit us. We had to start laying people off, we had to start thinking how long we can continue doing this for. We had debts that were beginning to pile up. And so if you imagine that we are now in 2023, our first release came out in 1995. We're now almost thirty years old, and only five years of that was growth. It's a fucking wonder that we're still here at all.

Jane McKeown (vocals/bass, Lung Leg): I still to this day have low-key imposter syndrome – it's not as if I'm any great shakes or anything, we're a very low-level cult band, but I never believed myself to be any good at anything. Because of the second coming of Lung Leg, which has been happening the last two years, we're obviously back together. And we're going to be recording a new album. So the band's not even over yet. It's actually an ongoing process, which I love. The interesting evolution is that we've got some younger girls in the band. And what I love most about it is since we've come back, and we've only played a few gigs, for the last gig we played at Hug & Pint, we asked this all-girl band Curdle to play – an all-girl band, because they had contacted us through social media and bought our t-shirts and stuff. And speaking to them was just so incredible. They were so pleased to be playing with us. And I could see that we were being inspirational to them. And I love that. It reminded me of when Lung Leg got asked to support The Raincoats. They were heroines to us. Obviously The Raincoats are way more successful than Lung Leg but same sort of vibe. And I love that. I'm very female-centric. I'm not saying I don't want to encourage men – I don't think they need any more encouragement – but if I can be encouraging to women and young women to be doing music or anything creative, I really fucking love that. We had a young band, The Warm Girls, cover one of our songs recently and put it out on a demo tape. They were in America and my friend highlighted them so we got in touch and they sent us the demos, and to be tangible to these younger people is incredible. It gives them the encouragement. It's like when people like [Sonic Youth's] Kim Gordon and The Raincoats became tangible to me, I just think it's brilliant. It's just so positive.

Pat Crook (Vesuvius Records): I'm proud of the label, no doubt. A hundred per cent proud. But significant? I don't know. The fact that The Yummy Fur and Lung Leg are still about is pretty amazing. They're still going, good on them. I just like to share the story of it. It's nice when you are proud of something. It's always been about sharing, for me. We weren't just focusing on Glasgow, it was that ethos but in different places. International, in particular the USA. Not that much elsewhere, but there is something about the DIY ethos of it. That talent you can recognise wherever you are. Your kindred spirit.

Final Words

Nothing in this book began with permission. It began with closed doors and a stubborn belief that music could still be played even when there was nowhere obvious to play it. That has always been the heart of Scotland's independent music culture – when no infrastructure existed it had to built.

The 1990s scene began as a continuation of what had come before. Postcard, Fast Product, the anarcho-punk networks, and the 53rd & 3rd axis had already proven that Scotland did not need approval from elsewhere to matter. Everyone featured in this book simply extended that logic but just used different sounds, different clothes and, importantly engaged that Scottish refusal to wait to be asked.

Vegan cafés opened and became places to meet, cellars became stages and collectives replaced promoters. The Glasgow and Edinburgh music collectives and the world built around the 13th Note didn't merely host music; they trained people how to sustain and grow it. They taught bands how to organise and how to fail safely, how to release records and how to survive.

From these places the music travelled far beyond where it was born in. What would later be framed as unlikely global success – most visibly in the rise of Franz Ferdinand – was not an anomaly but a logical extension of years spent learning how to operate without pay-to-play, and how to build audiences slowly, and how to trust process over outcome.

What travelled outward was a new view of Scottishness and a proof of possibility. *No Mean City* was replaced by monochrome record sleeves. This was how the outside world now saw and thought of Glasgow. Belle and Sebastian have done far more for a positive worldview of Scotland than Visit Scotland or Creative Scotland could ever do.

Popular music is still too easily treated as lesser than theatre, opera, or the officially sanctioned arts. This history exposes that hierarchy as empty. What these musicians built required composition, performance, organisation, economic risk and ethical commitment. They shaped international perception and they built functioning cultural ecosystems from almost nothing – and they had fun doing it.

Perhaps the most enduring achievement of this was access. There were no gatekeepers at the door and entry was reframed as being earned through showing up, helping out, putting your name on a poster, sharing a bill, being original; or just not being a dick. And this is something that should be taught in schools.

What endures most powerfully is not any single band or venue, but a way of thinking: that culture is constructed, not bestowed; that difficulty is not an obstacle; that success does not invalidate struggle; and that popularity does not erase origins.

For younger generations reading this now, the lesson is neither nostalgic nor cautionary. It is practical. You do not need to be chosen. Scenes still grow from contact, friction, shared spaces and stubborn belief. The tools might change but the principle does not.

Acknowledgements and Thanks

All the contributors, who kindly gave up their time for this project.
Zoë Howe
Angela Slaven
Douglas MacIntyre
Grace Fairley
Jill Adam
Iain Key
John Robb
Tayba Mason
Ian Smith at Last Night From Glasgow
Lee Brackstone
Pete Selby
David Keenan
Jessie McPhee
Albert McPhee
Barry McPhee
Kaye Kennedy
Monorail
John Reid and Richard Anderson
Love Music Glasgow
Murdoch Macleod
Alastair Braidwood

Bibliography

Blogs:
williampinfold.com

Books and Magazines:
Days and Diary Entries, Jer Reid, Gruf Witt, 2023
Spaceships Over Glasgow, Stuart Braithwaite, White Rabbit, 2022
The List, List Publishing Ltd.
'John Peel Wiki', John Peel, 8 October, 1994
Urusai Yatsura Interview, *Melody Maker*
Yummy Fur review, Andrew Collins, 1994

Film and TV:
Lost in France, director Niall McCann, 2016, Curzon

Photos

The Stretchheads c/o Graham Gavin
dawson/Glasgow Music Collective poster c/o Angus McPhee
The List advert for the Kazoo Club c/o *The List*
The opening night of the Kazoo Club c/o Pat Byrne
Urusei Yatsura c/o Andy Wisher

Back of the *Kazoo* LP c/o Alex Kapranos
The Yummy Fur photo c/o Graham Gavin
The Yummy Fur *Melody Maker* review c/o *Melody Maker*
Music By Walt Disney But Played By Yuri Gagarin EP cover c/o John McKeown
Lung Leg c/o Stuart Reidman
Lung Leg, *The Negative Delinquency* EP c/o band
The Blisters/Urusei Yatsura split 7-inch c/o Modern Independent Records
Kitten Frenzy fanzine c/o Graham Kemp
In Spelunca album cover c/o Marc Baines, Vesuvius Records
Pink Kross *Active Dalmatian* EP c/o Gordy Davidson
The Male Nurse c/o Paul Ro
The Male Nurse *Patrick Swayze* EP (Guided Missile) c/o Keith Farquar
'Le Pastie de la Bourgeoisie' c/o Johnny Muir
'Le Pastie de la Bourgeoisie' flyer c/o Stuart Murdoch
V-Twin *Gifted* record label c/o Martin Clark/V-Twin/Domino
V-Twin with Andrew Oldham c/o Michael McGaughrin
Sally Skull c/o Tom Worthington
Back sleeve of *Tigermilk* c/o Stuart Murdoch
Mogwai Young Team c/o Chemikal Underground/Mogwai
Country Teasers c/o Tom Worthington
The Delgados *The Great Eastern* sleeve c/o Chemikal Underground

In Memoriam

Alan Crichton

Mark Gibbons

Carey Lander

Geraldine Kane